BY-PATHS IN SICILY

"Roast Sheep!"

BY-PATHS IN SICILY

BY
ELIZA PUTNAM HEATON

Scatter now some bright praise for the island which Zeus, the Lord of Olympus, gave to Persephone, and confirmed to her by shaking his locks, that he would support prosperous Sicily, fairest spot of the fruitful earth, by the wealthy excellence of cities.—First Nemean Ode of Pindar.

NEW YORK
E. P. DUTTON & COMPANY
681 Fifth Avenue

Copyright 1920
By E. P. DUTTON & COMPANY

All Rights Reserved

Printed in the United States of America

PREFACE

ELIZA OSBORN PUTNAM was born in Danvers, Mass., a descendant of families long native to that region. Her education, begun in Danvers and Salem schools, and furthered by graduation in Boston University, where she was an honor student in the classic tongues, well fitted her for a writer's career.

After her marriage and removal to New York, Mrs. Heaton began newspaper work, in which she swiftly gained such success as was possible at a time when women in that profession were still few and looked upon as experimental; serving first as special writer and afterward as a managing editor in newspaper and syndicate offices, until failing health made arduous tasks impossible.

Marooned in Sicily by ill health a dozen years ago, the author turned for occupation to the study of peasant life, a study eagerly pursued until it was cut short by her death. Of that work the present volume can fairly be presented as completed.

CONTENTS

INTRODUCTION vii

PART I
THE OLD MAGIC

CHAPTER		PAGE
I.	ELFLOCKS AND LOVE CHARMS	3
II.	DONNA PRUVIDENZA'S LEMON	34
III.	COLA PESCE	66
IV.	THE CLEFT OAK	96
V.	THE HAIRY HAND	116
VI.	JESUS AS DESTROYER	137

PART II
FAIRS AND FESTIVALS

I.	CHRISTMAS	159
II.	TROINA FAIR	178
III.	ST. PHILIP THE BLACK	203
IV.	THE MIRACLES OF SANT' ALFIO . . .	228
V.	THE CAR OF MARY AT RANDAZZO . .	261
VI.	"RED PELTS" AT CASTROGIOVANNI . .	281

PART III
ISLAND YESTERDAYS

CHAPTER		PAGE
I.	Etna in Anger	297
II.	Messina Six Months After	312
III.	In the Sulphur Mines	327
IV.	Hearth, Distaff and Loom	339
V.	Speed the Plow	352

LIST OF ILLUSTRATIONS

"Roast Sheep" . . . . *Frontispiece*
                                                          FACING PAGE

The Flax Worker	3
Elf Locks	16
Door Charms for Evil Eye	48
Catania Boats Have Eyes	67
Lobster Pots and Fish Traps	85
The San Pancrazio	85
The Little Oak Tree	109
The Piper	163
Going to the Fair	195
Hotel at Troina	195
A Herdsman	195
Girls and Pigs	195
"Most Becoming"	195
The "American" Cart, and Detail Showing Lincoln	248
A Straw Hut	263
Tying the Boys in Place, and Detail of the Car	272
"White Wings"	292
Gossips at Castrogiovanni	292
A Pig Pillow	292
The Laundry	292
Driven by the Lava	305
Fruit Trees for Fuel	305
Ruined by Etna	305

LIST OF ILLUSTRATIONS

	FACING PAGE
How the Lava Advances	310
A Useless Vigil	310
Queen Elena's Village	318
"Kitchenette," American Village	318
Miners at Villarossa	329
"Carusi"	337
Child Labor	337
The Little Sulphur Miners	337
Gna Tidda's Loom	341
A Sicilian Kitchen	345
Plowman Homeward Bound	353
Threshing	355
The "American Houses"	358
More Houses of Returned Emigrants	358
Pictures Made for "Babbo in America"	363

INTRODUCTION

The author of this book was able to act in Messina after the earthquake as an occasional interpreter between Italian officers from the North and the local peasants. This odd situation may illustrate the difficulties that dialects threw in the way of her study of Sicilian customs and her success in mastering them. But the gift of tongues was not the only qualification for the task by which intimate acquaintance with the chosen field enabled her to profit. Of the 700 local dialects of Italy, those used in Sicily have a family resemblance. All draw more largely than those of North Italy upon Greek, Saracen and Spanish sources. Such skill in comparative philology as the author possessed, from Sanscrit down to the modern Latin languages, was a key to them all. A better key to confidences and frank speech was her neighborly sympathy. Probably there were few regions in Sicily where she did not gain true friends among the unlettered, as well as among savants and antiquarians.

Beginning her work with no plan beyond solacing

an invalid's leisure by the production of a book of tourist observations, Mrs. Heaton delved into the mass of material presented by the survival of old beliefs upon a soil largely pagan; by picturesque custom and poetic observance; by peasant steadfastness through centuries and the recent swift effect of new-world migration, until her projects widened to embrace several volumes. To these a capstone should have been set by describing the debt of the United States to the industry of the Sicilians, and the benefit Sicily in turn derives from the homecoming emigrant. Her study of island thought and work as affected by the "Americani" might have helped to make the industrious children of the sun better understood in the country which is enriched by their labors.

For this task much material was gathered and many hundred photographs taken of intimate Sicilian life. This remains material only. The author's projected study of the reaction of the old world to the new, through sea migrations more vast and more fruitful of change than were the Crusades, was interrupted by the war. She was one of those Americans who, protesting, were ordered home by Secretary Bryan in the early days of the great conflict; her health did not permit her to offer her services in war work, so that her observations upon a theme so deeply affected by the past five years would require rewriting from fresh inquiry, and must be counted lost.

INTRODUCTION

Nine chapters of this book were completed by the author. Those upon the August festival in Randazzo and the fairs of Troina and Castrogiovanni were finished from rough drafts. The account of the sulphur mines, of the Etna eruptions in 1910 and of Messina after the earthquake, are made up from letters home. Two remaining chapters of Part III were put together from notes and material left in unfinished form. The manner of a work thus gathered varies, from the fanciful treatment of "Donna Pruvidenza's Lemon" and "Jesus the Destroyer" to the more soberly descriptive later pages. Nor can a volume so compiled be wholly free from errors, which an author's revision would have corrected.

A very small part of the rhymes, invocations, charms and "'razioni" noted down by Mrs. Heaton in all manner of difficult circumstances, and at much cost of labor and discomfort, are printed in footnotes. These passages, with examples of familiar speech in the text, will furnish material for comparison with literary Italian to those acquainted with the most beautiful of all languages.

The Sicilian dialects do not differ so competely as to bar speech between provinces, as sometimes happens in the mainland. The doubling of initial consonants and the substitution of "g" and "d" for "l," and of "u" for "o," are the peculiarities most striking to the visitor. Thus "beautiful daughter"—if one could be supposed to tempt the evil eye by such a compliment—is "bedda figghia," not "bella filia." Anello (ring) is "aneddu"; castello (castle), "casteddu"; Mongibello (Etna), "Mungibeddu." "B" is frequently softened to "v," as in modern Greek.

Spanish influence is noted in many words; and diminutives and nicknames are universal, applied as freely to tourists as to natives, perhaps not always with their knowledge. For an American matron of years and presence to be addressed as Dear Little Missy, "Cara Signurinedda," is a compliment of friendship.

Naturally, Greek words appear, as in "cona" (icon), a sacred picture or statue; and there are places, like the ever memorable Plain of the Greeks of Garibaldi's heroes, where more than a little Greek is still spoken. Words of Arab or Saracen origin are common in place names, in the names of winds, of tools, of articles of ancient and common barter.

Nearly all the illustrations of the book are from photographs taken by the author, or from those made under her direction by Francesco Galifi, of Taormina. On her behalf it is proper to offer thanks to many who furthered her work by aid or encouraged it by interest; to the memory of the learned Dr. Pitrè; to the Advocate Lo Vetere and the Deputies Colaianni and De Felice; to Mrs. George H. Camehl, of Buffalo; the American-born Signora Baldasseroni, of Rome; the British-born

Signora Caico, of Monte d'Oro, and Miss Hill, of Taormina; to the courteous American Consular representatives; to a hundred Sicilians of humble station in life, many of them known to the editor only by nicknames; last and most, to the Signorina Licciardelli ("Nina Matteucci"); her brother, Major Licciardelli, and their family, in Taormina and Catania.

J. L. H.

PART I

THE OLD MAGIC

THE FLAX WORKER

CHAPTER I

Elf-locks and Love Charms

Amusing and caressing him (the babe in the cradle) they (the "Donne di fuora") sometimes touch his hair and mat it into a little lock not to be tangled, which goes by the name of woman's tress, "plica polonica." This tress is the sign of the protection under which the baby has been taken, and constitutes its good fortune, as well as that of its family. No one ever dares to cut it; certain, in case it should be cut, of incurring the wrath of the Signore, who would visit on the child cross-eyes, or a wry neck, or spinal weakness.—Pitrè.

It was early twilight of a bleak day at the end of December when I first saw Vanna, the Grasshopper-eater. I had left Giardini while purple clouds still scudded across the golden sky, and the smoke of Etna flamed in the sunset. In the cold hill shadows as I climbed the old road to Taormina the wind from the sea bit sharply, and the first brave clusters of almond blossoms shivered, pinkish-gray against bare gray-brown branches.

There passed me a couple of men muffled in shawls, their long cane poles bearing witness that they had been beating olives from the trees; then I was alone until at a sudden turn I came upon a group of women knitting and gossiping as they toiled up the bare lime-rock way, so hard at the surface, so soft and rutted where the crust has worn through.

"A-a-a-a-ah!" twanged one of them to an ass that snatched a hasty bite at the side of the path and then lurched ahead, its saddle-sacks bulging with the squeezed skins of lemons.

"A-a-a-a-ah!" The woman repeated the nasal call. But the ass refused to quicken its pace, swinging now right, now left, in the zig-zag track from step to step across the path where countless generations of mules and asses have trodden foot-holes and helped the rain to scoop channels.

Three hens that clung to the animal's back, their wings flopping nervously every time it heaved up a shoulder, so absorbed my attention that I started when a voice said, "Good-evening, your ladyship!"

An old woman had detached herself from the group and was waiting for me, lowering from her head to the wall a great bundle she had been carrying. "All sole alone?" she queried, looking curiously at me out of faded yellow-gray eyes that yet were the brightest I had ever seen.

In a country where shop girls still hesitate to go to and from work unchaperoned, a woman who walks by herself outside of her village is an object of scrutiny.

"Are there wolves?" I responded.

The old woman grinned comprehension. "The way is safe. Are we Christians, or are we not?"

she answered. "I have failed in my duty! I should have known that Vossia (Your Ladyship) understands her own affairs. But," she added, "I do not persuade myself that Vossia ought to make the road alone at this hour."

"My daughter, I am not alone," I said; "am I not with you?"

"Va be! Rest then a minute, and we will make the road together."

She was lean as a grasshopper but erect, and her cheeks, though sunken, showed a wholesome red. She had no visible teeth and her chin curved up toward her nose. She was barefooted, and her skirt, in faded checks of black and red, was pulled up at one side under the string of her blue apron. A yellow kerchief was tied over her head and another in pink and white covered her shoulders.

"Softly! The way is bad," she warned me, as presently we started forward.

"The way indeed is bad," I replied; and then almost I lost consciousness of her presence in the monotonous rhythm of the prayer she began to wail:

> St. Nicola, send away this gale;
> Sant' Andrea, beyond our pale!
> I walk with Mary, I walk the way;
> In the name of God and of Christ I pray
> Let wind touch me not as I walk this day.

The cracked voice went on and on. When it came at last to a stop I perceived that with Sicilian facility of rhyme she had finished her song with a twist in my direction:

> Joseph, Mary and our Lord,
> Give me health along the road;
> For Vossia's sake this prayer I say,
> May she meet good people by the way.

"How are you called?" I asked abruptly.

"Vanna," she answered, naming also her three daughters-in-law.

"'The Grasshopper-eater!'" I exclaimed, a nickname that I had heard coming suddenly to memory.

"First the nickname, then the name!" she returned, good-humoredly. "And Vossia is the American who talks as we others talk."

"You may use my nickname, if you like," I apologized.

"It suffices to say 'the little American,'" she responded, politely.

Thus completely introduced, we gossiped about our families until we came to the roadside altar that stands at the last turn in the way from which one looks back on Giardini. Here under the carob tree Vanna paused. Untying the mouth of her heavy bag, she took out a tight little bunch of the red carnations that are called "cobblers' flowers" and set them on the ledge of the picture in a rusty tin that once had held tunny fish in oil. Then she signed herself, kissing her fingers to the Mother and Child.

I had long been curious about this unbeautiful Madonna, at once neglected and revered. Old red paint shows behind the harsh blue of the altarino's broken masonry. Mary's face is long-nosed and anxious and her hands are as huge and clumsy as the baby's legs. Neither sun nor rain can soften the stark greens and yellows of the icon; yet offerings never fail of flowers, fading without water.

"Is she perhaps miraculous," I inquired; "this Madonna?"

"Yes," said Vanna, with a short positive nod; adding after a pause: "I make a novena to her for the return of my son from America."

"She will bring him?"

"Once before when I made it he came and stayed a year."

She retwisted the cloth that made a pad for her head, and bent while I lifted the great sack to its place on this "corona." As we resumed the way she said: "One rests well here, for Vossia knows it was here the Madonnuzza rested when she came to Taormina fleeing the Saracens."

The Madonna is seen so frequently at Taormina even to-day, in the visions of the old, that I asked, without surprise, even as to the Saracens:

"And St. Joseph, did he rest here also?"

Vanna looked full at me with her quick, quiet eyes that shone like a cat's with yellow. "No," she said. "The Madonnuzza sat on the wall and gave the feeding bottle to the Bambineddu while

San Giuseppe took his stick and went to find a hiding place."

Vanna's active step became that of a bent old man trudging uphill leaning on a staff.

"He went up past Taormina," she said, "until he came to the grotto where is now the church——"

We looked up, but the rock under the Castle of Taormina where stands the hermitage of the Madonna della Rocca was not in view.

"When San Giusipuzzu had found the grotto, he hurried back to the Madonna and the Bambinu, for the Saracens were coming, 'Pum! Po! Pum! Po!' "

Here the Patriarch's feeble step was changed to that of a tramping host as my companion continued to stamp, "Pum! Po! Pum! Po!"

St. Joseph and the Madonna climbed as fast as they could, but the Saracens climbed faster; so they turned aside into a wood of lupines but the lupines rattled their pods and made such a clatter that the Madonna did not dare to stop, though she was tired and the Bambineddu kept crying.

Vanna twisted her mobile old face and began to whimper like a fretted baby; stopping to say: "So the Madonna cursed the lupines, saying, 'May your hearts be as bitter as my grief.' " And Vossia knows how bitter are the lupines; one soaks them long before eating.

"They hurried through the lupines and came to a field of rye, but the rye refused to close behind them. It bent as they passed and would not spring up again, but left a track for the Saracens to see. The Bambineddu kept crying, and the Madonna cursed the rye. It is for this that bread made of it is not satisfying.

"The Saracens were close behind, coming Pum! Po! Pum! Po! So they hurried through the rye and came to a field of wheat. The good wheat closed well behind them and made no noise, and the Madonna blessed it, and they rested, and the Bambineddu went to sleep with its face in the Madonnuzza's neck.

"By and by they went into a vineyard, and the vines arched over them and twisted their tendrils and made a shelter like a straw hut; and there they stayed till it was dark, for the Madonna said: 'I can no more!' When it was night they went up to the grotto. Thus it was, Vossia."

"Did the Madonna stay long at the grotto?" I inquired.

"Yes; one day in a thunderstorm there came into the grotto a little girl who was minding two lambs, and the Madonna said to her: 'Pretty little girl, go down to Taormina and tell the archpriest to come up here.'

"The little girl said: 'I can't go; I must tend my lambs.'

"'I'll tend them for you,' said the Madonna.

"So the little girl went. The archpriest came

up to the grotto and the Madonna said to him: 'Excellency, I wish a church built here.'

"The archpriest answered: 'There is too much rock.'

"But the Madonna said: 'The rock will break away of itself.'

"The archpriest called the master masons, and the minute they went to work the rock did break away of its own accord. They built the church that Vossia has seen, but the grotto itself they did not disturb. These are things of God, Vossia; no one knows them but me."

Vanna looked at me again with her calm, shining yellow eyes. She set the tip of her forefinger against her forehead, repeating with deliberation: "I tell these things of God to Vossia; there is no one else who knows them."

It is true that the flight into Egypt through Taormina is known to no one but Gna Vanna; but the legend of the plants that hid and that refused to hide the Virgin is old Italian. As to the sanctuary of the Madonna della Rocca, there are those in Taormina who say that it was a boy, not a girl, who entered the grotto, and that he saw a beautiful woman spinning. Frightened, he ran away and told the story. The people who came to look found, indeed, no woman; but, instead, a miraculous picture of the Mother and Child.

In the gathering dusk we met fishermen coming down the hill to the sea for their evening's work,

ELF-LOCKS AND LOVE CHARMS

and there passed us a scrap of a boy driving a little Sardinian donkey. The child had been to mill to get a *tumulu* of wheat ground, for his father had land, he said; and almond trees so tall you could not get the nuts without climbing a ladder. While he boasted sociably of this phenomenon and of the clean, shivering ass, newly clipped because it had been "too dirty," Vanna lapsed into a silence so unresponsive that, when the lad had bubbled "bb-b-bb-r-rr-r" to the ass and had left us, I asked if the great bag was tiring her.

"No," she said, shortly, straightening herself and stepping out more smartly. Although she was old, she could work in the fields and carry burdens with the best of them. Of course the bag was heavy. In it there were chick peas, cauliflowers, lemons and chestnuts. Some of these things she had earned picking up olives as the men beat them from the trees, and others people had given her out of respect. It was fortunate that people did respect her and give her food, because her husband had a heart "like the claw of a devil fish"; he was so stingy he never gave her anything. In the bag there was food for several days, and her grandchildren would be glad to see her coming. Of course it was heavy, but she could carry it, because the Madonna, St. John and the sainted souls of the beheaded bodies helped her. It was natural that she should be helped, because she was good. She worked, she brought food from the country, and she had no amusement except to stand in her doorway.

The monologue ran along until a mysterious "they" aroused my curiosity. The respect and help on which she was enlarging seemed to involve other personages than the Madonna, St. John and the sainted souls of the beheaded bodies.

"Who are 'they?'" I interrupted.

She gave me no answer and continued to talk of her merits and their rewards. But it was not long before the flood of her own words swept her to revelation. Setting down her sack, she glanced quickly around and took off her head kerchief, replacing it instantly as a couple of women came in sight at the turn.

"What long hair you have!" I exclaimed. I had had a momentary glimpse of grizzled braids, thin as a string, wound many times round and round her head and held in place by the knifelike blade of a silver dagger.

"Si," she replied with finality, as if there were something I ought to understand. And suddenly there came to me a recollection of old men I had seen in mountain villages among whose scant, short locks there stood out long matted wisps of gray hair. Such "trizzi," tangled by elfin fingers while a baby lies in the cradle and never cut—how would one recognize them on a woman? Were Vanna's protectors those impish little sprites, half fairy, half witch, the Women of the Outside?

ELF-LOCKS AND LOVE CHARMS

"You have 'the tresses?'" I inquired.

"Si," she said, with short positiveness.

She would tell me nothing more, for we had passed the chapel of the Madonna of the Mercies, and already we heard the stir of the village as we climbed the last long slope under the walls of Taormina. Some day she would show me her hair, she promised; but these were secret things not to be spoken of except when we were alone.

Vanna the grasshopper-eater had just moved into my own street, and I marked the house she pointed out to me. But next morning when I passed it going to the Corso the door was shut, for Taormina was shivering at a temperature of not more than fifteen degrees above freezing, and the fiend was riding in the wind. It was not until New Year's Day that, noticing hens hopping casually across her threshold, I followed them inside.

The room in which I found myself was so dark and smoke-grimed that in spite of the partly opened door I did not see at first that I had stumbled on a family gathering. Vanna's house has a window opening, but for economy of heat its wooden shutter was closed. Vanna and her daughter-in-law Rocca, a red-cheeked young woman, were making macaroni, and Vanna's greeting was more ready than cordial.

Vanna's husband, too, was at home. He of the claws of the devil-fish proved to be a little half-blind old man whom I already knew as Domenico the dwarf. With a rusty long cap pulled down over his head, hairy sandals resting on the "conca" where perhaps a little warmth lingered in the white ashes, chin bent on his two hands that nursed the top of a stick, he looked sunk in chilled misery. Ordered to kiss my hand, he yielded dumb obedience.

Vanna set a chair, lifting from it a bundle of clothes wet from the wash, and wiping it with her apron while she shrilled "sciu! sciu!" to a lean brown fowl that flew upon the bed to get at the macaroni. A less enterprising bird was settled in a nest of rags and brush under the fireplace.

"Do they lay well?" I asked.

"They eat and do nothing!" scolded Vanna. "Uncle January sends us cold weather. The hens dirty the house," she added; "but what can one do?"

Let those criticise Vanna's housekeeping who have themselves kept house and reared live stock in one room. Beside the cold fireplace were heaped brambles and roots of cactus fig for the cooking fire. A disordered table, a long brown shelf against the rear wall and a chest at the foot of the bed held most of the family possessions. Behind the great bed and in the corners stood old baskets, boxes, water jars and tall coops made out of rush-woven fish-traps. A hen with a broken leg and a cock moped in these cages, and from some burrow in the litter appeared at moments dirty white rabbits.

While Vanna railed at a peevish child that tumbled about on the floor, I studied the walls and their smoke-dimmed icons. The Madonna of the

Rock, the Madonna of the Chain, the Black Madonna of Tindaro, S. Pancrazio, Sant' Alfio and his brothers, S. Filippo the black, S. Francesco di Paola, S. Giovanni the beheaded, the sainted souls of the beheaded bodies——

I had not finished counting the Lares and Penates when Vanna found an interval of quiet in which to tell me how she had set the hen's leg, which "he" had broken with his stick. Furtively she thrust out towards her husband her first and fourth fingers in the sign of the horn, her gesture and the gleam in her pale bright eyes spelling warning.

While she talked Vanna did not neglect the macaroni. Rocca held on her knees a board carrying a lump of dough, from which from minute to minute she pinched off bits. Rolling these between her hands, she passed the rolls one by one to Vanna, who sank into each a knitting needle and re-rolled the paste on the board to form the hole. Each short piece as she slipped it off the needle she hung to dry over the edge of a sieve that balanced on the rolled-up mattress at the foot of the bed. When enough for supper was ready she tied the rest of the dough in a kerchief and shut it into the chest, throwing the crumbs to the cock with a "chi-chi-richi! cu-cu-rucu!"

This work finished, Vanna picked up the dark mite of a child and began crooning, "ninna, nan-na——" interrupting herself to kiss the tear-blurred face. "Pretty boy! He has fifteen months,

Vossia. His grandma's wee one! Ninna, ninna, nanna——"

The brown eyes shut, and after a minute Rocca carried the baby away, his shaven head drooping over her arm.

I was rising to follow when old Micciu, who beyond grunting once or twice, "I am not content!" had sat hunched in his chair seemingly oblivious of his surroundings, struggled to his feet.

Vanna repeated the sign of the horn, forming with her lips the words, "Zu Nuddu is going out"; and, in fact, "Uncle Nobody," picking up his shoulder bags of black and white wool, scuffed toward the door.

"An accident to you!" exclaimed Vanna. "Eccu!" she said, with satisfaction, as the door closed behind the old man.

Left alone with me, she took off her kerchief after some urging, displaying again her fleshless head, where the skin clung to the scalp like parchment. Gold hoops hung in her ears, and wound in rings like a mat around the back of her skull were grizzled strings of hair. Pulling out the pins, she let down this mass, undoing with her fingers the upper part of two braids and releasing a scanty lot of gray old woman's hair that hung loose and ragged to her shoulders.

Starting from this short mane and falling to Vanna's feet, even lying on the floor, dropped two dark tails that, felted with dust, had more the look

ELF LOCKS

of strands of sheep's wool than of what they were in fact, matted locks of her own hair.

"Eccu!" she repeated.

These tails were the "trizzi." Never cut, never combed, treated with the respectful neglect which is their proper care, they marked Gna Vanna as a person living under a spell; the protegée from birth of the mysterious "women of the outside," or "women of the house"—the little "ladies" who have many names. Her fearsome pixy locks set Vanna apart as one who, taught by witches, possessed some at least of the seven faculties of the witch summed up in the jingle!

> She can embroil the peaceful moon and sun,
> Fly through the air fast as the wind doth run;
> Through closed doors she knoweth how to go,
> The man most strong she maketh weak and slow;
> She leadeth closest friends to fight with knives;
> Her will makes husband wrangle with their wives;
> She striketh men and women sore and lame,
> To have no rest and suffer cruel pain.

Vanna's "Eccu!" was said with pride. She looked over her shoulder at the tails and then smilingly at me.

"What would happen," I asked, "if they were cut?"

"I should die."

It is a number of years now since Vanna said this to me, and I am as confident to-day as I was then that she meant it. She believed and still believes in the sanctity of her elf-locks, while fully realizing their value as an asset.

"But if you combed them?"

"Something would happen to me."

With much dramatic gift the weird old creature told me how sometimes in the night she waked to see in her room twenty-four lovely little "women of the house," ladies and fairies.

When the "ronni" appeared the whole room glowed with light. They wore bright, beautiful clothing and sometimes they sang. Sometimes they talked in tiny little voices, but mostly they were mute. Sometimes they played games. One of their favorite tricks was to pitch "the old man," whom they did not like, out of bed. Once when "the old man" would give her nothing to eat they showed her the key of the box where he kept bread and wine. Sometimes they caressed her hair and made new tresses.

Lifting her gray locks she pointed out little curls against her neck, sacred like the tresses. But even she was not safe from their anger. Sometimes, if she went bare-footed, they gave her beatings because they insist on cleanliness. She pulled up her skirts to show her white, well-kept flesh.

Oftenest of all they danced.

I looked on dazed while Vanna the grasshopper-eater whirled around the room in a wild dance in imitation of the ronni, her brown, wrinkled face full of uncanny animation, yellow eyes glowing,

ELF-LOCKS AND LOVE CHARMS

elf-locks swinging, her grotesque hops scaring the hen out of the nest under the fireplace.

Not scanning details too closely, I did not doubt the good faith of words or actions, because I have long understood with what literal truth Pitrè says that in certain environments we cannot listen to tales told in all honesty without remaining uncertain "whether these men and these women are a prey to continual visions, or whether we ourselves are dreaming with our eyes open." Rather through this woman so garrulous and so secretive, so simple and so shrewd, so vindictive and yet so kindly, so credulous and so positive, I seemed to catch glimpses of an obscure brain-life like that of a witch of the fifteenth century.

Up to a certain point she would believe in herself and others would believe in her. Witches have always carried magic in their hair, and hence the foes of witches have cut it off. Sibilla herself was unkempt and her hair tangled like a horse's mane.

I wondered if any trace attached to this skeleton-thin "Grasshopper-eater" of the evil eye fear expressed in the saying:

"A grasshopper has looked on thee."

Ceasing her gyrations, Vanna put the cackling hen to the door and sank out of breath on the dark old chest, bringing the warm egg and dropping it into my hands. While she coiled her hair once more around the dagger, she repeated her former self-congratulations that she could work, although she was old, by the help of the ronni. "Because of their favor, too, people brought her gifts, desiring her prayers." That very morning she had received the unhappy cock in the fish-trap and two rotoli of flour to make pasta for the New Year. These things were fortunate, because she had no one but the ronni to provide for her.

"I am an orphan," she concluded; "I have no father, mother I have none. I have no one. I must live. Do I speak well?"

She replied to her own query with a complacent nod.

Knowing what sorts of prayers are in request from reputed "wise women," I suggested: "People ask your 'razioni against witchcraft?"

"Si," she answered. Only a few days before a woman had sent for her whose bread had come out of the oven full of ugly bubbles and "twisted as if it had been struck by lightning." Even a blind woman must have seen that this was the work of evil eyes. She had not used oil, salt or incense, but she had said a prayer:

> Four loaves and four fishes,
> Away forever with ill wishes!
> God is moon and God is sun,
> Harm this bread there can no one.
> Christ Jesus died, Christ Jesus rose,
> Out of this oven malocchio goes!

Next morning the woman baked sixteen loaves and they came out as beautiful as bread could be.

She cut a big piece and gave it to Vanna to eat, all hot as it was, seasoned with oil and garlic.

"These are things of God, Vossia," Vanna continued. "The priests speak against these 'razioni, but they themselves cannot help the people. What do priests do but say the mass and eat and sleep? If people want help they must come to me; therefore they respect me. I cannot read prayers out of a book, but I have many written in my mind. Always for good, never for evil, are they. Loose? yes; bind? No! Are we Christians or are we not? Vossia is persuaded?"

Relieving me of the egg, she lifted the lid of the chest as if to put it away; questioning as she did so. "In Vossia's country hens make themselves by machine; it is true?"

"By machine?" I repeated.

"Si; one of my sons brought home from America a machine for making chickens; but the hens make them better. He lost everything, and now he has not pennies to go again."

Taking out of the chest two or three other eggs, she pressed them all on me, saying: "They do not give to eat to Vossia such eggs as these, eggs of the house, all made to-day."

A suspicion that Vanna meant to save herself from bare feet and beatings by enlisting me as a respectful giver of shoes grew larger in my mind, but fortunately I concealed it. To me, at least,

Vanna has always been a friend more disinterested than a ronna.

To cover my uncertainty I picked up a strip of faded silk that lay on a pile of stuff in the open chest; it proved to be a man's necktie knitted in pink, through which ran a line of black embroidered lettering.

"What does it say?" demanded Vanna. I read to her. It was in correct Italian: "I love thee, thee always have I loved, thou wert the first."

"To wear at festas the poor thing gave it to him!" exclaimed Vanna.

"Who is he?" I demanded, scenting a story.

Vanna took out of the chest a pair of coarse blue socks and two or three men's kerchiefs. These things she turned over for some time on her knees before she brought herself to the point of telling me that they belonged to a young man called Peppino who had refused to marry the girl to whom he was promised, on the ground that his mother objected, and that the poor girl's father was threatening to kill her. The girl's mother, who lived not far away, had sent for Vanna the day before, and had asked her to make a "recall" of the youth to the girl he had abandoned.

I fingered the pink necktie with fresh interest. "You are going to do it?" I questioned.

Vanna said she didn't know. The poor girl cried all day long; it broke one's heart to hear her. She would gladly do something to bring the mother to such a good will that she would say to her son: "Take her." But never had she heard of such a hard-hearted mother-in-law. And they had not given her money enough to buy candles. To make the recall she must light seven candles every night for nine nights in succession, and if anything went wrong, she must begin again at the beginning. Every candle cost half a lira, so that she ought to have at least nine lire.

At this point the door opened and Rocca entered with a little girl, perhaps four years old. Glancing at us curiously, she demanded: "What do you talk about so long?"

"Things of God," replied Vanna, shutting the chest and warning me with a glance of her quiet shining eyes. "I tell Vossia things of God of which she may think in these days of rain when she must stay indoors."

Rocca snorted good-humoredly.

Bidden to wish me "good-evening," the child, as I rose to go, proffered a timid "buona sera."

"Listen to her!" cried Vanna delightedly. "She says 'buona sera!' instead of 'buna sira' like we others. That comes of going to school!"

The brown little curly-head was made to speak a piece:

> Giovannina is my name;
> I am not pretty nor too plain,
> I do not know how it can be
> That everybody's so good to me.

"Beautiful, eh?" cried the proud grandmother, fishing a soldo out of the big pocket that hung at her waist. "Beautifully she speaks! Run, buy a biscotto!"

It was some days before I again saw Vanna, and I might never have known more of the poor "zita" at Santa Venera, if I had not chanced to pass her door one afternoon just as she was inserting the key. A little book that I carried caught her attention. Taking it from me as she invited me indoors, she turned the pages with interest, putting on spectacles to see the better. Finally, giving it back to me, she asked:

"What does it say?"

The book happened to be an Italian version of the old Sicilian Greek, Theocritus, and it opened to the page I had been reading. I turned into the vernacular what Andrew Lang has better phrased: "As turns this brazen wheel, so, restless under Aphrodite's spell, may he turn and turn about my door! My magic wheel, draw home to me the man I love!"

Vanna looked puzzled. She asked: "Is it a book of prayers? There was a lame man who lived above Giarre who had an ancient book of 'razioni. He is dead now, but to all who went to him for help he would read out of his book. I cannot read, I have no book, but in my head I have many 'razioni. What more does it say, Vossia?"

I began the second idyl, but when I had reached

the words, "Wreathe the bowl with bright-red wool, that I may knit the witchknots against my grievous lover, who for twelve days—oh, cruel!—has never come hither——" she interrupted, exclaiming:

"It is a love prayer!"

"Yes," I admitted; "is it like the one you were going to say for the poor deserted girl at Santa Venera?"

"Mine is more better," she boasted.

It may have been the wish to prove that the prayers in her head were "more better" than those written in my book that procured me a matinee rehearsal of the charms she was saying nightly for the abandoned sweetheart. For she had reached the middle of the novena. The difficulty about candle money had somehow been overcome.

Opening the chest, she took out Peppino's socks, necktie and kerchiefs. "The wool must be white," she said, going to a sheepskin that hung from a nail on the wall, and pulling off some flocks. Before proceeding, she fastened the door.

The "recall" could not be made, she said, except when the moon was waxing and on a night when the stars were bright. The first step was to light seven candles. She nodded towards the table, where seven spots betrayed that seven drops of melted tallow served as candle bases. Then, taking the wool, she carded hastily a little, using a hand contrivance supported on a chair. Next, spinning a thread with the distaff, she braided a cord of three strands, explaining that if this "lacciu"—lassoo or noose—were made just the length of Peppino, that would add to its virtue.

Taking the cord in her hands, she tied in it three knots while reciting as fast as her tongue could run:

> Peppino, two are they that watch thee;
> Of them that bind thee, ten there be.
> I bind and do not loose the knot
> Till what I wish from thee I've got.
> 'Tis thee I bind and thee I make
> Thy promised bride to wife to take.

Laying down the knotted cord, Vanna put Peppino's kerchiefs on her head, piling above them the socks and necktie. Having thus put herself into communion with him, she rushed on:

> Peppino, I look at thee,
> Thou look'st at me.
> All things else out of mind must sink,
> Of pledged wife only must thou think.

Dropping Peppino's property beside the cord, Vanna next took a little salt and stirred it with the forefinger of her left hand around and around in the palm of her right hand; but before she could begin the new prayer I begged her not to gabble at such a speed.

Glib recitation of formulas was no more essential in ancient Roman sacrifice than it is to-day in Sicilian incantations. Unless a spell is said, fast and smoothly, without mistaking a syllable, it must be repeated from the beginning. A trip is a bad omen. It results that no conjuror can get through her formula at all except at top speed.

"Softly! Softly!" I would entreat of Vanna. "I don't get half the words." Then she would break, stumble, begin again and in a minute rattle faster than before. While stirring the salt she said:

> Turn salt!
> Turn bread!
> Turn pine cone!
> Turn wood!
> Turn Peppino's head.
> All things else from his mind must sink,
> Of his sweetheart only must he think;
> For I hold true faith that come he must
> His troth to keep, for this is just.

Opening the wooden shutter of the small window and looking up, Vanna said that the next 'razioni must be said while gazing at the moon:

> Vitu, dear saint of Mountain Royal,
> To you there comes your servant loyal;
> I come to you to ask a grace,
> As if kin we were of blood and race.
> It is your dogs that you must lend;
> To hunt Pippinu you must them send.
> The beast so savage that has eyes,
> Like a butcher's dog "A-a-a!" that cries,
> Let him seize Pippinu by the hair
> E'en to his pledged wife's door to bear.
>
> With no woman may he speak,
> No man's counsel may he seek.

> In thee I trust, strong is my hope
> To hear dogs bark, bells ring, doors ope.

Saint Devil, concede me what I wish. I will not respect you as Devil, if you do not concede me what I wish. I will respect you as Devil, when you concede me what I wish.

With a face as placid as if she were knitting a stocking Vanna concluded this invocation. Then, dropping on her knees at the window, and surveying the heavens as if she were choosing a star, she declaimed:

> Shining star, powerful star,
> Heedless of me still you are?
> Bright angel of the good light,
> In three words bring him to my sight.
> Well come, well go; take him by the feet,
> And he comes thither fast and fleet.
> Devil of Mt. Etna dread,
> Peppino seize by the hairs of his head,
> Thou devil of the mouth awry,
> Peppino take and bring him nigh.
> In Holy Trinity its name,
> When sounds Ave Maria bring him home.

It spoiled the congruity of Vanna's charm that from force of habit she tacked a Holy Trinity tag belonging to some other 'razioni to an invocation of the devil. More to myself than to her I commented: "Why does every love-charm call up the evil one?"

"He has great power," said Vanna, pulling herself to her feet, and confirming her answer with a positive glance and nod. She was beginning an account of Satan's subjects—unbaptized babies who die while yet pagan and scream forever in the darkness, and dying sinners whose hair "the black man" clutches, shouting "Come on!" while they howl, "U-u-u-u-u!" when I brought her back to Peppino.

The "recall" ended, she said, with a prayer, to "the sainted souls of the beheaded bodies," followed by nine paters, nine aves and nine glorias. During these and after the finish she made "the listening" standing at her window to catch the night sounds of the village. If this listening brought to her ears music or laughter or the ringing of bells, or the opening of doors, or if a cock crowed or a dog barked, her prayers were answered. But if an ass brayed or a cat miaued, or if she heard quarreling or the splash of water thrown into the street, these were bad omens.

She folded away Peppino's goods and began cutting up lettuce leaves and throwing the green ribbons on the floor as she told me that, for her, the best sign of all was the appearance of a little white puppy that sometimes came and lay on her knees. When she saw this shadow dog, her 'razioni never failed. Lacking the puppy, she observed whether the star to which she had prayed "shut and then opened again," for this meant that it heard, thought and said "yes." Our stars, she said, give us the grace we ask of them.

"It is a great labor," I said; "this recall."

"Yes," she admitted; "but it never fails."

While the hens fought for the lettuce she asked to hear my prayer again, and I read: "Do thou, my Lady Moon, shine clear and fair, for softly, Goddess, to thee will I sing, and to Hecate of hell. The very whelps shiver before her as she fares through black blood and across the barrows of the dead. Hail, awful Hecate! to the end be thou of our company——"

When Vanna realized that my 'razioni, as well as her own, included knots, a turning spell, dogs and invocations to the moon and to a ruler of hell, she agreed that for a book prayer it was not bad.

I continued to read, and we were still comparing notes when there came a thump at the door. "The old man!" sighed Vanna, going to let him in. "He swears by the Holy Devil," she said, "if he finds the door shut."

Instead of swearing, the old man scuffed and stumped across the floor and hid himself in a chair behind the bed. But our séance was over. When I asked Vanna to complete the recall by reciting her prayer to the souls of the beheaded—criminals who, expiating their deeds by the forfeit of their lives, have acquired power to work miracles—she was absorbed in the pot of basil on her window ledge. She must put a wet cloth over it at night, she said, to make it grow better. She offered me a few fragrant sprigs together with a double lemon —two lemons merged in one except for their twisted ends.

"It is against malocchio; it makes the horns," she assured me, tucking it into my handbag.

My first thought on reaching home was to look up an old prayer to S. Vito that I happened to have copied long before. The chief function of this saint is to protect from the bite of mad dogs; he also casts out evil spirits, and his underworld connections are such that for centuries lovers have appealed to him. Gna Vanna's prayer, in fact, is a time-battered fragment of an old charm, included in a manuscript book of "secrets for making gold, constraining devils, evoking and divining the future" that was taken from Dr. Orazio di Adamo and used as evidence against him in his trial for witchcraft at Palermo in 1623.

This 'razioni was to be said in a garden by moonlight. At the end a knife was to be stuck into a tree.

Dr. Pitrè gives a charm practically identical with Adamo's as still in use; but I have come upon nothing more than fragments which have undergone many changes. Once, for example, while a good-natured dealer in antiques was turning her drawers upside down for me in search of some trifle, there fell out a crumpled paper scrawled over with characters so illegible that it was with difficulty I recognized the prayer to S. Vito. The first six lines ran like Vanna's; then, as to the dogs, it continued:

> You must "sick" them into S——'s heart,
> Hard as the pain of my grief's dart.

And there it stopped. On the other side of the paper was a charm to be said in church. Smoothing out the sheet before us, my friend informed me with hesitation that to use it one must enter the church with the left foot foremost, hiding a red cord under the shawl. At the moment of the consecration one must make three knots in the cord, saying:

> I do not come to mass to hear,
> Nor yet to worship Christ so dear.
> I come to bind with this my noose;
> I bind, I tie, I do not loose
> Till my love does all my pleasure.
> His feet I tie with this my noose,
> His hands I bind, I do not loose
> Till my love does all my pleasure.

"It was a woman in Catania," said my friend, "who gave me these."

"A wise woman?" I suggested.

"Yes," she confessed; "but I don't use them. Sometimes when my husband is away on his business trips I should like to know—but I don't believe in charms. And yet—do you know X——? He used to beat his wife till all the neighbors heard, and now he takes her out in an automobile. They say she puts drops of her blood in his coffee. Some things don't seem true and yet—— But charms can't be of any use, else every man in Taormina would be married to a rich tourist."

Elf-locks and incubators! Love-charms and automobiles!

CHAPTER II

Donna Pruvidenza's Lemon

John Bly and William Bly testified that, being employed by Bridget Bishop to help take down the Cellar-wall of the old House, wherein she formerly Lived, they did in Holes of the said old Wall find several Poppets, made up of Rags and Hogs Brussels, with headless Pins in them, the Points being outward.—*Cotton Mather. Wonders of the Invisible World.* Testimony against Bridget Bishop, executed, Salem, Mass., June 10, 1692.

On the eighth of May, 1913, there appeared in the "Giornale di Sicilia," of Palermo, an item which I abridge as follows:

Yesterday an old man and woman, red-faced and out of breath, followed by a crowd of excited women, burst into the procuratore's office, crying: "We have found it! Look, Signore! Look!"

"See!" shouted the man; "see what killed our daughter!"

The man laid on the table two parcels, one containing locks of chestnut hair, the other something made of wool.

"Here is what killed my daughter!" screamed the woman, shuddering with terror. "Here is the witchcraft!"

The two people were Emanuele Malerba and his wife Antonina Bracciante, whose daughter died some time ago, a few months after marriage. The parents have suspected the girl's mother-in-law, who opposed the match, of making away with her by witchcraft.

All the furniture, including the marriage bed, which the

DONNA PRUVIDENZA'S LEMON

girl had carried as dowry to her husband, was restored in due course to her family; and the old mother, picking over the mattress, pricked her hand. Searching inside the bed, she found something in the shape of a doll into which were stuck a large needle, two safety pins, one black and the other white; and two other safety pins on each of which was transfixed a seed of a nespolo (medlar).

"Here is the witchcraft!" she thought.

As soon as she had recovered she ran to tell her husband and the neighbors. The quarter was thrown into commotion. To die at eighteen years by the will of God is one thing; to perish through the brutal malignity of a mother-in-law is quite another.

One of the women explained: "When the seed dried, poor Rusidda died."

"You see," said another, pointing to the doll without daring to touch it; "there is a seed at its stomach, which means that the witchcraft was made in the stomach of Rusidda."

"It is true," shuddered the mother; "my daughter complained always of stomach pains."

The two old people denounced the fact to the police, and when their complaint was not received seriously, they betook themselves to the public prosecutor, who also met their demand for justice with good-natured laughter.

The father and mother, once again at home, allowed a brave young neighbor to cut open the image. When there came out more nespoli seeds mixed with sawdust they returned to their belief in the strange doll's errand of murder.

"There is no justice!" they raved, glaring at the bystanders; "there is no justice!"

There were thousands of years when learned judges did not laugh at such dolls, and ignorance does not yet laugh at them.

Twelve hundred years before Christ, in the reign of Rameses III, a steward of the king was prosecuted in an Egyptian court of law for causing paralysis to men and women by making wax figures of them. As late as 1692 the finding of "poppets" stuck full of pins was admitted in Salem, Mass., as evidence in a witch trial. Even now, maltreating an image to harm a man, if not actionable in court, and if not as usual everywhere as it may be in Amoy, where bamboo and paper "substitutes of persons" are sold ready-made, is certainly not a form of imitative magic confined to the primitive Bakongo.

"Substitutes of persons" are not uncommon in Sicily; but oftener than into a human figure, simple like those of Amoy, or elaborate like those which thirteenth century black art modeled with the features of an enemy and baptized with his name, Sicilian magic stabs its jeers or its threats into an egg or a lemon, a potato or even a piece of meat.

The first lemon of this sort that ever I saw in Taormina was a "substitute" of Donna Pruvidenza, and I had sight of it, as it were, by accident. If Donna Pruvidenza's confessor had not chanced to be at a church convention in Malta, she would have taken the "making" straight to him, after the manner of the more devout, to beg that he read a prayer over it, first putting on his stole. It was the absence of the priest that sent her to the kindly family who exorcised the lemon, much as he might have done, perhaps, by assuring her that it could do no harm; and who suggested that she bring it to me.

It was on the terrace outside the dining room

that Donna Pruvidenza found me; and no sooner had Pietro set a chair and brought a second coffee cup than I saw that hers was no ordinary visit; for though she drank with appreciation and was lavish of morning compliments, her manner was at once uneasy and that of a person even more conscious than prim little Donna Pruvidenza commonly is of her own importance.

"Dear little Missy," she said when the coffee was finished, "can we not withdraw to some location less public? What I have to say to you is consequential."

"Let us go to my room," I assented, for beyond the long window stood Pietro, arranging flowers for luncheon by putting into each glass blossoms of as many different colors as possible.

As he opened the door for our retreat I saw him glance at a cloth Donna Pruvidenza carried, for it hurt Pietro's sense of the proprieties that parcels brought to me were apt to hold gifts of carob pods, dried chestnuts or hard little salted olives, beneath the dignity, as he considered it, of the dining room.

In the quiet of my chamber Donna Pruvidenza untied the kerchief and laid it on the table.

"Ah," I said, seeing among the folds of the cloth the shape of a lemon; "have you brought me some fruit?"

"Cara Signurinedda!" There was horror in Donna Pruvidenza's voice, and in the gesture of her hands.

Looking closer, I saw that the lemon which lay on the kerchief was livid with black and purple spots, exuding moisture and at the same time drying and warping out of shape. Stuck into it were nails, the rusty shanks of which were beginning to show as the fruit twisted, shrinking away from them.

"What is that? A fattura?" I exclaimed, guessing at the meaning of the ugly thing.

The parchment of Donna Pruvidenza's brown face crinkled with indignation. "It is a brutal surprise that I have brought the Signurinedda!" she ejaculated, her hands denouncing the authors of the injury; "a surprise for me, an orphan who have no one to vindicate me, who am dedicated to the service of God, and who look for nothing but his graciosity and the protectorate of good people!"

"Where did it come from?" I questioned.

Donna Pruvidenza began her account of the lemon with praise of her grandparents. While in quaint, high-flown phrase she extolled her family, I drew the kerchief to my side of the table. "The Signurinedda must not touch the 'gghiommaru'!" she interrupted herself to warn me.

Why instead of lemon she said "gghiommaru," which means anything round like a ball of thread, I can only guess. Donna Pruvidenza never uses a common word when she can find an uncommon one.

I had counted three needles, seven pins and five screws piercing the lemon, and had reached the thirty-first nail when she came to her own childhood.

"I called my progenitors 'father' and 'mother,' as did Jesus Christ, and morning and evening I asked their blessing, kissing their hands. While in the days of to-day the very offscouring of the streets scream 'Papa!' 'Mamma!' as if they were ladies and gentlemen! . . . Madonna mia! The Signurinedda must not touch the thing!"

"Where did you get it?" I reiterated, pushing the kerchief away from me.

"It is of the devil! Of the brute beast!"

Donna Pruvidenza would not be hurried. Half-listening to the ills of life that had reduced a person of her worth to the one inherited room that was her sole remaining property, I noticed that the nails ranged from cobbler's tacks to blacksmith's sizes and even to crooked board nails.

In spite of all reassurances, my guest was ill at ease; but no hoodoo could lessen the innocent satisfaction with which, pursing her lips and arching her brows like an old-fashioned New England spinster, she pouted out the river of her talk until she came at last to the great discovery.

Someone had hidden the lemon in her oven. There it might have stayed, she said, till the viaticum was brought and the passing bell was tolled for her, since she never had flour with which to bake, if she had not touched it accidentally while reaching for a brush she kept inside.

Donna Pruvidenza is old, nearly hump-backed and half-blind. She is poor, short of temper and sharp of tongue, the butt of many a brutal jest; but pride and an applauding conscience brought a smile of conviction to her lips as she said she must have been attacked because of envy.

"Dear Missy, I am envied," she assured me; "and where there is envy there is witchcraft, or there is the blow of the eye."

Someone must have entered her room while she was at mass, she thought, or receiving the evening benediction; some evil-minded neighbor who saw that, even if she was poor and condemned to live in a bare and squalid nest, good friends when they had a nice dish to eat often sent for her to enjoy it with them. Because of her friends some envious person must have said, "How she is respected! This morning So-and-So has sent her salted codfish! Such-a-One has given her a dress for the festa of San Pancrazio!"

There flashed through my mind a vision of the cast-off dinner dress left by some tourist to a charity fund in Taormina, which Donna Pruvidenza had trailed with dignity through the dust of the Corso.

"Dear little Missy," she concluded, "can any but the envious think me greedy if I accept now and then a cup of broth or even a little meat? Surely a person worthy of respect, an orphan without father or mother, ought not to suffer!"

"The family you mentioned," I ventured, "are not your friends?"

"Bad people!" It was not a month since Donna

DONNA PRUVIDENZA'S LEMON

Pruvidenza had begged her confessor to tell the man's wife that if she must throw at respectable neighbors words as hard as dog-killing stones, at least she should throw them gently! gently! And this was the answer—to hide in her house a charm, as if she were a witch!

"It is not that I fear!" she protested. "Not a leaf moves without the will of God; but"—she pushed her chair farther from the kerchief—"who would not shudder at the malignity that fills a lemon with nails?"

Through the open window there came the cry of a peddler! "Sixty brass pins for a soldo! Four yards of tape for a soldo! Look, females; Look and buy! 'Tis a sin to leave them!"

"Sixty pins for a soldo!" groaned Donna Pruvidenza; "and this is stuffed with nails!"

Her emphasis led me to ask, "Are nails worse than pins?"

"Signurinedda!" Donna Pruvidenza was shocked. "Nails fastened our Lord to the cross! Never before have I seen a 'gghiommaru' filled with nails!"

In the end, Donna Pruvidenza gave me the lemon. It was not likely to harm me, she said, since the sending was not against me; and as to herself, she was not afraid, though it would be well if I would promise not to throw it away but to burn it, first taking out the nails. These points settled, she pulled up her rusty black shawl around her shoulders and trotted away—a pathetic little figure, pursing her lips and smiling with the discreet happiness of those conscious of well-doing.

At the door she turned to say, "Cara Signurinedda, let all this remain between you and me."

I had no thought of betraying Donna Pruvidenza's secret, but an hour later when I returned to my room the box into which I had shut the lemon was on the floor, and Tidda the Bat, dusting cloth in hand, was gazing at the evil looking fruit with horrified curiosity. "I did not touch it," she said in explanation; "it went down."

Tidda 'a Taddarita has a way of bumping about the room as aimlessly as her namesake, the bat. This morning, whether dusting or bringing water, or lowering canvas screens against the May sun, her motions were even more hit-or-miss than usual. She did not pick up the lemon, and she could not keep her eyes away from it; she revolved around it, striking against whatever stood in the way. It was not until she stood at the open door, her tasks done, that she said, turning for once her brown and peaked face in my direction:

"Scusi; was that made against the Signurinedda?"

"No," I answered, stopping to pick it up.

"Jesus, Joseph and Mary! Jesus, Joseph and Mary!" Tidda crossed herself hastily, backing into the hallway. "For the love of God! Little Missy, don't touch the bewitched thing!"

I dropped the lemon into its box. "But since it is not against me——"

DONNA PRUVIDENZA'S LEMON

"For the love of God!" Tidda's face worked convulsively. "One sees that the Signurinedda does not understand such things!"

Tidda is a forlorn creature with high red cheekbones, shiny little African eyes and a low forehead covered with black hair. By trade she is a carrier of water. Morning, noon and night, an earthen quartara on her head, her small black-clad figure comes to our door. Sometimes when the domestic machinery stalls I find her at work inside.

Shutting the door with a blow of her broom, she poured out a flood of tales. Years ago there was a good woman in Taormina, she said, who used to give food to the prisoners in the jail. One day when this woman felt ill, a woman in the jail who was a witch asked her many questions and then begged her to bring an egg when she came back next day. The sick woman brought a fresh egg, laid by one of her own hens; but when the witch broke the shell it was full of broken glass. The sick woman at once felt well.

"That was long ago," I commented.

"But it's not six months," returned Tidda, "since my chum found thorns in an orange stuck into the wall beside her door; and who knows what might have happened if she had not asked the priest to bless it?"

"At least nothing did happen," I suggested. "Someone is ringing."

"Something happened to Vitu 'u Moddu," Tidda

persisted, shaking her head impatiently as a bell sounded from a neighboring room.

"The Signurinedda knows Vitu the Soft, steward for the English in the villa? Two years ago Vitu fell so ill that no medicine could help him. Month after month he lay groaning in bed till one day a hunter thought he saw a bird fly into a hole in the rock above Vitu's house. The Signurinedda knows the place, under the hill on the path to Monte Ziretto? So the hunter climbed up and put his hand into the hole; but it was not a nest of sparrows that he pulled out; it was the head of a kid full of pins. Vitu's wife called a priest to undo the spell, and Vitu has been as well ever since as he was before."

Again the bell rang, but Tidda had plunged into the case of an uncle saved from death by a witchfinder's discovery of a thorn-filled potato. From the uncle she jumped to the tale of a bedridden woman who walked as soon as her son had dug in a place pointed out by a passing stranger. "Your ills are before your door," the stranger said, and indeed they found the dried liver of an animal.

"Bad people do these things," she concluded, as a third time the bell jangled; "witches who ought to die like dogs! Why does the Signurinedda handle things made by witches?"

After luncheon a fear that Tidda might gossip about the lemon was confirmed when Pietro detained me in the dining-room to see a photograph of the palace on Staten Island inhabited by his brother. The "palazzo," which looked like a brick tenement, was distant from New York one little hour by train-in-air, steamship and train-of-fire; and to it he wished to send a package for which would I please write the address?

Pietro did not approach abruptly the topic of Donna Pruvidenza's lemon. The parcel was to contain razors, for Pietro's brother is a barber, and in New York razors cost too much money. There were to be stockings knitted by his signora—Pietro's wife is his "lady"—and a loaf of baked "ricotta," which is curd sun-dried and browned in an oven. For his brother's children there was a quantity of a hard almond sweet called "torrone."

It was while we were planning the packing of these articles that Pietro began a gently superior discourse on Tidda's cowardice and my curiosity as to lemons. A lemon turned into a pincushion was only a lemon. He ought to know, for had he not paid more than four hundred lire for the finding of a piece of meat stuck full of nails? And had it done him any good to have the nails taken out? Not a particle! Once he had believed such foolishness, but now he knew better.

"Four hundred lire!" I exclaimed; for Pietro is a plodding man of fifty, careful of his money.

"Four hundred lire!" he repeated with mild cynicism; was he not then a judge of such matters?

The thing had happened some years earlier, he

said, when he had given up his profession as a waiter, because his signora had tired of starching shirts and collars. "A waiter," he exclaimed, with a glance at his linen, "must always be clean."

So he had opened a shop for the sale of salted codfish, oil, wine and macaroni—such things as people need. But trade was not good, and to make matters worse a great oil jar leaked one night, and the oil ran over the floor and even into the street. Now to spill oil is a bad sign, and for days his lady was ill with worry.

Just at this time there came to their door one morning a woman who begged food. When she had eaten and rested, the poor woman seemed grateful, and offered to search the house for the evil influence that interfered with sales. When he and his signora understood that she had such power they agreed gladly. So for days she searched, eating always of the best, until at last she declared the place was haunted by a demon.

"We believed her," said Pietro with melancholy scorn of past credulity, "because, though we never saw anything, we often heard a 'pum! pum!'"

"E-e-e—I think now," he added with hesitant utterance that was not yet a stammer, "that she may have made the noise herself."

The woman carried away a suit of Pietro's clothing, which she said must be burned. "It was a good suit," he sighed reminiscently.

One night she led him and his lady to a lonely

place behind a church, when she made them dig at the roots of a clump of fichi d'India. The charm was buried there, she said; but they found nothing. The next night she took them down to the sea and walked into the water until it reached her knees. There she searched a long time, and when she came back she brought a bag that held a piece of meat full of broken glass and nails. This, she said, was the source of their misfortunes; some rival had pierced the flesh as if it had been their bodies.

The woman took the nails out of the meat and burned it. Then she sprinkled salt and water in the house, repeating charms. She demanded much money because she had found the charm in the sea.

"That proved her clever?" I questioned.

"Yes," conceded Pietro; "at least she said so."

"Of course," confirmed Tidda, who had bumped into the room and was picking up dishes. "The Signurinedda sees that a charm hidden in a house may perhaps be found quickly, and so do little mischief; but what is lost in the sea only a person of great power can find. It goes on working until it kills the one against whom it was made. For a charm thrown into the sea there is no pardon; God cannot forgive such wickedness."

"Business was no better," said Pietro skeptically, comforting himself with bites at a medlar. "I gave up the shop and came back to waiting."

Before the day was done I took the lemon to the padrona's sewing room, begging her to check

Tidda's tongue, though I had no faith that our silence would prevent the spreading of Donna Pruvidenza's news.

The mistress of our house is so wise in the lore of the people that whatever of interest I hear is submitted to her judgment. Looking up from her mending, she regarded curiously the discolored lemon, which was still leaking juice and bulging and shrinking around the puncture of the rusty nails. Poking it with her plump thimble finger, she told me fresh tales of haps and mishaps with charms. Often as she had heard of such things, never before, she said, had she seen one.

"But fear of witchcraft," I queried, "is not yet forgotten?"

The padrona looked long toward the courtyard beyond the terrace, where her husband and the cook were bowling. "Fear of lemons like this, yes," she said finally. "If a woman's neighbors think her a witch and threaten her with this counter-witchcraft, one sees the threat is harmless, because such people do not know the proper words to use when sticking in the nails."

"What proper words?" demanded Maria, the laundress, checking her song, "The sun which goes to-day returns to-morrow," as she came in from the terrace with an armload of folded towels.

Maria told us the tale of a girl who once picked up a lemon from the ground, when teased about her betrothed, and in a joke began pricking it with

DOOR CHARMS FOR EVIL EYE

DONNA PRUVIDENZA'S LEMON

thorns. "This in his head!" she said. "This in his arm! This in his leg!" The girl was washing at the riverside, and no sooner had she and the others reached home with their bundles of dry clothes than she heard that her betrothed had come from reaping seized with terrible pains. Running back to her washing stone, she found the lemon and pulled out the thorns. Next morning her lover was well.

"What words did that girl know?" laughed Maria, as she took up her song again and started towards the garden to pick towels from the flowering bushes. "The thorns are the thing!"

In Sicilian magic few acts are performed without accompanying incantations. The padrona's reminder, therefore, of the need of words decided me not to touch the nails until I knew whether their extraction required a formula. I did not hope to learn the putting in of nails. "Release, yes; bind, no," is a saying in the mouth of every adept. But if to black magic no one would own, in the white magic of undoing a spell someone might instruct me.

Gna Angela, called the Fox, who censes houses to drive out the evil eye, and Gna Vanna, the Grasshopper-eater, who claims uncanny powers, because of her protection by the "ladies," were the women I planned to consult. I should not have thought of Za Tonietta, whose dealings with the unknown are more limited, had I not come across her next morning, crouched in a recess of the ivy-clad wall near my own door. Indeed, at first nothing was farther from my thoughts than magic, for Za Tonietta's grizzled hair stood up in moist rings, her kerchief was open at the throat, and she was gasping "As God wills," bent double with asthma.

I sat down beside her in the flickering shade of the pepper trees, and after a while, when the struggle for breath became less violent, she told me that she was on her way to a house where a death had occurred, to sprinkle holy water, which she had taken from the three fonts of the Matrice, the mother church. In her lap there lay a bottle which still carried a Worcestershire-sauce label.

While we rested there came in sight a swarm of children playing a favorite game of our street—conducting a saint's procession. Down the winding road, carried on the shoulders of ivy-crowned boys and girls, advanced a toy Vara, adorned with candles and flowers, and holding, instead of a church image, a rude print of Sant' Alfio and his brothers. Ahead marched a tiny boy ringing a bell to stop and start the bearers. Behind flocked children shouting vivas.

"As God wills!" wheezed Za Tonietta, when the procession, to which she had hardly lifted her eyes, had gone its way. Sant' Alfio was a powerful saint, but it was to our own San Pancraziu, great father of the people, that she prayed:

[1] To the ten thousandth time we raise
San Pancraziu's high praise;
We praise him daily when we wake,
Who Taormina safe doth make,

she recited, smiling drearily. She had prayed much to be well, but at night she could not lie in her bed.

In Za Tonietta's windowless house asthma is not as God, but as building custom wills. Waiting till she dragged herself to her feet, I rose also; and then, remembering my errand, showed her the lemon.

The result startled me. At sight of the shrunken, ominous-looking thing Za Tonietta dropped back into her seat, clutching at the bag of amulets pinned under her dress, and racked by a spasm of coughing that shook her bowed old figure. When at last she panted that the lemon was "to die! to die!" I had had more proof than I liked that it could do mischief.

As Za Tonietta moved wavering down the road with her holy water, and I turned towards Gna Vanna and the village, I could think of nothing but the cruelty of fear which ages of life had not driven out of so radiant a world.

In the morning sun the gray-green mountain wall above the town drew so close that I could follow the movements of men and goats up and down the zigzags, to and from the old castle of Taormina, and the church of the Madonna of the rock.

[1] A la decimila vota
Lu ludamu San Pancraziu;
Lu ludamu la matina
Ca prutiggi Taormina.

Over the gray walls between which winds our road, purple flower clusters hung from the patience trees. From cypress and cedar, and even from tall eucalyptus dropped curtains of honeysuckle. Olives were blossoming green, and the lemon gardens in white bloom scented the air.

The village was out of doors. As trees gave way to gray-white houses, I came up with Cola the rope-maker, who had planted his wheel in a shaded spot and was rubbing down yellow lengths of cord with halved lemons.

Beside their doorstones were the gossips, washing, knitting, spinning, making nets and nursing babies. Men, too, had brought out chairs to the cobblestones, where they plaited fishtraps, cobbled shoes or, seated on the ground, twisted with fingers and toes store of rush twine against the wheat binding. Even the tinsmith had littered the street with petroleum tins to be knocked down to usable sheets of metal.

I found Gna Vanna standing over a wandering tinker who was drilling holes in the fragments of a thick earthen basin. "Have a care!" she warned the swart young Calabrian, as he raised and lowered the rude cross-bow contrivance that turned the point of his drill. "Have a care!" she repeated while he patched together the huge dish, straddling wire pins from hole to hole and poking in cement as a final operation.

Vanna looked cross, and as I stepped indoors to

avoid the tilt over pennies for the mending, I saw that an upset house had perhaps upset her temper. The once smoke-blackened walls were wet with whitewash, and in the middle of the spattered floor were heaped goods and chattels.

"Badly have I done!" she fretted, bringing in the big dish and setting it down anxiously. "The house was too dirty, but five lire they made me pay! Bad Christians! They broke the basin, and in a week smoke and flies will make things worse than before!"

There is a vent above Vanna's fireplace which smoke never finds.

Without the name of its owner the charm did not soothe Gna Vanna. As I took the cover off its box she signed an impatient cross or two, looking from it to me with irritation. The victim must be suffering pains in the ears, eyes and stomach, she asserted; and whose was the blame if I refused to take her to the house, so that she might drive out the witchcraft by her prayers?

"Vossia knows that I understand these things," she pursued with the air of an unappreciated genius, planting the tip of a skinny forefinger in the middle of her forehead. "There is no one else who understands them. Let them call me witch! Vossia knows that I am respected because I have broken many evil charms."

Whether in the end she would have relented and taken out the nails, I cannot tell; for as she jerked a chair from the piled up furniture, there crawled from some cave underneath her grandson Micciu and the white-faced kid, Sciuriddu. Fresh almond leaves satisfied "Little Flower"; but Micciu ranged the floor, dragging the kid by the red rag at his neck, scrambling after a dish of raw, shining fish and tugging at his one garment, a dingy little shift.

"Nanna," he teased, "take it off, grandma! It's hot!"

"Fui! Fui! Run away!" scolded Vanna; and the child, seizing a fish, darted towards the street, bumping into a fleshy, middle-aged woman who appeared in the doorway.

At sight of me, Comare Alfia, Vanna's sister-in-law, came forward with hesitation. Lowering herself into a chair, she sat in heavy silence, her round, not unkindly face set in lines of dissatisfaction. My chance was gone, and I was rising to yield the field when, responding little by little to complaints about the price of whitewashing, Comare Alfia gathered confidence, and put into Vanna's hand a thick knotted cord braided of red and green rags.

"What is it?" asked Vanna, glancing sharply from the braid to the lumpy face of her sister-in-law.

"I want to know," answered Comare Alfia; "what is it?"

Her suspicious eyes fixed on the cord, Comare Alfia explained that she had found it an hour before among the vine cuttings with which she was feeding the fire in her oven. It might be harmless, but she could not feel safe unless Vanna undid the knots, for her head ached and her stomach felt as if it also were tied in knots. It was just such a sending that two years earlier had killed her husband, and she knew well the wretches who had twisted the spell. On that very street they lived, not many doors away. They had quarreled with her husband over the price of two hens, and now perhaps they had braided this cord to twist and tie her vitals also. The law ought to punish such assassins.

Gna Vanna studied the braid which had been made the more deadly by three knots drawn tight. "It may be," she agreed, "a fattura."

Restored to good humor by her sister-in-law's openly expressed dependence, Gna Vanna asked me to show the lemon. At sight of the nails Comare Alfia displayed something like animation, while I tried to look wise over the charms. A fellow feeling being thus established, I was allowed to stay while Vanna conjured the harm that might have been planned against her sister-in-law's bowels.

First muttering formulas of which "name of God" was all I heard, she picked at the first knot until she had loosened and untied it, repeating the while:

> Hair of God and Mary's hair,
> Be called home this witchcraft sair!
> Let there be praised and thanked
> The most holy Sacrament

> And God's great Mother Mary
> And all the heavenly company.
> In the name of God and for Jesus' sake,
> Let this woman no harm take.

Comare Alfia, who sat hunched forward in her chair by Vanna's side, paid dolorous attention as Vanna smoothed the kinky strands and passed to the second knot, reciting while she tugged with persistent fingers,

> The ass, the ass, he came on feet four;
> It was St. Mark on his back he bore.
> In the name of God, for St. Pancras' sake,
> Let this woman no harm take.

The third knot was more difficult. "The knife!" called Gna Vanna impatiently. "Micciu, the knife!"

Micciu, who had strayed back to the doorstone, brought her from the table drawer a knife and the loaf he found with it. "Always bread in your mouth! Devil's face!" she ejaculated, kissing him as she cut a big piece. Then slashing the knot, she proceeded:

> Four loaves and four fishes,
> Out, I say, with ill wishes!
> Bright angel of the good light,
> In three words I break evil's might.
> In the name of God and of St. John,
> If there's harm, I cut; 't is gone.

While Vanna unbraided the strands she continued to recite charms for good measure. Comare Alfia brightened enough to twitch her white kerchief straight, so that the knot came under her chin. When I left the house she was gathering the red and green rags to burn, and Gna Vanna was repeating,

> [2] Star of the Eastern light,
> Never back but forward bright.
> To the three, to the three, to the three,
> And even to the twenty-four.
> Now this witchcraft is no more.
> In Jesus' name I undo the charm;
> Never more shall it work harm.

Though Gna Vanna had recited nothing over the lemon, I felt sure that, if I had been able to take her to Donna Pruvidenza, her procedure, as to the nails, would not have differed in essentials from her conjuring of the knots. It was to get, if possible, a different method that I set out in the afternoon to find Gna Angela, the Fox, who is perhaps wiser in old lore than Gna Vanna.

May in Sicily is summer and the town was taking its siesta. Shops were shut as I passed through the Corso, streets empty. Nothing stirred but dart-

> [2] Stidda di lu luveri,
> Veni avanti e mai arreri!
> A li tri, a li tri, a li tri
> E sinu a li ventiquattru;
> Ssu malunatu è sfasciatu.
> Pi lu nomu di Gesu,
> Sciogghiu ssa fimmina;
> E nun mi avi nenti chiu.

ing lizards. Even the blackbirds were silent in the many cages ranged against the house walls. But while I climbed to the high under-the-castle quarter of Taormina, a little breeze began to wake the sea. Its effect was magical. Heavy black wooden doors opened, and from under round-arched doorways came women carrying water jars that lay slantwise on their heads as they started towards the fountains. Women appeared on little iron balconies taking in dry clothes from long cane poles. The tottering old people at the Hospice crept out on their terrace. Sounds arose of chatter and singing.

From a distance as I approached Gna Angela's house I saw her across the way from her door, sitting at her netting beside the wall towards the sea. She was alone; but even while I hurried forward, there appeared two women coming over the hill from an opposite direction. They reached her first. There was a moment of gesticulation; and then, picking up the chair in which she had been sitting and another over which were folded the brown lengths of her net, Gna Angela crossed the road with the newcomers.

It was too late to retreat; but instead of following the three into the house, I sat down on the doorstone, watching the chickens that old Zu Paulu, Gna Angela's husband, was taking one by one from under a tall, rush-woven cage and protecting from evil eye by tying red rags under their pinfeathery wings.

The two women, who looked like mother and daughter, were telling their errand when Gna 'Angela came to the door to wish me good-day; and so it chanced that I overheard their anxiety about the younger one's husband. Desperately ill he was, the mother said, in New York. The news had come a week before, and now for seven days they had had no letter. Was he getting better or was he dead? Would Gna Angela tell them?

More than once I had heard Gna Angela, the Fox, pronounce on the health of absent relatives, so that her agreement to this request did not surprise me.

Drawing her chair into the breeze at the doorway, she sat almost at my side, clasping her hands about her knees and composing herself to immobility. Little by little her faded eyes became veiled, and her queer animated old face put on a mask devoid of expression. Surreptitiously I pulled out a pencil, for I guessed that she would recite the so-called "paternoster of San Giuliano," protector of travelers.

Presently, crossing herself, she muttered "Jesus, St. Joseph and Mary!" and then words began to pour from her lips in a rapid, colorless stream. Faster and faster, becoming almost inarticulate, ran the river of sound. It seemed a long time before, suddenly as it had begun, the flow stopped. The gray old figure straightened itself. Gna Angela's eyes brightened, and her half-opened mouth snapped shut with a look of satisfaction.

"Your spouse is well," she said to the younger woman. "You will soon hear from him."

"Are you sure?" the two demanded. There followed a hubbub of questions.

"It is certain," replied Gna Angela in the tone of one who finishes a simple matter. "It is not I who tell you; it is San Giuliano himself, the miraculous saint who never mistakes. Did you not hear? The words came quick and smoothly; I said it three times through without missing a syllable. It is San Giuliano himself who says it: Your spouse is well."

As Gna Angela spoke she rose, dismissing her guests. Old, sinewy, a little bent, she seemed, as she leaned against a doorpost, indifferent as a sybil to the doubts of the ignorant.

"Come, daughter," she said, touching my shoulder to indicate the turn of another client.

The women were impressed. Dropping coppers into her hand, they came out of the house, bidding a cheerful good-by to Zu Paulu as they trudged down the road, two black figures in the white Sicilian sunshine.

"Come, daughter," repeated Gna Angela, inviting me into the bare little room.

By repute Gna Angela is a witch, able to call up spirits of the dead; but the trade, if such it is, yields her little more than the bed, the bench and the chest of the old song of the dancing master:

> Trois pas du côté du banc
> Et trois pas du côté du lit;

Trois pas du côté du coffre
Et trois pas—revenez ici.

Driving out a hen from the heap of stones that served her as fireplace, Gna Angela questioned me with a look as she sat down before the broken chair that held the unfinished net.

"Won't you say the paternoster again?" I begged, for I had not succeeded in writing the half of the old charm, which for who knows how many centuries, anxious women have invoked for news of travelers.

"Again?" she queried.

I showed my pencil. "Please; say it slowly for me."

"Ah," she said good-naturedly; "you will tell it to the wise in your own country. Listen then, daughter."

Dropping again the reed netting needle, she loosened her neckerchief, uncovering her corded yellow throat. Then she looked meditatively at me and away again, and the flood of words recommenced. I could not keep pace with it, and a request to repeat caused Gna Angela's jaw to drop and her brown and yellow mottled face to look hopelessly bewildered.

That old gossip, Pliny, says that in order to ensure the exact recital of certain Roman public prayers, one assistant read the formula in advance of the celebrant, while others kept silence in the audience and played the flute to shut out extraneous sounds. A slip in the prayer spoiled the omens.

Gna Angela had no help, and a slip in the paternoster was disastrous. To ensure success she rushed to the end on impetus. If she paused, the thread broke.

As nearly as I could catch it, what she recited ran:

> Come the true cross to adore
> Which down from Calvary they bore;
> May grace and light our spirits foster
> To say St. Julian's paternoster.
>
> Once St. Julian went to the chase;
> In his hand his good stick found its place.
> To Mary, great Virgin, chance him led;
> Great St. Julian spoke and said:
> At this court good friends we be;
> From evil foes deliver me;
> From doctors, too, and jails unkind
> And from misfortune's cruel mind;
> From raging demons set me free,
> From mad dogs' bites safe let me be.
> Should any wish to do me harm,
> May a dead man's heart inspire his arm;
> But mine the heart of a lion strong
> That wreaks its wrath on doers of wrong.
>
> This morn I rose up from the sod,
> And my right foot with speed I shod.
> St. George's sword to my side I girt;
> Mary's mantle shielded me from hurt.
> Then down I went unto the sea,
> Where one and all my foes met me;
> Down on their faces they fell in the mould,
> While I stood up like a lion bold.

> Be it on the road, or indeed safe at home,
> Come with me, Saviour, where'er I roam.
> Be it on the road or indeed by the way,
> Come with me, Mary mother, I pray.
> Be it on the road or indeed on the plain,
> Come with me ever, St. Julian.
> Be it on the road or when danger is near,
> Come with me ever, St. Antonine dear.

This St. Julian is he of whom the Golden Legend says that, having slain in ignorance his father and mother, he did penance in long wanderings. Indeed Dr. Pitrè gives a form of the paternoster which begins:

> His mother he slaughtered, his father he slew;
> St. Julian he to the mountain flew.

I have heard a similar version from a woman who, instead of resorting to a witch, had memorized the charm and would retire into a corner, shut her eyes and recite it whenever her husband, whose business took him much from home, failed to return at an expected time.

When Gna Angela had resumed her netting and I with apologies for my many questions, had produced the lemon, I discovered a witch's limitations. Gna Angela could cure headache by driving away its cause—the evil eye; she could tell me of the life or death of friends beyond the ocean; but before the lemon she confessed ignorance.

Touching gingerly the nails which, as the skin of the fruit grew dry, began to stick out like chevaux de frise, she said it would take strong magic, the magic of a book, to undo such a spell. Once she had known a priest who had a book of the fifteenth century. (Fifteenth-century charm-books are most esteemed.) She had no book. I must ask a priest to read a prayer over it, first putting on his stole.

My second call having proved even less satisfactory than the first, I planned as I left Gna Angela's door to submit the lemon as a last resort to a witch of whose powers I had heard much—a woman who lived at Piedimonte at the foot of Etna. But the notion was short-lived. I had not yet reached the flight of steps at the head of my own street when an urgent voice said, "Cara Signurinedda!" And there was Donna Pruvidenza harnessed by a string to a packing case which she was dragging through the Corso with a serene disregard of on-lookers.

"Dear little Miss!" she repeated in a tone of importance and uneasiness. "That badly educated, the wife of —— screams maledictions against all who respect me! You have destroyed the lemon?"

Donna Pruvidenza's apprehensions had so increased that it was not until I had promised immediate action that she demanded admiration of the packing box. "Firing for weeks! Hot food I shall have!" she exulted. "Ah, Missy, ——'s wife has reason to envy me my friends!"

The lemon went to the kitchen fire. I have kept the pins, the needles, the screws and the nails. For

DONNA PRUVIDENZA'S LEMON

Donna Pruvidenza's sake I recited as I pulled them out, a revised edition of one of Gna Vanna's charms:

> Star of the Eastern light,
> Never back but forward bright.
> To the three, to the three, to the three
> And even to the twenty-one;
> Now this lemon is undone.
> Thus do I take out the nails,
> And thus the spell of all harm fails.

CHAPTER III

Cola Pesce

> The king seized the goblet—he swung it on high,
> And, whirling, it fell in the roar of the tide:
> "But bring back that goblet again to my eye,
> And I'll hold thee the dearest that rides by my side;
> And thine arms shall embrace as thy bride, I decree,
> The maiden whose pity now pleadeth for thee."
> —*"The Diver." Schiller.*

It was at his sister Brigida's wedding party that Cola asked why I did not come oftener to the marina to fish with him.

"The Taormina boats are blind," I said; "I like better the fishing boats of Catania, because they have eyes, and they are painted with saints."

"We carry our saints in our hearts," retorted Cola, "instead of painting them on our boats."

Then he left me to take his place in the tarantella. Brigida was dancing, a brown girl with almond-shaped Arab eyes; and the bridegroom and others of the fisherfolk. The clear space for the dancers had but the length of twelve bricks of the uneven pavement; the musicians had barely room for their elbows; but the "Sucking Babes" played—it was the "Babes" and not the "Rats," I think, who sent

CATANIA BOATS HAVE EYES

music; the "Babes" and the "Rats," conservatives and radicals, do not mix at weddings any more than in politics—till the floor shook, and the basket-work fish traps that hung in clusters from the ceiling, shook also.

It was hard to move without stepping on plates, and Brigida's mother was still dishing roasted kid and spaghetti to be sent to the neighbors. Brigida's sister served wine and "Spanish bread," which is a powdery sponge cake; and later, when the day declined towards sunset, and we had helped Brigida out of her cotton house dress, and into her dove-colored wedding silk and white scarf, and had stood about pretending not to see her weep as she kissed the hands of her father and mother in good-by, we walked in procession through the narrow streets conducting Brigida and Santu to the little whitewashed upper room that was to be the new home.

It was after we had admired the knitted counterpane of the big white bed and the fine oil lamp and the colored prints of saints and the royal family, and the band had played at the door, and we had said good wishes to the couple that, as Cola and I walked away together, he said, "Signorina, Occhietti, who fishes from Giardini, has a Catania boat; I shall borrow it, and my father and I will take you fishing to-morrow morning."

"After all, I prefer the Nuovo Sant' Alfio," I answered.

Cola's boat, the New Saint Alfio, was an old and

leaky tub as long ago as when I first saw Cola perched on the wall by the highway above the beach at Isola Bella, kicking together his hard little-boy heels and hailing every passing tourist with, "Voli battellu? Andiamu a li grotti?"

The poor old boat has been fishing by night and taking tourists to the grottoes by day from then until now, when Cola has done his military service and feels himself a man; so I repented that I had scorned so tried a friend as the sea-worn saint and had longed for painted boats with eyes.

"We'll ask Occhietti to come with us," said Cola, "and bring his boat, the San Pancraziu."

And so it happened that when I opened my door at three o'clock next morning a dark figure that stood leaning against the wall on the opposite side of the Via Bagnoli Croce started towards me from under the red-flowering pomegranate tree, and there was Cola, carrying a little lantern and a big basket, the padded rim of which was stuck full of the many hooks of a baited trawl.

"Why have you brought the trap?" I asked, for setting a trawl is not lively fishing. "Let us lift some pots for lobsters."

"We shall lift lobster traps," said Cola. "Come on! Father has gone down already."

There were stars in the blue-black sky, and the Fisherman's Path, which drops sharp and steep from Taormina to the sea, is cut for the most part against the bare rock face of the mountain; but when our stump of a candle flickered out, I could have wished for another to relight the tiny lantern, for the zig-zags are rough, and here the heavy leafage of a carob tree, and there a miniature pass, left us in thick warm darkness without vision. Even on the blindest turns Cola's bare feet trod boldly as if it were noon; but my groping hands made sad acquaintance in the long steps down from stone to stone with dusty brambles and the harsh stubble of cut forage, or the dry white stems of wormwood, for it was mid-June, when the Southern world is burnt and gritty. There was not a growing thing along our way except thistle heads and the pink blossoms of an oleander shrub. But at last we passed under the walls of the inn that stands by the high road and so down to the water, just as a low pale streak in the East began to hint the dawn.

At the little curving harbor between Isola Bella and the rock of Capo Sant' Andrea we found grizzled old Vanni, who is Cola's father, and Turriddu, his cousin, putting rollers under the bow of the New Saint Alfio and the equally battered Madonna della Rocca, and drawing the two boats down the beach. Occhietti's long Catania-built boat, the San Pancrazio, was just coming up to the landing rock through the narrow clear way between the stones.

Occhietti, like his boat, is named Pancrazio; but his little twinkling eyes make him Occhietti as inevitably as Turriddu's thirst makes him Acquafrisca. Occhietti had been spearing fish all night by the light of a gas torch, many-branched, like the horns of a stag, a light of which most of the older fishermen strongly disapprove.

"Very beautiful, Vossia!" he said exultingly, holding up to view in the yellow flare, a big poulpe, all stomach and arms.

"A beauty of a polyp!" exclaimed Turriddu.

"Splendidu!" cried Cola.

"Magnificu!" I echoed as in duty bound.

"Beauty of a torch!" growled Vanni, who is not moved often to such ill-temper. "Vossia knows that the light goes down into the water and burns the fish, so that they do not taste good; and little fish that are not caught are burned so that they never grow well."

"Beautiful pennies to pay for the gas!" taunted Occhietti, dropping the devil fish and poising his long-handled trident. "Some boatmen have not the heart to put out the money!"

"A stomach-twisting to you!" snarled Vanni.

"Did you ever hear," I asked in a hurry, "of the old Greek of Syracuse who ate a poulpe a meter long and ached so with colic after it that his doctor told him to dispose quickly of his affairs? 'I have disposed of all but the head,' he groaned, dying; 'and if you will bring it, I will dispose of that also.'"

"It is true the stomach must be strong," grinned Occhietti; "but a good eating of polyp is worth a twisting of the inwards."

"Come on!" he said sharply to the boy who stood

at the oars; and the San Pancrazio slid away over the warm black water to lie in wait for more poulpes under the rock shadows of the Beautiful Island.

"Deaf doctors to you, and dead druggists!" muttered Vanni, angry at the desertion.

Turriddu had hung two great fish-traps shaped like beehives to the bow-post of the Madonna della Rocca; he pushed out leisurely behind Occhietti. Cola brought oars from the fish-house on the beach and a longish cane with a hook at the end and a heavy spear. Then we, too, with Vanni, climbed aboard, and the tubby Nuovo Sant' Alfio took the water last of the three. Cola's trousers were rolled up to the knee, and as he stood pushing forward his clumsy oars tied each to its single oar peg, his dark figure took just the attitude of the rower in one of the Herculaneum pictures.

Like most of the Taormina boats, the Nuovo Sant' Alfio is heavy and squat, hardly more than fourteen feet long, with three thwarts and decked a little at the bow. Her sea-keeping furniture is as dingy as her planks—two traps swinging at her bow-post, tangles of net like mops stowed under the bow seat, cheek by jowl with a basket for bread, a fat jug for carrying water, and a flask for oil; and in her side cleats, and under foot, knives, stones for weighing fish and coils of rope twisted of rushes so roughly that the ends bristle at every joining.

We were outside of Isola Bella, and Vanni was setting the trawl when we began talking about Cola

Pesce. It takes time to put out four hundred hooks, passing each through the hand to make sure it is running true and is well baited. First, Vanni threw overboard one of our rope coils. A stone tied in a loop went to the bottom, and at the other end floated slices of sea-bleached cork strung on the rope like little islands. Near these floats he tied the trap. Each drop line with its hook was two meters long, perhaps, and each was separated by several feet from its neighbors.

The pale streak in the East was turning crimson, but the sea was blacker than before. Turriddu had put out a trolling line at each side of the Madonna della Rocca, and had headed North beyond our view. In the distance towards Naxos gleamed the drifting lights of a dozen torches. From the beach beyond Capo Sant' Andrea came the distant shouts of men hauling a seine.

Of a sudden one of Vanni's hooks, as it went overside, caught in floating pumice, such as is driven at times through the Straits of Messina from Stromboli. We took aboard some spongy pieces, for the floors of Taormina are scoured and the hearth for the winter fire is lined with pumice.

"Do you often find it like this in open sea?" I asked.

"Oftener at the beach," said Cola. "When the current sets North it will wash ashore at our marina."

"Like the body of Cola Pesce?" I suggested.

COLA PESCE

"Like Cola Pisci," to my surprise assented Cola.

At Messina I once went fishing with an old man who prattled of the legendary diver who inspired Schiller's ballad as of a hero well remembered; but though tradition says that the body of Nicola, the Fish, who plunged into the whirlpool of Charybdis to gratify a whim of Frederic II, the Suabian, was cast up at Taormina, and though the tale itself is one of the commonest told in Sicily, never before had I heard his name among our fishermen.

"Just where did they find Cola Pesce?" I pursued.

"How should I know?" returned Cola, who is of the newer days, scornful of old fables. "It is my father who talks of Cola Pisci," he added.

By this time the trawl was set, and Vanni was dropping the buoy and anchor. I was silent until he had finished; then, as the Nuovo Sant' Alfio, now half a mile beyond the island, turned slowly towards its outer ledges, I said, "Aren't there dolphins out yon? They remind me always of Cola Pesce."

Vanni is taciturn when his son is with us, and I glanced towards his end of the boat without much hope of drawing an opinion. "They bring bad weather," was his only response at the moment; but after a little, pulling off his sun-faded cap and scratching among the curls of his grizzled hair, he went on slowly:

"In the days of to-day there is no one who speaks of Cola Pisci. The young men have never heard of him. But my mate and I reason together about him once in a while, because we are of the old times. My 'cumpari' does not wish to believe it, but I hold that Cola Pisci deceived the king."

"You think," I asked, "that he was not drowned?"

"No," said Vanni. "There are those who hold that he swam away under the sea, because he was half man and half fish; but I say that he deceived the king. My chum says that the king threw into the sea a cup of gold; but my grandfather, who died very old, always told me that it was a golden plate that twinkled with precious stones."

Vanni spoke deliberately, planning his argument.

"And the king threw this plate into the round whirlpool that they call the 'Carnation'?"

"Yes, Charybdis. And the king said to Cola Pisci, 'If you go to the bottom and bring it up to me again, it is yours!' And Cola threw himself into the sea and brought back the king's plate in his hand. 'There it is, Majesty!' he said. And the king gave it to him as he had promised. But then the king threw in a ring, and told Cola he must go down a second time and bring this up also.

"Why?" demanded Vanni, his bronzed wrinkled face asking the question as earnestly as his tone. "Why did the King say to Cola Pisci, 'Again you must go down and you must fetch me this ring?'

"Because," replied Vanni to his own question, "my grandfather said that when Cola brought back the golden plate he had not been to the bottom. How did he know? My grandfather's ancients said that Cola had not been gone long enough to get to the bottom; and they were fishermen. A fisherman always knows the depth of water. The boatmen of Messina must have told the king how many fathoms deep is Charybdis. And then the plate——"

Vanni finished the sentence with his hand, rocking it to show the dipping motion with which a flat object sinks slowly, like a falling leaf.

"Understand, Vossia?" He repeated the dipping motion. "It was still near the surface when Cola reached it. It was for this that the king sent him down again, to go really to the bottom, which Cola did not succeed in doing. You persuade yourself, Vossia?"

Vanni did not argue as a partisan. His heavy grizzled brows shadowed his puckered face, and he smiled good-humored admission of the perplexities of the case as he reasoned his way through it; but at the end he lifted his head with the air of one whom logic has satisfied. His "You persuade yourself, Vossia?" was less a question than a chance for me to affirm my conviction.

"But Cola's body," I queried, "where did it come to land?"

"My grandfather's ancients told him nothing of that," he answered. "Somewhere at the beach; or it might be yonder at the Grotto of the Bats."

In the tourist season the Grotto of the Bats becomes the Grotto of the Doves, and there are those who count its changing emerald lights more beautiful than those of the Blue Grotto of Capri. Looking across at its mouth in the wall of Capo Sant' Andrea was like regarding the grave of Poseidon; for Cola Pesce, who, according to Messina, was a marvelous diver who explored the bottom of the straits, and according to Vanni was a man who deceived the king, was but another phase, according to Dr. Pitrè's folklore studies, of San Nicola, and of Neptune, and even of Old Nick of Northern sailors.

"How deep is the water over there?" I wondered.

"Outside the grotto, six fathoms, perhaps——"

Vanni was marking "braccie" with outstretched arms when Cola, weary of his namesake, interrupted: "In the days of to-day men go under the sea in diving bells; but as to the past, such tales are fables. Ecco, our floats!"

Vanni and I were silent, a little shy before Cola's young wisdom. The Nuovo Sant' Alfio was now under Isola Bella, and just ahead floated another set of cork buoys. We had come to lift traps in search of bait for the larger traps that are set for lobsters.

Vanni took my place at the stern; and, fixing in place a small block and wheel, he seized the rope the corks supported, and passed it over the pulley. One hairy leg inside the boat and one outside, his sun-bleached shirt and trousers gray in the growing light, he presented a lean and still sinewy figure as he began to haul. The huge baskets came up slowly. As the first appeared at the water's edge, he redoubled his efforts, bringing it dripping into the boat, where it stood nearly three feet tall, its funnel-shaped entrance defended against escaping fish by a chevaux de frise of rush ends pointing up from the broad bottom.

Unpinning from the thimble top the small round cover, he shook into the boat a dozen or more of the tiny black fish that are called "little monks." Then, fastening the cover again with wooden pins, he rinsed the hive-shaped trap and tossed it at my feet, the very pattern, perhaps, of Pliny's "osier kipes" for taking "purples" for making dye.

But Pliny's traps were baited with cockles. In Vanni's there was nothing. "The little monks do not go in for food," he answered to my query. "They take delight in the traps; they go in to play. We do not bait them."

The little monks did not seem on pleasure bent that morning. One by one Vanni hauled traps until the boat was piled with them, as with a towering load of bubbles; and still we had taken little—a few monks, a few dozen shrimps, some wee red "ruffiani" and half a dozen "coralli," striped orange, white and green.

It was not until nine or ten traps were up that Cola pointed to rising bubbles. "Eels!" he exclaimed.

Vanni was working too hard to speak. He puckered his lips as if to whistle.

"The eels do like children with their mouths," explained Cola; "they whistle."

Bubble after bubble came to the surface and at last appeared the trap, which held two conger eels, each of six to eight pounds. The last trap should have held an eel, also, but instead there was a hole in its wicker side.

"Robber!" said Cola disgustedly. "He ate the monk and then bit out a hole and got away."

When the traps were all up, Vanni put them down again one by one, while the boat moved just enough to float them apart, the floats marking as before the end of the long rope on which they were strung. The two fresh traps that swung from the bow-post went down in place of the torn one and another which we carried away to be cleaned and mended.

By this time the stars had faded. The dark red streaks in the Eastern sky had paled to pink and gray, and the morning clouds were like delicate wings brushing the sky. In the clear dawn-light the straits narrowed up sharply to the North of us towards Messina, and the saddle of the mountains of Aspromonte was defined to the smallest detail. At one side of us was the rocky Isola Bella, at the other the red marble ridge of Capo Sant' Andrea. Behind us rose the hills of Taormina, parched and brown, more bare and rigid than in winter. The sea was smooth and silvery.

As the boat slid leisurely back to the trawl we had left almost an hour earlier, the pink in the

East brightened again until it was saffron. One held one's breath in sharp suspense waiting for the sun. Minute by minute the saffron became more vivid and the waiting more tense, until at last a knife-like gleam flashed above Calabria.

"Does the sun come up just the same in your country?" asked Vanni, while we watched the red crescent become a globe and slowly lift itself from the horizon. "They say it is the earth that moves; it does not seem so, but Vossia, who has been in many places and perhaps understands the seven languages of the world, should know."

The trawl as Vanni stripped it did not net us many fish. From the four hundred hooks we took not more than half a dozen "uopi," or "bo-opi"; brilliant little eye-shaped fish spotted with red; ox-eyes, according to their name, like those of Hera.

"Thieves!" again exclaimed Cola. "The fish eat the bait, and if they don't bite hard, they get away."

Turriddu's boat was now again in sight. He had taken in his trolling lines, and we headed out to meet him without bait-fish, for he was ready to haul the lobster pots sunk in deep water.

Before we reached him we could see that the trap refused to come. His straining figure silhouetted against sea and sky put forth its strength to no purpose. The powerful current running South from the straits must have twisted a rope, Cola said, under a rock. When we came up with the Madonna della Rocca he stepped aboard of her and took the oars, pushing at top strength against the tide, while Turriddu continued to haul.

The cousins were much alike, with the brown skin, straight nose and fine features of Arabs. Cola was much the younger, and his crisp hair, almond eyes and flashing teeth made him as he bent to his work, a swarthy model for a statue of labor.

There were sixty fathoms of water under the boat, Vanni said, and it would be hard to free the trap before the tide turned. Vanni measures the depth of water as the Romans used to do, by "braccie," though the Roman braccium was under five feet, while nowadays, it has become a fathom.

We left the two men at the task and headed south of the island. The men who had been fishing by torch-light had finished their work, and their boats scattered over the sea as far away as Capo Schizò were putting ashore. Over the water came the monotonous, long-drawn wail of their song:

> ". . . Quantu beddu star cu te.
> Lasciu patri,
> Lasciu matri,
> Lasciu casa
> Ppi star cu te."

At the beach South of Capo di Taormina some twenty men were hauling a "sciabica," a net that may be an eighth of a mile long, and that was ancient in the days of the Phœnicians. As the two files of men, leg-deep in water, pulled in the

red folds and coiled them in heaps on the sand, the
boat that had cast the seine followed it to shore.
Behind the arms of the net trailed its deep pocket,
which as it was drawn up and emptied, seemed to
hold but little, though a night or two earlier a net
had taken, between sunset and morning, more than
twenty-six hundred pounds of anchovies.

"To-night, maybe," said Vanni, "they will not
take the value of fifteen lire, and of that a third
goes to the net. But that is fishermen's luck. I
myself have paid ten soldi for bait and taken eleven
soldi of fish; and with one soldo how does one give
food to a family?"

He hesitated, then went on: "I am but one, and
if I were really to fill myself, I could eat all alone
five and a half soldi; that would be only half a kilo
of macaroni. The rich strangers who visit our
country pick a little of many things, but we eat
all we can get of one or two things—bread and
macaroni, or bread and beans. It is only at weddings," he finished confidentially, "that we arrive
at sweets."

As Vanni sent the Nuovo Sant' Alfio in among
the rocks that fringe the south side of Isola Bella,
he dipped a reed into his oil-jar and let fall on the
water a drop or two of oil. Then he put overboard
a tangle of net, dragging it across the bottom by
the hook on his cane rod, keeping within the circle
of the oil mirror. After a little he lifted the net
and took out of it, enmeshed by their spines, half

a dozen big brown sea urchins, such as sell two or three for a soldo.

"Shall we eat?" he suggested, bringing out the basket with bread and cutting the "fruit of the sea" as one might slice off the top of a lemon.

It was a pleasant place to breakfast. Isola Bella lies half way betwene Capo Sant' Andrea and the slate-black crag of the Capo di Taormina, which rose across the little bay to our south, broken into the rugged walls of miniature fiords, rough with jutting rocks, the haunts of rooks and wild pigeons, where even in the morning light the green and violet waves were somber.

On the other side of the boat, almost within hand reach, dropped the dark green leaves of a leaning fig tree, rooted in a crevice of the island rock.

There was little depth where we floated. At one minute through the crystal-clear, radiant water every breath of the bottom life was visible; at the next the rock reefs were hidden by streamers of many-colored sea weed. High overhead circled swallows. In the air was a clean, pleasant smell of salt and algæ.

"It's good here," said Vanni. He dipped a last morsel of bread into the cup of a sea urchin, and picked up again the handful of net and the pole.

With the urchins there came up presently a red starfish. Vanni laid it out on a thwart, separating its five points carefully.

"Fine and red," I commented. "It is against evil eye."

"Yes," he answered reservedly.

"You don't believe in the evil eye?"

"But, yes," he said, with a considering smile such as he had given to the case of Cola Pesce. Straightening his bent figure, he wiped his shaggy eyebrows with a red handkerchief. "Would the priests fumigate the altar and the people if there was no evil eye?" He seemed reasoning with himself as well as me. "The people see the priests swing the censer and they argue about it. They see that the fumigation is against evil eye."

"And the starfish——" I pursued.

The starfish was for my pleasure.

I spoke of a door that I passed almost daily, where a horseshoe was nailed between two starfish, and he said that now and then a family that had suffered a misfortune would pay a soldo or two for one large and red. Mothers asked for cowrie shells to hang at the neck of teething babies; papery white sea horses, too, would sometimes bring soldi; but these were not to be had often.

We talked of a hundred things—of the dogfish with teeth "like a mule," for fear of which the fishermen dare not nap in the boat in the long summer nights when they are afloat from evening until sunrise; and of the great tunny, which the Taormina men take at times in open sea, looking well not to get a slap from its tail. And minute by minute it grew hot even in the shadow of the wild fig trees; so hot that I had grown sleepy when of a sudden Vanni dropped his cane rod and began to row at full speed out to sea.

As the boat shot forward, I strained my eyes to find the object of this chase, but the sea was empty, white and shimmering. It was some minutes before I caught sight of an upstanding black fin. Giving one last powerful shove as we came within striking distance, Vanni dropped the oars; and, seizing Cola's heavy lance-headed pole, he cast it while the boat shot past what looked like a great black wheel. A streak of blood stained the water, and the wheel began to plunge and wallow.

We had speared a huge basking sunfish, better named in the Italian—a "mola," millstone. It was not easy to get it into the boat, for it was more than two feet in diameter, and may have weighed sixty pounds. At last it lay at our feet, to the eye a headless, tailless mass, inchoate but for its big black back and belly fins.

Vanni was more elated than he wished to show. The rough shagreen hide was thick and good for nothing, not even for leather, he said. The fish would be two-thirds waste, and the rest would sell for soup; it would fetch no more than a few lire; but as he took a long drink of water from the fat-bellied jug, and headed the boat again inshore, his eyes shone with satisfaction. Cola was the

LOBSTER POTS AND FISH TRAPS

THE SAN PANCRAZIO

cleverest lancer, he boasted, of all Taormina, though when he himself was young——

Cola could not beat him yet, I protested.

Fish were plentier in his young days. As a lad he lanced the mola for sport, he said; nobody would have eaten it. Did I know the "palamati"—the beautiful young tunny fish all blue and silver? Years ago the Taormina men caught them as now they catch anchovies, by the boatload; and sold them for good prices. But in the days of to-day when Christians eat meat, even on Fridays, like Turks, the few fish you get you must give away almost for nothing.

The Madonna della Rocca was still where we had left her. Cola and Turriddu must have had a hard time freeing the traps, for though the boat was piled high with them, the last were not yet in.

"She's all bubbly domes," I said; "like a floating mosque."

"A mosque? I don't know," returned Vanni. "When the tramontano wind blows we can't lift traps; the boat would be carried out to sea."

When Cola saw us approaching, he shouted, "You got the mola?"

"Yes," replied Vanni, with assumed indifference. "How many lobsters?"

"Eight," said Vanni, holding up in each hand a big red lobster. "Are there lobsters in your country, Vossia?" he demanded, as we came alongside.

"Ours are green," I said, "before they are cooked."

"Then they are not so beautiful."

Turriddu was baiting the last trap. Cola tossed him two or three little monks strung on a rush and he twisted it across the trap on the inside and pinned down the cover. They would follow us to the beach, they said, as soon as the nasse had been put overside, stopping on the way for another look at the trawl.

As we approached the landing rock we saw fish peddlers waiting with baskets and scales. The fishermen do not market their own fish, but sell at the water's edge, weighing in balances, each man against his own set of stones. Knives were at work in a minute, hacking the tough black skin off the mola.

It was not much past eight o'clock, but sky and sea were white with scirocco, and the chain of my watch was so hot that it scorched the hand. Their fish disposed of, the men would clean out their boats, light a fire on the beach, cook the remains of their bait fish, if there were any, and eat before going up to Taormina.

I walked along the curve of the tiny beach, for while we were skirting Isola Bella I had noticed through an opening in the rocks, a pocket overgrown with acanthus; and I had a mind to have a closer look at the flowers. It hardly costs a foot-wetting to pass the ford that makes the broken rock an island. Split by storm and sun, eaten by the waves, Isola Bella is fantastic, a caprice of nature. There is only a handful of it, and it rises not many meters above the water, but its crags and precipices, its beaches and caverns, are as picturesque as they are lilliputian.

The little refuge it afforded from the heat was rock shade, for the scanty leafage of its sea-gray olive trees allowed the sun to pass almost without hindrance. In a cleft of the rock grew an aloe with a flower shoot twenty feet tall and thick as a young tree. Beyond this in a tangled glade surrounded by a thick scrub of resin-scented "scornabeccu"— the lentisk of Theocritus—rioted acanthus. The spikes of its white, purple-veined flowers rose above my head, mixed with Queen Anne's lace—wild carrots.

I do not know how long I had dallied, dreading the hot climb to Taormina, when there came a mutter of thunder. At sea level, rain in June is almost a prodigy. Under the rock parapet that skirts the shore it was impossible to see Etna, the barometer; but over the sea the sky had grown threatening. Cola and Vanni were still at the beach, and I hurried back to the fish house, taking a stool in the doorway to await developments.

To my query, "Is water coming?" Vanni answered, "With difficulty."

Ammazzacarusi was of a different opinion. His nickname, "Boykiller," handed down from who knows what incident, through who knows how many generations, belied the mild, white-haired old fisherman whose boat, the Santa Liberata, was drawn up beside Cola's. Glancing at the purple and gray cloud masses through which the sun still managed to dart an occasional beam, he said gloomily:

[3] "June rain;
Ruin in train."

"In my country," I ventured, "summer rains are good for the crops."

Patiently, painstakingly, speaking each in turn, they explained to me that this is impossible. Warm slow scirocco rains mildew the flowers of the olive and the vine, while the hail that comes with a thunderstorm cuts whatever it touches. If in my country it rained often in summer, how could any crops be raised?

"You understand?" concluded Vanni.

I assented, though I had scarcely listened. I was studying the pictures on Occhietti's boat. He had come ashore before us at daylight, and had left the San Pancrazio nearer the fish house than any other of the dozen boats in line, so that I could measure her against the tubby Taormina craft and see that she was ten feet longer than our boats, though smaller at that than many of her build at Catania, where the barche mostly carry sails.

But it was her shining colors that caught my eyes —her checker-board sides gleaming in yellow, red

[3] Acqua di Giugnu
Ruvina lu munnu.

and green. At one side of her curved bow-post was painted our black San Pancrazio, at the other his companion of Taormina, San Pietro. Her short stern-post carried San Giorgio, young and valiant; and, backed against him, a group of souls in the streaming flames of purgatory. Under the right bow Agramonti led a file of crusaders; under the left, Italian soldiers of to-day who fought in Tripoli. At the stern a fight between lion and gladiator vied with Judith cutting off the head of a limp and bloody Holofernes. Rows of cherubs enlivened the freeboard on the inside.

Most fascinating of all were the San Pancrazio's eyes. Since the days when Egyptian lords voyaged in painted barges on the Nile, boats have had eyes against the evil eye. At Siracusa the blue-painted boats that cross the Porto Piccolo wear pictured horns against witchcraft, as well as eyes with queer looped brows. At Catania there are boats with sharp protruding beaks like those of swordfish, and the eyes of these are round and fishy. But the eyes of the San Pancrazio, with winking lids and bushy brows, were grotesquely human.

"Fine, eh?" said Ammazzacarusi, noting my gaze.

I had scarcely answered, "Very beautiful! Even in the darkest night the San Pancrazio sees!" when there came forked lightning and a rattle of hail. Vanni was whittling pins for fastening the covers of his traps. The sight of his knife and of his figure in the doorway blotted out the boats and brought back to mind a June storm of the year before.

In memory I saw myself sitting in the doorway of the church of the Madonna della Rocca at Castiglione on the slope of Etna. Beside me there had been a bent little man who walked slowly with a stick. Behind us above the altar, smiled one of Gaggini's soft, smooth Madonnas, a golden chain falling between her hands. In front, I looked out on gray and yellow roofs of tumbled tiles pelted with hail. The bells of many churches were tolling.

Of a sudden there had come a blinding flash, and the old sacristan had shrunk behind the worm-eaten, iron-bossed door, tottering forward again after a minute and peering into the blackness to spy out the direction of the squall. I could see again his shaking arm as, opening a knife, he signed with it in air three great crosses, finishing with a furious stab towards the wind, his lips moving, his faded ayes agleam.

"That is a prayer?" I asked; every "scongiuro" goes by the name of prayer.

"Yes," he answered; "to cut the squall."

He had evaded telling me the words of the charm; an incantation is not taught to a passing stranger. "Three Fathers, three Sons, and three Holy Ghosts" was all I could coax out of him. But later, when the weather had lifted and his rheumatic old wife hobbled into the church and he had asked her with a man's superior smile, "Wert thou frightened?" he turned to me with pride, saying:

"The knife cut it; you saw. I have more than eighty-two years, I have seen many things and I know much that I tell to no one."

"What did the knife cut?" I persisted.

"The dragon's tail," he had said concisely. Waterspouts, whirlwinds and sometimes hail clouds are dragons because of their tails.

"The malignant spirit," his wife had added.

[4] Fraser says that the South Slavonian peasant shoots at hail clouds in order to bring down the hags that are in them; but for these two old Sicilians I fancied that the dragon itself was the evil spirit— had some such personality as had the south wind for the Psylli who, Herodotus says, went out to fight it because it had dried up their reservoirs.

Thinking of these things as I watched Vanni's knife, while we sat in the doorway of the fish house, I asked him if he knew a 'razioni to drive away the hail, or to cut the tail of the waterspout that so often on these coasts brings terror to fishermen.

"No," he said. "There are such 'razioni and they are useful, for there is peril in storm; but I do not know anybody who is skilled in them."

The scudding clouds dropped showers here and there over the sea, but on our beach there fell little water, and after no long time I was rising for the

[4] "Balder the Beautiful." Vol. 1, p. 345.

homeward climb when Ammazzacarusi lifted his brown weazened face with a friendly smile.

"If it is true," he said, "that before long Vossia must cross the sea to her own country, this knowledge would be useful to her. There is one who cuts the tail of the dragon for us; she is Filippa 'a Babba."

I thanked him, asked to have the lobsters brought up for me by the long way past the octroi, and took the shorter path.

It was not until next morning that I went to find Filippa 'a Babba, who is Filippa the Idiot—only by the sort of inheritance that makes Ammazzacarusi the Boykiller. Filippa must live in the short Via le Mura; but who wants her seeks her at the wall above the old steep road that comes up from Giardini past the chapel of the Madonna delle Grazie; a perch commanding every man, woman and ass that climbs out of the valley and giving a broad outlook over the sea.

It was at the wall that I found her with two or three comari, putting a black patch into a blue apron. In presence of the other women I did not venture questions about whirlwinds or waterspouts, but contented myself with looking at the light smoke which rose idly from the black cone of Etna.

The rain of the day before had been heavy on the mountain, for a long yellow tongue of roiled water streamed from the mouth of Alcantara, and on sea and slope the play of blues and greens was as vivid as in winter. The air was so still that the lemon gardens of Capo Schizò were doubled in the water.

One of the comari who sat on the gray round-topped wall was knitting the sole of a stocking for her husband in America. I picked up the leg which had lain at her side.

"Why is it?" she asked, "that in your country stockings make themselves in one piece?"

"Why do they make themselves here in two pieces?" I countered.

Comare Lia smiled indulgently at my ignorance. "One knows," she said, "that an American stocking is good for little because when the foot is worn one must throw the whole away. With us when the sole is gone one throws away only the sole. One unsews it and puts in a new one."

"But who will sew extra feet into the stockings of your husband in America?"

"Who knows?" returned Lia so soberly that I was glad to hear the melancholy call of a peddler "The lupine man is passing!" which broke up the party.

In the Via le Mura there had appeared the scraggy mule of an old peasant who comes to town with saddle-bags full of lupines, soaked till they are sodden to take out their bitterness, and from the doorways flocked women with plates and bits of paper, bargaining for one soldo's worth, or two.

Even when Filippa and I were left alone together,

we gossiped of twenty things before I had courage to say "dragon" to the plump comfortable looking old body whom I had associated always with cleaning and fine ironing. But she told me readily enough that an old fisherman had taught her grandmother how to cut the tail of the dragon.

"Sometimes when there is bad weather," she said, "the water goes up and up to meet the sky, and the sky comes down, down to meet the water, to destroy boats and trees and houses. But if you do as I shall tell you, the water will fall and the tempest become calm.

"You must take a white-handled knife of the sort used in pruning the vine shoots; wait," she said, "I will show you."

She hurried away up the street and came back after a minute bringing some of the dried vine cuttings that are used for firing and a knife so small that I asked if my white-handled penknife would not answer.

"Perhaps?" she said, looking at it doubtfully.

"You must sign three crosses in air," she continued, turning towards the sea, knife in one hand, a bit of vine in the other; and making three sweeping crosses such as I had seen at Castiglione. "And you must say:

"Whither goest thou, ugly fate?"

" 'I go to a bourne lone and far,
Where never singeth hen,
Nor shineth moon or star.'

"There drop the water without wrong.
Father, Son and Holy Ghost,
I cut the tail; remains the song."

As she reached the words, "I cut the tail," she slashed the vine shoot viciously.

"You have a knife," she concluded; "do you wish that I give you some vine shoots to take on board ship when you go to your own country?"

CHAPTER IV

THE CLEFT OAK

In a farmyard near the middle of this village stands at this time a row of pollard ashes which by the seams and cicatrices down their sides manifestly show that in former times they have been cleft asunder. These trees when young and flexible were severed and held open by wedges while ruptured children, stripped naked, were pushed through the apertures under a persuasion that by such a process the poor babes would be cured of their infirmity. As soon as the operation was over the tree in the suffering part was plastered with loam and carefully swathed up. If the part coalesced and soldered together, as usually fell out where the feat was performed with any adroitness at all, the party was cured; but where the cleft continued to gape, the operation, it was supposed, would prove ineffectual.—*Gilbert White's "Natural History of Selbourne,"* letter 28, Jan. 1776.

FOR a day or two after the festa my neighbors along the Via Bagnoli Croce talked of little but Sant' Alfio. The greatest miracle of the day, they agreed, had been worked for the dumb child in blue whom we had seen weeping at the altar. In the church she had not spoken; but later, on the car of the saints, she had said, "The bells of Sant' Alfio are ringing." One or two of the people claimed to have been near enough to hear her voice.

THE CLEFT OAK

"Now Vossia knows," they said with satisfaction; "now she has seen with her own eyes."

I was standing among a group of women at the door of Zu Saru, a bronzed fisherman who sat mending a fish-trap plaited of rushes. "Are there any Taormina children," I inquired, "whom Sant' Alfio has liberated?"

"But yes," said Zu Saru's wife, Lucia, who is blue-eyed like her husband, and whose yellow hair is sun-bleached to the color of tow. Her tone was one of surprise. "Here is Vincenzinu of Cumari Tidda. He was ruptured, and Sant' Alfio did the miracle two years ago."

Vincenzinu is Gna Vanna Pipituna's grandson. He was then a thin, silent four-year-old, brown as a Moor, with big, sober bright eyes. Zu Saru dropped the trap and caught him as he trotted clumsily past, riding a stick, and pulled up his one garment to show that his flesh was whole and smooth.

So it happened that when I passed Gna Vanna's door, and she called me inside to see the naked, uneasy chicks which her two white pigeons had hatched in their nest behind the bed, I inquired of her about Vincenzinu. She, too, caught the solemn youngster by his petticoat, and bribed him with green almonds to stand still for exhibition.

It was not true, she said, that Vincenzinu owed his liberation to Sant' Alfio. Tidda had indeed taken him to Trecastagne not only once but two years in succession. He had lain on the vara, and his father had sent money from New York to buy a two-pound wax candle. She herself had given a white kid, the one she had called "the little flower." But the saint did nothing. Tidda, her daughter-in-law, had been in despair. "But I understand such things," she concluded; "I said we must wait till the vigilia of San Giovanni."

Gna Vanna was cleaning hens' heads to make broth for Vincenzinu's sister, who was ill. She had bought three heads for three soldi and three "interiori" for five soldi, and was so scandalized at the high cost of living that she wandered from the subject.

"Bad Christians!" she ejaculated, three red combs dangling as she shook three necks venomously. "Bad Christians who ask so much from me! I am a poor unfortunate! I have no father; mother I have not; I have no one. I go barefoot, I must live. I cannot pay so much."

The orphan planted the tip of a long, lean old forefinger in the middle of her forehead, the gesture that calls attention to right ways of thinking; and her pale, keen eyes snapped as she appealed to me; "Vossia persuades herself? Do I speak well?"

"But the vigilia of San Giovanni?" I suggested.

"San Ciuvanuzzu? Ah, si; Vincenzinu. We passed him over the tree."

"Over the tree? You made Vincenzinu pass over the tree?" I thought I had not heard correctly.

"Yes, through the trunk of an oak."

"Through the trunk of an acorn tree? Did passing through an oak make Vincenzinu well?"

"Of course!"

It is often Gna Vanna's pleasure to assure me, when speaking of the spells and charms which she calls prayers, "These things I know; no one else knows them, no one at all; and I tell them only to you. When I die no one in the world except you will know them. Daughter I have not; you are my heir."

As one thought worthy to pass the old wisdom on, I seldom express surprise at any revelation. In the matter of the oak tree I asked, as if the answer were a matter of course, "At midnight?"

"Yes; down at the shore."

She told me at some length how she and her daughter-in-law, and a party of friends had taken the ruptured child down to the shore at Isola Bella, where they had made a slit through a young oak, and then under her direction had passed him three times through the gash. "Three times they made him enter." Then they tied up the tree and ate and drank toasts as if it had been a baptismal festa. Vincenzinu slept under the tree, and in the morning he felt better. After a year they had visited the oak and had found it healthy and grown together. Vincenzinu's hurt had grown together also; he was no longer ruptured.

"I wish you had told me at the time," I said; "I should have liked to go with you."

Gna Vanna promised that if ever she heard of another child who needed to pass through the tree, she would tell me in season; but the twenty-third of June came and went, and I heard nothing more about the matter. I learned by inquiry that this old, old cure by sympathetic magic is still well known in Eastern Sicily. My landlady gossiped to me about a neighbor who had been subjected to it in childhood, but who nevertheless had not been sound enough to do his military service. The ceremony seemed not uncommon, but I had given up hope of ever seeing it when, a year later at the approach of San Giovanni, Gna Vanna beckoned me mysteriously inside her door one morning to announce that only the night before her services had been spoken for in behalf of a lad, whose parents had not been able to take him to Trecastagne. She had already sent a message to her cumpari, Vanni Nozzulu, John of the olive stone, to ask if he would help her, as he had done in the case of Vincenzinu. Would I really like to make one of the party?

The Sicilian ritual requires that the ruptured child be handed through the tree by a man and woman who "make their names" on St. John's day; that is, who are called Giovanni and Giovanna. Gna Vanna's repute as a witch makes her an especially appropriate Jane to act as mistress of such a ceremony.

I did not accept at once my invitation, though I did not doubt Vanna's good faith. Whether she or her compare, or the parents of the child had any substantial faith in the ancient formula they proposed to repeat, who could know? That the force of tradition, dying but not dead, would make the experiment seem to them perhaps useful, certainly not harmful, was beyond question. I held acceptance in reserve only to make sure that nothing should be added to the function or taken away from it because of the expected presence of an outsider.

From day to day Gna Vanna chatted of the preparations. This time they were going into the hills, not down to the shore. Petru Barbarussa, the boy's father, had already found a likely tree. It would be moonlight; they would take bread, cheese and fish, and make a supper after the ceremony. Cumpari Vanni would bring wine. In the late afternoon of the twenty-third she reported that everything was ready, except the supper; she would like to give that herself; "but I am scarce" she concluded with a shrewd eye-glance. It was then that I agreed to come and to supplement her scarceness of money, if she would buy for me the peas, beans, nuts and seeds necessary to complete the festa.

Peter of the Red Beard is a fisherman. His Pippinu I had known from the child's babyhood. Pippinu was at this time a white, sickly sprout of a six-year-old, red-headed, pale-eyed, ill-fed; yet withal an ingratiating little soul. When I stopped hesitatingly at his door at nine o'clock that evening his shy grin of welcome made me even more ashamed than I had expected to be of gratifying curiosity at the expense of such a weakly mite of humanity.

Pippinu lives at the foot of the broad "ladder" that goes up from a confusion of narrow ways to the street known of all tourists, the Via Teatro Greco. His is the usual house of one room, its smoky wall lighted only from the doorway, its floor of broken bricks littered with water jars, brambles for the fire, confused heaps of nets and dingy household utensils. Gna Vanna had not yet come, and in the dim interior Barbarussa, a gaunt man of forty with a red stubble beard, barefooted, wearing cotton shirt and trousers, was preparing lanterns, ropes and the like for our excursion.

Donna Catina, Pippinu's mother, was putting down children for the night; two boys on one side of the room, two girls on the other, the pallets partly screened by ragged sacking. The big marriage bed stood as usual in an alcove at the back, cut off by worn red curtains.

There was not much other furniture: Two small tables, a chest, chairs, a washtrough full of soapy water, a rack holding bottles and dishes, prints of the Madonna and saints, family clothing.

Donna Catina was pretty once; she might be pretty now, if her straggling hair were ever combed and her untidy dress were ever buttoned at the throat. She is not yet thirty, but her oval face is thin and faded, and her smile flickers anxiously. While we waited, she showed me by the light of an ill-smelling lamp the two treasures of the household, a "snapshot" of her husband's first wife taken by some tourist, and a wax image of the baby Christ, framed in a wooden box with a glass front.

At last Cumpari Vanni appeared, a rugged contadino, better-nourished than the others. His straw hat was so huge it interfered with the big basket he carried on his shoulder. Behind him came Gna Vanna, limping with a touch of rheumatism, and Pippinu's aunt, Donna Ciccia, whose good brown face, framed in its yellow kerchief, beamed in anticipation of the adventure.

When our party of seven started at ten o'clock, the moon was not up; and, once outside the village, we lighted two square lanterns not bigger than water glasses. Our way took us past the Messina gate and then down beyond the Campo Santo into a rough path that dips into a fold of the hills, a shortcut to the shore north of Taormina. It was a black descent; the circle of mountains almost cut out the sky. There was not a breath of air. The hot earth exhaled an aromatic smell of pennyroyal.

The two men walked ahead, talking in low tones of the scarcity of fish, of the drought, of the light wheat crop. Donna Catina came behind them with Pippinu clinging mute and frightened to her hand. Next came Donna Ciccia with the second lantern, flashing it now and then to discover a sprig of the tall-growing shrub; "for the presepio," she said. Pennyroyal gathered and dried on the eve of San Giovanni blossoms fresh at Christmas.

Gna Vanna grasped my arm, groaning, "My leg hurts enough and too much. I cannot walk. I cannot sleep. There has gone from me the love of eating. To-day I cooked myself one soldo's worth of spaghetti, one soldo's worth and nothing more. I want to die, for I cannot suffer any more."

She interrupted her lament to point out a big toad that hopped across our path, calling it a good omen; then went on, "They call me lame, I who, Vossia knows, have always walked better than any of them." And she stepped out so vigorously that with difficulty I kept up with her.

After perhaps half an hour we dropped the basket under a big walnut tree, left the path, and began scrambling up the parched mountain side. It was a familiar slope, where in autumn blossom narcissus, cyclamen and Jack-in-the-pulpit, which Sicilian children call the pipe; but in the blackness I could not recognize a landmark. Barbarussa had come by daylight to choose us an oak, but Gna Vanna refused to accept the gnarled, stunted little tree he had pitched upon. Though small, it was old, and would not augur long life for Pippinu.

The men climbed higher while we women clung together. A screech owl hooted; Gna Vanna crossed herself, and Donna Ciccia muttered, "Beautiful

Mother of the Rock, deliver us!" Donna Catina touched something in the bosom of her dress.

After a long wait the men came back. They had found a better oak, but high on a cliff side so steep that without Gna Vanna's help I should have been slow in reaching it. "My leg hurts," she mourned, as she dragged me up the baked and crumbly steep. There was no vegetation but bunches of a wiry grass on which the feet slipped, and which cut the hands.

The new oaklet stood on a narrow shelf with a few dwarf fichi d'India and wild plum trees above, and at one side a recently planted baby olive. It may have been four feet tall, a straight slender stem carrying at top two waving brushes of the small, close-growing, much indented leaves of the Sicilian oak. We sat down beside it.

It was not yet half-past eleven; nothing could be done until midnight. To save oil for our return we put out the lanterns, and stuck a candle atop of a stone under the oak, whose dark glossy leaves rustled without wind as if it shivered before coming pain.

Pippinu went to sleep in his mother's arms. The yellow point of candle flame made blacker the black outlines of Monte Ziretto and Monte Veneretta that loomed silent on the opposite side of the ravine. There was no sound but the sleepy "Frisci, frisci, frisci" of a belated cicala.

"What does the cicaledda say?" I asked.

"I am wrong, I die," answered Donna Ciccia; and she told us the tale of the idle cicala and the industrious ant, as she had heard it from her elders; as they heard it from their "ancients"; for on the lips of the South some of the old Greek tales have never died.

The silence that fell again was broken by the hoot of the cucca. "Some one must die," shuddered Donna Catina.

"The cicaledda," suggested Vanni.

Gna Vanna settled her bad leg more comfortably, announcing, "When there passes the pain in my leg, I shall carry two candles to the dear Madonna of the Chain."

She told us again how Vincenzinu, her grandson, had passed "over the little oak" and how much better he had felt the next morning. Vincenzinu's father, Turiddu, who had made already two voyages to New York, was about to sail again. "He says," she continued, "that they call our cucuzzi 'squashes'; is it true, Vossia?"

I praised Turiddu's English, and confirmed his tales of "treni in aria" and "treni suttu terra"—elevated and subway trains. Turiddu had told his mother that in America one does not enjoy life, for there is no music in the piazza on Sunday. The air, too, is not so fine as in Sicily, and the fish have not the same good taste.

"That would be true," said Barbarussa, "for even the fish taken at Catania, one hour from here, have not the same good taste as the fish of our own sea of Taormina."

A few minutes before twelve by Cumpari Vanni's watch Gna Vanna gave the signal for us to sign ourselves with the cross. Then the party repeated in unison three paternosters, three aves and three gloria patris.

When these were finished Cumpari Vanni took the little tree by its two poor leafy branches, and slowly and dexterously split it with his hands. To use a knife, Gna Vanna said, would be unlucky. When he had opened it two-thirds of the way to the ground, he put one side of the top into my hands and the other side into Barbarussa's. By traditional usage this made me cumari—co-mother—with the parents of Pippinu. We stood North and South of the oak.

Pippinu began to whine as his mother delivered him, cold and sleepy, to Gna Vanna, who unbuttoned and pulled off his short patched breeches. Custom prescribes that the child be naked; but Pippinu's screams became so shrill, and his thin, dusty legs waved so protestingly that she left him his shirt and cuddled him, cold, sleepy and afraid, in her old arms, promising sweets to eat in the morning. She had taken off her white headkerchief, and the yellow hoops of her earrings gleamed in the flickering candle light that brought nose and chin grotesquely close together. She would have looked a witch, if she had not looked a good grandmother.

The split in the tree ran East and West. When Pippinu's sobs had subsided into disconsolate little chokes, Cumari Vanni and Cumpari Vanni placed themselves in front of it and behind, making a cross with Barbarussa and me. Then Vanna, holding out the boy, began:

"Cumpari Vanni!"

He answered, "Cumari Vanna!"

"Cumpari Vanni!"

"Cumari Vanna, What do you wish?"

Vanna replied:

> [5] Pigghia stu figghiu
> E lu passa cca banna;
> A nomu di Sanciuvanni,
> Lu dugnu ruttu, dammilu sanu.

At the word "pigghia" Gna Vanna passed Pippinu feet first across the split betwen the two halves of the tree into the hands of Vanni, who, when he had received him, began in his turn, "Cumari Vanna!" They repeated the formula until Pippinu had passed from one to the other through the tree three times. There was no attempt to be impressive and nothing like jesting. They made a plain working conversation.

When Vanna had received the child back for the last time, she set him on his feet, still frightened

[5] Take this child and pass him back to me again; In the name of San Giovanni, I give him you broken, give him me sound.

THE LITTLE OAK TREE

THE CLEFT OAK

and shivering, a wee pathetic smile dawning on his face. Holding him at her side, her hands on his shoulders, she finished her incantation:

> Praised and thanked be the most holy Sacrament, the great Mother of God, Mary, and all the (heavenly) company. San Giovanni, in the name of Jesus close this flesh. In the name of Jesus, blessed San Giovanni, close this hurt; and may Pippinu suffer nothing more. Take away all the peril and the evil suggestion, dear good San Giovanni. Praised and thanked be the most holy Sacrament, the great Mother of God, Mary and all the heavenly company!

A little dazed, the child wavered across to his mother, who dressed him while Cumpari Vanni bound up the tree, winding the new rope that Barbarussa had provided in a continuous coil to cover the entire length of the slit, while he and Vanna repeated together: "As this tree closes, so may Pippinu's rupture close."

If the tree healed within a year, Vanna said, Pippinu would heal; if not, Pippinu would not get well.

Vanna does not know how passage through the tree was to help Pippinu. To her, Gaidoz, whose monograph aims to prove the root idea to be a shifting of trouble from Pippinu to the tree; or Frazer, who thinks that an escaping Pippinu leaves a pursuing malady caught in the cleft; or Baring Gould, who sees a new Pippinu reborn free of old ills, would be equally meaningless. She does not need to speculate about the matter; she has inherited a practice that comes down to her perhaps from the elder Cato, who advised that a green split reed be tied to a dislocated limb during the recitation of a spell, the two then being tied together to heal in sympathetic harmony.

Vanna's invocation is a prayer. People call her a witch, but they are wrong, since she works only "things of God." Many a time she has said to me, "It is always for good and never for ill. Release (from evil) yes; bind, never! Am I a Christian, or am I not?"

If the priests do not approve of certain practices, it is because the priests have not the devotion. Her thought does not separate religion and magic; each is an appeal to superior powers; but in daily life, since the priests refuse to make appeals of various necessary sorts, wise people must make them, or cause them to be made, for themselves.

After rendering first aid to the oak, we slipped and slid down the hillside to the path, where under the walnut tree we laid out the baptismal supper. Barbarussa had brought three big round brown loaves of bread, a few early figs and a plate of little cold fried fish, and Cumpari Vanni had added a small form of sheep's milk, cheese and two bottles of wine. Vanni cut the bread with his evil-looking knife. We hung our lanterns to the thorn bushes and ate with satisfaction. Gna Vanna had not forgotten the feast.

It was time for the moon to be up; this we knew

by a faint light above the mountain tops; but she never gave a real look into our cup among the hills. My new honor as godmother gave me the first easy time-worn toast:

> [6] Good and fine is this wine;
> A toast to Pippinu, this is mine.

Pippinu's father followed with the second:

> Good as bread is this wine;
> Vanni made it from his vine.

I have yet to see the Sicilian who could not rhyme toasts as long as breath held out.

Dawn was in the sky before we reached home. As we climbed out of the gorge Donna Catina stopped to touch the ground, and then kissed her fingers, saying, "I kiss the earth; God save us from traveling again this fearsome road." She opened the bosom of her dress to show me, stitched into her clothing, the flat thin gold cross she had worn as protection against the evil spirits that infest the night.

"You and I saw the botta, Vossia," said Vanna, shaking her wise old head reassuringly; "that toad may have been a 'donna di fora,' one of the little people."

Within a few days I left Sicily, and it was more than a year before I saw Pippinu again. Time had

> [6] Chistu vinu e beddu e finu,
> Facciu brindisi a Pippinu.

not changed the house at the foot of the great scalinata, except that, hung to the side of the bed in the alcove, was now a cradle, made of a piece of sacking that swung by ropes from the bedframe.

Donna Catina was not at home. Barbarussa said she had gone "To make the day's expenses (for provisions)." More gaunt and good-humored than ever, he was sweeping the floor. "I am making the cleaning of the house," he added, explaining an occupation not unusual among the fishermen. .

After a few minutes Catina appeared carrying in her arms the tenant of the cradle, ten-months-old Giovanninu, named for the saint we had invoked when his brother passed over the tree. "Four teeth he has," she said proudly, as soon as we had exchanged greetings, prying open the youngster's mouth to show me his four new teeth. "He creeps, and he can stand alone."

She coaxed him to smile, smoothing his red hair, tapping his plump rosy cheeks. He was indeed a fine boy compared with his thin hungry-looking sisters, grown too large to be nourished with their mother's milk.

"But where is Pippinu?" I asked finally.

"At the cobbler's," said the little girls in chorus, darting from the house to fetch him.

My godson, being now seven years old, had become one of the men of the household. He was apprenticed to a cobbler, who, being cumpari with Barbarussa, asked no fee, and sometime would pay wages. Meantime he did not give food, as seemed obvious when Pippinu sidled bashfully into the room, white and frail as always.

While the children were gone Catina had been rummaging in the big wooden chest to find the certificate of Pippinu's marks in the Taormina school. He had finished the second elementary class, and pointed out with small leather-stained fingers how well he had done in reading and writing. Would he ever go to school again? Perhaps; they hoped he might go one more year.

That afternoon Pippinu's aunt went with me to inspect the tree. It was not the first excursion Donna Ciccia and I had made together, and I do not know a better companion. Her brown, leathery face and sun-strained eyes, her brows arched in a perpetual question, bear witness that life has not handled her gently; but to every buffet she opposes a jest. I have never seen her wear shoes, though she saved money for months to buy a pair for mass on Sundays. She says the cobbler—he to whom Pippinu is apprenticed—made them too tight; perhaps her good muscular feet rebelled at confinement. Even for this visit of ceremony, she left them in her chest, that family hold-all.

It was late July. For that very afternoon Hesiod might have written of the summer resting time, "When the artichoke flowers, and the tuneful cicala, perched on a tree, pours forth a shrill song ofttimes from under his wings." The white smoke of Etna rose straight and slow into a white and cloudless sky. The sea was blue-white. There was a bluish haze over all the world. It was a day of powerful heat, when the stones baked under foot, and the long walls scorched the hand. Even in the rock shade of the fold among the hills the leaves of the almond trees were turning yellow before the fruit had ripened, and the thick fleshy leaves of the fichi d'India were drooping.

We found the little tree still wound tightly. It showed a long, dark scar well closed. Its crown of leaves was thick and vigorous. It had grown a trifle, was more than four feet tall. It held its head up courageously in face of the scorched mountains opposite, which showed their bleakest summer aspect. The drought for a year had been extreme. Again there was nothing green under foot; the air was heavy with the pungent smell of pennyroyal.

We rested in the warm silence. The air was so still we might have thought Pan had not yet waked from his siesta. Donna Ciccia pulled her knitting work out of the pockets of her apron, and I read to her the words of the goatherd in Theocritus: "We may not pipe in the noontide; 't is Pan we dread, who truly at this hour rests weary from the chase."

By and by Donna Ciccia dropped her needles. "I used to come here when I was a girl," she said, "to pick up wood. Nowadays my Christian has a vote, but they have not left us any place to pick up wood."

Again for a long time we said nothing. In one of her pockets she had brought green almonds; with her strong teeth she cracked them easily. It was nearly five o'clock, and there was a faint air stirring, when we rose to begin the homeward road. We knew the hour because on the path below fishermen were going down to the sea.

"The tree has come good, it is healed," said Donna Ciccia. We did not take off the cord, lest Pippinu should take off his bandage. It has been agreed that while the tree wore a truss Pippinu should wear one also. "It has come good," she repeated; "but as to Pippinu one does not yet know."

But perhaps when he is older, a little surgery may help us find out about Pippinu.

CHAPTER V

THE HAIRY HAND

Fe! Fi! Fo! Fum!
I smell the blood of an Englishman!
Be he 'live or be he dead,
I'll grind his bones to make my bread!

THE moon was coming up large and round over the shoulder of Monte Tauro. The air was heavy with the scent of jasmine. The summer evening was peaceful and still. "If the war lasts——" said the Signora L——, drawing forward a chair for me in the doorway of her shop. She did not finish the sentence, but I knew she was thinking, "there will be no tourists next winter, and no work."

Donna Peppina's Mazza, trudging homeward from vespers, paused a minute to say, "I have taken the holy benediction!" Her brown, wrinkled face expressed well-considered self-satisfaction. "But— what is that? Thunder?"

"Cannon," answered the Signora.

It was that August evening when the German ships, Breslau and Goeben, leaving the port of Messina, ran the gauntlet of the French and British fleets. Not two hours earlier we had watched the silent passage, one by one, of dark, low war-vessels.

"A verra?" pursued Donna Peppina. "Is it the war? It can't last long." But the tone was not as cheerful as the words, and the little bent figure, muffled in its black shawl, hurried uneasily away.

A neighbor's child sat down at our feet, stuffing her fingers into her ears, as from the quiet, moonlighted water there came another sullen boom, "Sarina," I suggested, "ask the Signora to tell us a story."

The Signora smiled indulgently. In those tragic days we whiled away with stories many an evening. She thought a minute, following with her eyes a man who was hurrying supperward, carrying cracked ice on a folded kerchief. Then she began, "When I was a little girl in Caltagirone and my grandmother used to tell me stories, the one I liked best of all was 'The Hairy Hand.'"

"Once upon a time there was a poor man who had four daughters. Every morning he went into the country to gather soup greens to sell. When summer came and the great sun burnt the country bare, the poor man's children must have died of hunger, had not the neighbors given them sometimes a glass of wine, sometimes a little oil, sometimes a bit of bread.

"One day when the poor father had found nothing at all to put into his shoulder bags except a few wild blackberries, he saw in the field on the other side of a hedge of fichi d'India a fine plant of wild fennel. He scrambled through the thorny hedge, but no sooner had he reached out his hand to gather the most beautiful plant than he heard, 'Cing-a-li! Cling-a-li! Cing-a-li!' a sound as of something dropping. He looked with all his eyes, but could see nothing. He pulled again, and again he heard, 'Cing-a-li! Cling-a-li! Cing-a-li!' as if a little bell were ringing or money dropping. He looked again, but could find nothing. The third time he pulled the plant up by the roots, and he saw a hole which grew and grew until it became the mouth of a great cave and out of the cave there came a giant fierce and monstrous. He was a wicked dragon, who killed every person that passed and ate the flesh. If he was not hungry, he would cut off head and hands and throw the body into a great locked room.

"At first the dragon did not see the poor father. He stood in the mouth of the cave and said:

> What a good smell of Christian meat!
> If it I see, I'll swallow it neat!

"The poor father said, 'Give me your blessing, your Excellency.'

"Then the dragon said, 'Come in, good man; sit down.'

"The poor father went into the cave and looked about. He saw rich furniture and bags of money. 'Eat,' said the dragon, 'if you are hungry; eat as much as you like'; and he set out bread, wine, pasta, cheese and fish.

"When the poor man had eaten, the dragon asked, 'Where do you come from, good man?'

"The man said he had been gathering minestra to support his family.

"'Are you single or married?'

"'I have four daughters,' replied the poor father.

"'Four daughters!' said the dragon. 'I have nobody; I live alone.' He asked the poor father to give him a daughter to be his wife, promising that she should have plenty to eat and fine clothes to wear, and he gave him a fistful of gold.

"The poor father promised to bring his eldest daughter next day, then he said, 'I salute you; I kiss your Excellency's hand'; and he went home.

"That night he showed his four daughters the money. 'Eat,' he said; 'eat, my children, if you are hungry; eat as much as you like.' He told his eldest daughter that a prince had asked for her hand in marriage, and next morning he took her with him to the cave. The *drau* received him kindly and gave the poor father another fistful of gold.

"When the man had gone home the dragon gave the girl the keys of all the rooms in the cave, telling her she was mistress of the place to do what she pleased, except that one door she must not unlock; he pointed towards the great dark room where he kept the bodies of the men he had slain. Then he called, 'Hairy Hand!'

"'What do you want?' replied a voice, and there appeared a great hairy hand. It was black and

knotted, and its fingers were like the claws of——' "
The Signora hesitated. Sarina gulped with suspense. She no longer heard the sullen booming from the sea.

"Like the claws of the one that dances," continued the Signora finally; "the claws of a bear."

" 'Do you see the hairy hand?' asked the dragon. 'You have to eat it. If you eat it, you shall be my wife; if you don't eat it, woe to you! I shall cut off your head. Will you eat it?'

" 'Yes, I will eat it,' said the eldest daughter.

" 'I give you three days,' said the *drau*, and he went away. The dragon had vast estates; he was always busy traveling through his properties.

"When she was alone, the eldest daughter looked at the hairy hand. 'How ugly it is!' she said to herself; 'I am afraid; this thing I cannot eat.' She hid it in a big chest, and went about the work of the house. On the third day she took flour and made home-made macaroni. She killed a hen and made a stew. When the *drau* came home the table was set, and there were roasted onions hot from the bread oven.

" 'Have you eaten the Hairy Hand?' he demanded.

" 'Yes, I ate it,' she answered.

" 'It seems to me you did not eat it,' he said; and he called 'Hairy Hand!'

" 'A-u-u! What do you want?' replied a voice.

" 'Where are you?' asked the dragon.

" 'In the big chest,' replied the Hand.

"So the dragon knew that the girl had not eaten it, and he said, 'Woe to you! I cut off your head!' And he cut it off and threw her into the great locked room.

"Now when the poor father had spent all the money the dragon had given him he came again to the cave, and inquired for his daughter. Said the dragon, 'She is having a good time; she is with my sister who thinks her pretty.'

"The dragon complained that he was again all alone, and asked the poor father to bring another daughter. 'Eat,' he said; 'if you are hungry, eat as much as you like.' And again he set out food and brought a fistful of gold.

"Next day the father brought his second daughter, and the dragon said to her, as he had to the first, that she was mistress of everything in the cave except the great locked room. He showed her the hairy hand, and told her she should be his wife if she ate it. 'If not, woe to you!' He gave her three days and went away.

"The second daughter looked at the hairy hand, and said to herself, 'This thing I cannot eat,' and she threw it into a cask of wine.

"When the *drau* came home she had done up all the work of the house and the pasta with tomato sauce was on the table.

" 'Well?' he demanded; 'the Hand? Have you eaten it?'

"'Yes,' she said; 'I ate it.'

"'I don't believe you ate it,' answered the *drau,* and he called, 'Hairy Hand!'

"'A-u! What do you want?'

"'Where are you?'

"'In the wine cask.'

"So the dragon saw that the second daughter had not eaten the hairy hand, and he cut off her head and put her with her sister.

"When the poor father was again out of money and came back to the cave to inquire for his two daughters, the dragon said the second girl was visiting his brother. He was alone, quite alone, and the father must bring yet a third daughter. The poor man did as he was told, and to the third girl everything happened much as to her sisters. She hid the hairy hand in the oven, and the dragon cut off her head. Where the father came back to ask after his three children, the *drau* said the third daughter was with his sister-in-law. The poor man agreed for another fistful of gold to bring his fourth daughter, but he warned the dragon not to send her to any of his relatives, because she was the very last.

"Now the youngest daughter was more clever than the others. She received the order not to meddle with the door of the locked room, and she promised to eat the hairy hand. But as soon as the dragon had given her three days' respite and had gone away, she unlocked the forbidden door, and found the bodies of her three sisters and of

THE HAIRY HAND

all the other murdered people. She was frightened, and she thought, 'He will kill me, too; I am as good as dead.'

"On the third day when it was time for the dragon to come home, instead of setting the table, she took a piece of cloth and made a pocket and sewed the hairy hand inside."

The Signora folded a corner of her apron to show Sarina just how the youngest daughter had made a bag to hold the hairy hand. Then she went on:

"The youngest daughter tied the bag across her stomach with a rag and went to bed. When the dragon found her groaning, he asked, 'What ails you?'

"She complained: 'I don't feel well.'

"'Did you eat the hairy hand?'

"'Yes; I have eaten it.'

"'Hairy Hand!' called the *drau*.

"'What do you want?'

"'Where are you?'

"'At the mistress' stomach.'

"'Va be,' said the *drau;* 'Since you have eaten it you shall be my wife.'

"When the dragon saw that the youngest daughter was ill, he went away, and she got up at once and went back to the forbidden room. This time she heard a sound as of someone trying to breathe.

"'U-h, a-u-h, uh, a-u-h!' It was like this," said the Signora, moaning as if hardly alive.

"In the dark corner of the room the youngest daughter found a man in an iron cage. He was dying of hunger. 'Help me,' he wailed; 'for I am the son of the king.'

"The youngest daughter killed a pigeon and made broth. She put a spoon to the bars and fed the man, who lifted his head and began to move his hands Then she minced the flesh of the pigeon fine like meal, and fed that to him. By and by he said, 'I feel much better.' He told her to send for a shepherd with a mule.

" 'But the dragon,' she objected.

" 'He is gone away.'

"When the herdsman came, he filed the bars of the cage with a piece of iron, and the king's son and the youngest daughter climbed into the mule's saddle-bags, one on each side. The shepherd stuffed the bags with wool, for it was the time of the shearing of the sheep, and rode away towards the palace of the king.

"They had not gone far when they met the dragon, who asked, 'What have you got in those bags?'

" 'Wool,' said the herdsman.

"The *drau* thrust his sword into the saddle-bags, and looked at its point. There was no blood on it, nothing but a bit of wool. So the *drau* believed the shepherd was telling the truth. He struck the mule with the flat of his sword and said, 'Get on with you?' and off went the mule to the king's palace.

"Now the king's son had been gone two years, and when he reached home there was great rejoicing. He kissed his father's hand and said, 'Your majesty, bless me. Father, grant me a wish; give me this girl for my wife.'

"Now the youngest daughter had left at the window of her room in the cave a figure dressed in her clothing, so that the dragon might think her at home and attend to his mule before coming indoors. The hairy hand she had thrown into the rubbish heap. When the dragon saw the doll at the window he called, 'What ails you? Why don't you speak to me? Come down.' Then as the figure did not move, he came upstairs and discovered the trick.

" 'Hairy Hand!' he called. 'Where are you?'

" 'In the rubbish.'

" 'Then the mistress didn't eat you?'

" 'She didn't eat me.'

" 'Then why did you say she did eat you?'

" 'I said I was at the mistress' stomach, and forgot to say whether I was inside or out.'

" 'Where is the mistress?'

" 'Fled with the son of the king.'

"Even in the king's palace the youngest daughter feared the dragon and she told the servant who kept the door to pretend to be deaf in case he came. The dragon did come, and to all his questions the old woman answered, 'You want onions and beans? Down yon they sell them'; and she pointed to a shop down the street."

But of course the dragon got into the palace, and hid himself inside an enchanted clock to work mischief; and equally of course he was killed by the king's son, and the three older sisters were brought to life, and everybody lived happy ever afterward.

Sarina drew a long breath of satisfaction when the tale was finished, and begged for another.

"Enough," said the Signora; "it's time for you to go to bed." But in the end she was coaxed to tell us about a dragon's wife, a "mammadrava." A little wind stirred Sarina's short light hair. She leaned her head against the doorjamb, her eyes fixed blissfully on the Signora's face. She had forgotten the cannon.

"They tell and they retell," began the Signora; "that once upon a time there was a woman who went to the fountain to wash. There came by a 'mammadrava' who said:

"'What a beautiful smell of Christian meat!
If it I see, I'll swallow it neat!'

"There is nothing that tastes so good to a dragon or a she-dragon as the flesh of us Christians.

"'Spare me!' cried the woman.

"The 'mammadrava' spared the woman because

she was with child, and said, 'I'll eat what you have within you when you have brought it forth.'

"The woman gave birth to a beautiful daughter, but she did not give her child to the 'mammadrava.' One day the she-dragon saw the little girl passing and called to her: 'Pretty child, tell your mother that I want what she promised me.'

"The child told her mother, 'I saw the "mammadrava," and she said, "I want what your mother promised me."'

"The mother replied, 'Tell the "mammadrava," "Take it where you see it."

"When the little girl had given the message the 'mammadrava' said, 'Come here, my child; I have some sweets for you.'

"The little girl was afraid; for you must know that a dragon does not talk as do we other Christians; they drawl in a terrifying way through the nose."

The Signora bent towards Sarina, giving to every word a harsh nasal twang.

"The 'mammadrava' took the child to her house and put her into the 'cannizzu' to fatten until she should be big and tender enough to eat. (In a Sicilian house a tall cylinder of woven cane is an ordinary receptacle for grain or beans. It has a small hole near the floor, stopped commonly with rags.) She fed the little girl with pasta, fish and sweets, giving her every day as much as she could eat. After a time she said one morning, 'Stick out a finger.'

"The child poked a finger through the hole.

"'You are still too little to eat,' said the 'mammadrava,' and every day she gave her more pasta and more fish and more sweets. As the child grew she became clever; and she thought, 'If she sees that I am now good and big, she will eat me.' So she killed a rat and cut off its tail, and the next time the 'mammadrava' said, 'Put out a finger,' instead of a finger she poked out the rat's tail.

"The 'mammadrava' was cross and hungry, for it was a long time since she had tasted Christian flesh. She fed the girl as much as she could eat, but always when she asked to see a finger the child put out the rat's tail. At last when the girl was eighteen years old she thought, 'Now that I am really good and big I shall soon be strong enough to get the better of the old she-dragon.' And one day instead of the rat's tail she put out her flesh-and-blood finger.

"At sight of it the 'mammadrava's' mouth watered. She took the girl out of the 'cannizzu' and looked at her. 'How fine and fat you are!' she exclaimed, licking her lips. 'We'll make a festa to-day because you have come out.' She built a fire in the oven, for she meant to roast the girl as a dinner for herself and her husband, the dragon. When she thought the oven must be hot enough she said, 'Go, look into the oven and see if it is ready.'

"But the girl answered, 'I don't know anything about the oven; I've lived all my life inside the 'cannizzu.' Go you; I'll set the table.'

"When the 'mammadrava' stooped to take away the balata (the sheet of iron that closed the mouth of an oven) the girl took her by the feet and threw her inside and put the balata in position. Then she set the table and brought out wine.

"Towards Ave Maria the dragon came home. 'Where is my wife?' he asked.

"'She has gone to market. She is making a festa to-day because I am good and big and have come out of the 'cannizzu.' She is roasting a fine sheep. Do you want to see?'

"The girl opened the oven and the dragon sniffed the roasting meat. 'Would you like to taste a little bit now?' she suggested.

"The dragon was greedy. 'Yes,' he said; 'my wife has such an appetite she'll eat it all and I shan't get a bite. I'll eat a leg.'

"The girl gave him as much as he wanted of the flesh of the 'mammadrava.' When he had drunk so much wine that he was sleepy, she took all the goods that God had given the house, and ran away home.

"Now you must surely go to bed," said the Signora to Sarina.

The Corso was deserted. The men who throughout the evening had been standing in the Piazza Sant' Agostino, looking out over the sea, by twos and threes had gone home. The houses were dark and quiet.

Sarina looked across the narrow way to a shop where a light still burned. "My sister," she said, "has not finished ironing. Just another little short one. Tell us about the thirteen robbers."

"But you know it," replied the Signora.

"I don't," I suggested.

"Once upon a time," recommenced the Signora patiently, "there was a mother who had two beautiful daughters. One day she was obliged to go a long way from home to bleach her flax. She asked an old woman to sleep in the house with her daughters that night, and to let no one in for fear of robbers. 'Lock the door as soon as it is dark,' she said, 'and hang the key on the nail.'

"The old woman agreed, but as soon as the mother had gone, she sought out the chief of a robber band; and told him that if he would knock at the door at midnight, he might get possession of everything in the house. The robber chief gave the old woman a purse of silver, and at midnight precisely he rapped at the door. The old woman snored as if she were fast asleep.

"'Open, I am your mother,' called the master thief.

"The older daughter would have opened, but the younger was more clever. She said, 'Mother would never come home at this hour.' So the two beautiful girls climbed up into the hay-loft and pulled up the ladder.

"There were thirteen of the robbers, and they broke down the door. But the younger daughter threw blocks of rock salt on their heads until she had killed twelve. Only the robber chief remained alive, and to avoid discovery he carried away one at a time the bodies of all his men.

"When the mother came home next day the old woman pretended to have slept soundly all night and to have heard nothing. The robber chief was determined to avenge himself, so he asked the mother to give him her younger daughter in marriage. The clever girl knew that it was the head robber who sought her, and guessed that he meant to kill her; but she said yes, and they were married. On the day of the wedding she made a figure as large as herself, dressed it in her own clothes and put it into the bed. Then she hid underneath.

"When the head robber came into the room and saw the dummy, he thrust his dagger through and through it, shouting, 'Thus do I take vengeance for the death of my brave lads! Thus do I drink the blood of the murderess!' And he drank of the liquid that ran from the pupa. No sooner had he done so than he started to his feet, crying, 'How sweet is my wife's blood! I repent me that I have killed her! I will kill myself!'

"He began to sob and groan, and he would have

thrust the knife into his own heart; but the younger daughter jumped from her hiding place and said:

> 7 "'A sugar doll has bled at your knife
> And you and I are husband and wife.'"

"Is that the end?" asked Sarina. "Did they make peace?"

"Yes," said the Signora; "they made peace. And when my grandmother told me that story she used to say,

> 8 "'Now husband and wife are rich and contended,
> But we poor folks are sadly stinted.'"

Sarina's sister had finished ironing and came to fetch her. It had been a long hot day for the laundress, and while she rested with us in the evening air, she, too, begged for a story. The Signora tried to tell us about The Beauty of the Seven Veils; but she couldn't remember it, and gave us instead, The Enchanted Mirror.'

"Once upon a time a wicked woman had a beautifull step-daughter whom she beat and kept in rags. One day she asked an enchanted mirror whether the girl was fortunate or unfortunate.

"Fortunate," answered the enchanted mirror.

> 7 "'La pupa è fatta di zucchero e mieli,
> E nui siamu maritu e mugghieri.'"

> 8 "'Ora sono ricchi c cuntenti,
> Ma nuiautri restiamu senza nenti.'"

"The step-mother flew into a rage, and commissioned a bad old woman to take the child a long way from home and leave her in a place from which she could not find her way back; but the little girl guessed what was going to happen, and filled her pockets with flour; then as they walked she dropped a little here and there. After they had gone a long distance they sat down in a thicket and ate two pieces of bread. The child was so tired that she fell asleep, and the old woman stole away.

"When the wicked step-mother asked the mirror whether or not the girl would come back, the mirror said yes; and indeed after a couple of days the child came home. The step-mother treated her worse than ever, and after a time inquired again of the mirror whether the girl was lucky or unlucky. The mirror repeated that the girl was lucky, so the step-mother sent her away again with the old woman, feeling her all over before they started to make sure there was no flour this time in her bag. The old woman walked and walked, and when at last they sat down in a wood the girl was so tired that she fell asleep before she had tasted food.

"When she awoke alone, the beautiful girl did not know which way to turn. Not far away she saw a cave. A latchstring was hanging out, so she opened the door. Inside she found bread and cheese and eggs and oil and wine, and she saw men's clothing hanging from pegs, but nothing belonging to a woman. She knew the men who lived in the cave must come home to eat, so she gathered minestra and cooked it, and she killed a hen and stewed it with onions and olives and basil. Then she set the table and hid in a corner.

"When the twelve brigands who lived in the cave came home and saw the table they thought at first some other brigand must have been there but the head brigand said, 'These are not men's doings, they are the doings of a woman.'

"'If the woman were here,' said the other brigands, 'she should be our sister.'

"When the girl heard this, she came out from her corner. The head brigand made her sit by him and fed her from his own plate. The men told her she should truly be their sister to cook the food and make the beds and attend to all the work of the cave. They gave her fine clothes and became very fond of her.

"But after a time the wicked step-mother asked the enchanted mirror whether the girl was alive or dead, and the mirror answered that she was alive and had twelve brothers. Then the step-mother sent for a witch who gave her an enchanted ring that had power to throw into a sleep like death any person who put it on. This ring the step-mother entrusted to the old woman, who went back to the wood and offered it to the girl, who put it on her finger and fell at once asleep.

THE HAIRY HAND

"When the brigands came home, they mourned their beautiful sister as dead. They put her into a box of carved wood, with a purse by her side, and carried the box to the top of a high mountain. One day a prince who was hunting found the box. When he had opened it, he called his men to carry it to his palace, for he was wiser than the brigands and knew that the beautiful girl was sleeping. In the palace the prince's servant noticed the ring and watched her chance to slip it off the girl's finger, saying to herself, 'What a pretty ring! I'll take it myself!'

"As soon as the ring was off her hand the girl awoke and asked for her brothers. She told the prince about her step-mother and the old woman, but as to her brothers she refused to say anything except that they lived in a cave. The prince guessed they must be brigands and gave his word to pardon them, 'for,' he said, 'you are to be my spouse.' So they were married and the prince gave the brigands much land.

"Then again the wicked step-mother asked the mirror whether the beautiful girl was alive or dead. 'She is now a princess,' said the mirror; 'she is the wife of the king's son; she lives in a splendid palace and wears fine clothes.'

"'Then how can I avenge myself?' screamed the step-mother.

"The mirror did not answer. It had spoken in the past, because the beautiful girl was fortunate, her happy fate was certain to be fulfilled. But now destiny was accomplished. She was a princess and happy. What more was there to say?

"The step-mother broke the mirror in her rage; it never spoke again."

CHAPTER VI

JESUS AS DESTROYER

Another time, when the Lord Jesus was coming home in the evening with Joseph, he met a boy who ran so hard against him that he threw him down. To whom the Lord Jesus said, "As thou hast thrown me down, so shalt thou fall, nor ever rise." And that moment the boy fell down and died. . . .

Then said Joseph to St. Mary, "Henceforth we will not allow him to go out of the house; for everyone who displeases him is killed."—*Apocryphal books of the New Testament; First Gospel of the Infancy,* Chaps. XIX and XX.

IN spite of the fervor of the Bambino cult, the most important person of the Sicilian Holy Family is the Madonna, because she is not only powerful, but in her relations with man she is almost uniformly benign. Caprices of ill-temper are indeed attributed to her, as in case of the old charm against colic:

⁹ Vine branches out, vine branches in,
Straw and grain.
Away in no time goes this pain.
For Jesus' sake
No more of this ache.

⁹ Fora sciarmenti, intra sciarmenti,
Pagghia e frumenti;
Si nni va stu duluri tempu nenti.
Pi lu nomu di Gesu
Mi ci passa e nun mi nni avi nenti chiu.

Once upon a time, the tale goes, the Madonna was cold and begged of a neighbor cuttings pruned from the vines. The woman refused, saying she had none; but the Madonna knew that she had and cursed her saying, "May you twist in pain like the prunings that are twisting under your oven." Whereupon the woman writhed in torment until the Madonna thought she had been punished enough and charmed away the pain with the prayer now in use.

But in spite of such trivial outbursts, the Madonna appears in the folk tales as the world's great kindly Mother. San Giuseppe, too, is a wholly benevolent patriarch; but there are aspects of the Lord Jesus which remind one of the anecdotes of a vindictive Child Christ related in the Apocryphal Gospels of the Infancy.

As in more than one ancient trinity there figure the creator, the preserver and the destroyer-regenerator, so in the Sicilian trinity of father, mother and child one is tempted to place the child as the destructive force, thwarted and controlled by the mother. In old stories still current, as in songs newly manufactured, the Lord Jesus is shown as wrathful against men as was the far-darting Apollo towards the people who neglected his altars.

On one of my first visits to Messina after the earthquake of 1908, I heard the wail of a cantastorie among the ruins, and bought a copy of the penny ballad the crippled, dim-sighted old man was singing

JESUS AS DESTROYER

to curiosity-seekers and to those who sought their dead in that great sepulchre. The song of forty-eight stanzas explained the catastrophe as an effort of Jesus to destroy the world· an attempt limited in its success by Mary. Said lu Signuri:

> . . . "For me the world is dead;
> Destroyed would I see the blue sky."
> So his mantle black of wrath he took
> To break man's back that he die.
> He called the earthquake quickly;
> To his command it ran.
> "Shake thou the earth this minute!
> Destroy perfidious man!"

The earthquake obeyed orders, and men ran from their houses calling on the Madonna. She was asleep, but the groans of the dying woke her and at once she bade earth and sea be still. They refused obedience, telling her that Christ had expressly commanded them to sink the entire earth:

> "This word from whom did you get it
> To destroy my people devout?"
> The sea it answered her promptly.
> "The command 't is of Christ, do not doubt."

Then the Madonna went to her son and besought him by her tears,

> Behold how many thousands dead!
> The innocent for help who cry!
> Forget your wrath, all-powerful son;
> Think of your bitter cross so high.

Jesus refused to listen, saying that man had been warned with floods and fire, but refused to respect either sacraments or gospel, and the time had come to make an end of him:

> See you not man, the ill-liver?
> His sins he does not repent;
> Even the lads of tender years
> New blasphemies invent.

Yet in the end the Madonna had her will. Jesus put off his black cloak, though grudgingly, and bade her do as she chose. At once she renewed her command to earth and sea:

> "O earthquake, return to thy corner,"
> Then said the great spotless Mother;
> "Calm the fears of these my devoted,
> And make no more pitiless slaughter.
> And thou, sea wave, get back also;
> From my son the grace I have got."
> So, but for the Virgin Maria,
> This earth as 'tis now were not.

But for Mary, the fate of Messina would have been the fate of the entire world.

Again after the earthquake at Linera in the spring of 1914 the "story-singer" sang of the wrath of Christ and the intervention of the Madonna to save man. In a ballad called "The Powerful Earthquakes in Sicily" Jesus Christ tells his mother that he can no longer endure the insults heaped on him, and that if he has called in the earthquake, it is no affair of hers. This time San Giuseppe came to his wife's help, demanding payment, if the earth was to go down in wreck, of the Madonna's dowry:

> First give to me the sun and moon,
> And stars and earth, then too the sea,
> Paradise, angels, archangels and saints;
> These must thou give me instantly.
> And next consign to me the crown
> Of my wife constant and divine;
> For these things are her dowry; of them
> She's mistress; hers they are and mine.

The price was found so great that man received his pardon.

This doggerel, lacking simplicity and sincerity as completely as it lacks the dialectic interest of the older ballads, is of value only as showing the mechanical continuance of a tradition through its own impetus.

It was a drowsy afternoon when I first heard this song of San Giuseppe and the Madonna, one of those August afternoons when even the sea is sunwhite, except where waving lines mark the track of a boat long past or the motion of currents. At Gna Vanna's doorstone in the Via Bagnoli Croce a group of women were shucking almonds. Zu Vincenzu Nanu, the dwarf, has thirty-four trees on his bit of land under the castle, and their fruit lay in sacks just inside the door.

Peeling the outside shell off rich brown mennuli is commonly a merry task, but this day we were very quiet. The drought was extreme. From where we sat we could look up at the castle crag above the town, gray and yellow, bleached and bare, hot in the sun. Clinging to fissures, dwarfed fichi d'India drooped their sapless leaves to the rock. On the steep lower slopes against the gray-white terraces stood out withering almond trees, Zu Vincenzu's among them, dropping discouraged yellow leaves.

Instead of splitting away in ripening, the shells of our nuts had dried to the stone, making it necessary to use teeth and bits of rock as well as fingers in shucking them. Mine was the only knife in the party. The nuts, too, were so small and poor that low prices stood out in prospect.

Then, too, that morning thirty young men had left Taormina to join the colors, and who knew whether or not next morning another manifesto would be posted, calling other classes, and who knew whether or not Italy was going into the great war? Probably yes; for both the Pope and the black pope were dead; God had called home his ambassadors.

"Woe, woe to us others," complained Za Sara, puckering tighter her brown puckered face. "Last year I earned a lira and a half a day for a month, shucking almonds; but this year there are no nuts. Without taking in soldi how shall we live?"

A breath of wind stirred her rough hair. Za Sara has only two teeth, though she is not an old woman; a yellow fang on one side of the lower jaw and a second on the other side of the upper.

I do not know how she keeps up with the other women biting off the outer shells of almonds.

"Woe, woe to us," she went, her eyes, drawn up small by exposure to the sun, lost behind puckers of anxiety. "God sends us thirst and war! It is the punishment of our sins."

"Does God send thirst and war?" I ventured.

"Thirst, yes," answered old Za Delfi Sittima— Aunt Delphia, the seven-months-child; "for the Lord rains when he will; but war is an affair of kings."

It was after this pronouncement of the separation of church and state that we heard the quavering lament of the cantastorie. A blind old man led by a boy was coming down the street singing of the destruction of Linera:

> To an earthquake mighty and strong
> Christ gave the order, you ken;
> But Mary the mother asked him,
> "What do'st thou, O Lamb, to men?"

When the singer had tottered away over the cobble stones to the next group of houses, I inquired, "Why is the Madonna kinder to us than the Lord Jesus?"

"Because she is the Mother," said Gna Vanna.

Bastianu, the youngest of her three grandchildren, had been fretting for a tomato. Pulling a round, brown loaf of bread out of the table drawer, he brought it to Gna Vanna, who cut him a piece, muttering as she struggled with the dull knife, "Hard as a mazzacani," a stone big enough to kill a dog. Bastianu got his white little teeth into it without trouble, and flung himself on the sacks of nuts whimpering for the "pumiduru," the golden apple, as the tomato is called.

Bastianu was ill. A tomato would hurt him. All night long he had fever. An ailing child is a great expense. Five pennies of milk she bought for Bastianu every day, three in the morning and two at night; while Vincenzinu, his five-year-old brother, contented himself with bread and wine.

Unmoved by this reasoning, Bastianu whined the louder. Gna Vanna's face sharpened; her bright eyes became steely. "Get out!" she screamed. "Get out of here! You dirty dog! You devil's face!"

The child began shrieking. Seizing Zu Vincenzu's stick, she took Bastianu by the slack of his dust-colored, faded clothes and cast him at our feet in the narrow, cobble-paved way. Gasping, he came back to her side, his dark eyes shining too big by half in his white little face.

"Why do you make the child cry!" screeched Gna Vanna, throwing back his stick to Zu Vincenzu, who sat as usual bent in his chair, his head tied up in a red kerchief, oblivious to everything that went forward. Kissing Bastianu, she gave him a tomato in each hand.

"The Madonna," she continued, turning to me, "is the Mother; she keeps us beneath her mantle.

You know, Signurinedda, how a mother is. If a child is bad, she gives him some good slaps, but afterwards she kisses and caresses him. The Madonna is like that with us. But the Lord Jesus, you know, Signurinedda, he is her son, and children have no judgment."

Zu Vincenzu, rousing himself, retreated to a seat behind the bed, his skin sandals making a scuffing sound as he crossed the cement floor. Gna Vanna made spiteful horns with her fingers behind his back; and then, shucking nuts faster than the best of us, she began telling us between bites a tale of how the Madonna thwarted Jesus.

The Ashes of the Sheep

"Once upon a time a boy was minding sheep when there appeared a man who said, 'You must give me the best lamb you have.'

" 'I can't give it to you,' said the boy shepherd, 'because they are not mine; they are my master's.'

" 'Then go to your master and tell him there is a gentleman who wants the best sheep there is.'

" 'Vossia, I can't go,' said the boy, 'because I have to mind my sheep.'

" 'I'll watch them,' said the man.

"So the boy went, and the padrone, who thought the man might take all his lambs if he refused one, told the shepherd to bid him take whichever one he liked.

"The man chose the best of the lambs and gave it to the boy saying, 'Hold it.' The boy took the lamb by its four feet and held it. Then the man said, 'Get me some wood.'

"The boy picked up what wood he could find and some light stuff for kindlings. Then the man said, 'Give me a match.'

"'Vossia, I haven't any,' said the boy; 'I don't carry matches.'

"'But you see that you have some; you do carry matches,' replied the galantomo, nodding towards the boy's pockets. The boy felt in his sacchetti and found matches. Then the man made a great fire and said, pointing to the lamb, 'Throw it in!'

"The boy threw the lamb into the fire alive, just as it was, with all its wool." Gna Vanna took off her apron and threw it by its four corners on to the nut sacks, as if it had been the lamb. "Alive with its wool," she repeated, her hooped earrings bobbing, her shining faded eyes expressing the boy's fright and horror.

"When the lamb was entirely burned, the man took a stick and scattered the ashes. As soon as these were cold he told the boy to sweep them with a brush of leaves. Then he said, 'Give me a handkerchief.'

"'Vossia,' said the boy, 'I haven't any; I don't carry a handkerchief.'

"'You see that you have one,' answered the man,

JESUS AS DESTROYER

nodding again towards the boy's sacchetti. The boy felt in his pockets and found a handkerchief."

Gna Vanna pulled up her faded cotton skirt and felt in the bag pocket that hung by its cords from her waist, drawing out a huge kerchief, at which she gazed with all the amazement of the shepherd boy.

"'You see that you do carry a handkerchief,' said the man. He made the boy hold it by the four corners while he poured into it all the ashes."

Gna Vanna's kerchief drooped in the middle with the weight of imaginary ashes, and she held it carefully with both hands, finally knotting together the corners.

"The gentleman made the boy tie up the bundle, and he said, 'Now you must go to the sea and throw it in.'

"'Excellency, I can't go,' said the boy. 'The sea is a long way off, your Excellency. I must mind my sheep.'

"'You must go to the sea and throw in the ashes,' repeated the man. 'I'll mind the sheep.'

"So the boy went. Half way on his journey he met a woman who said to him, 'Where are you going?'

"'I am going to the sea,' he answered, 'to throw in this handkerchief with the ashes.'

"'Where did you get it?'

"'A man gave it to me.'

"'Give it to me.'

"When the woman had looked at the handkerchief with the ashes, she said, 'My son! I thought so! At it again!'

"The woman was the Madonna, though the boy did not know it; and the gentleman was really the Lord Jesus. Because of the sins of man he meant to destroy the world. If the boy had reached the sea, and had thrown in the ashes, the world would have gone in ruins like Messina. But the Madonna took the handkerchief and put it under her arm, hidden by her shawl.

"'Because of his sins,' she said, 'I take away from man three things, bread, wine and oil; but let the world stand as it is.'

"Then she said to the boy, 'Greetings,' and she went away to her own house.

"The boy said, 'Vossia, give me your blessing,' and he returned to his sheep.

"When the boy reached the place where the fire had been, the gentleman asked him, 'Did you throw the handkerchief into the sea?'

"The boy said a woman had taken it away from him. The Lord Jesus knew that it was the Madonna, and he said, 'I salute thee; nothing but that; I salute thee.' The boy answered, 'Your blessing, Excellency'; and watched him as he took a step or two away. All at once the man disappeared. The boy went home and lay down on his bed. He died of fright.

"Children have no judgment," concluded Gna

Vanna. "The Lord Jesus wishes to unmake the world, but the Madonna does not permit, because she is the Mother. It is true that we are sinners, and that is why we have no food. The Madonna has taken away bread, oil and wine. It does not rain, and there are no crops; but the Madonna does not allow her son to make an end of us.

"Do I say well?" she demanded, tapping her forehead with a long forefinger, and glancing from one to another, confident of approval.

"Are these things excellent? I have no books, but I have all these things in my head. I know these things, and other people do not know them. The Madonna keeps us under her mantle. You agree with me?"

By this time Bastianu had finished eating, and was crawling under the table to get at a quartara of water. He mishandled the thick earthern jar, which rolled on its side, fortunately without breaking. "I'll knock you!" shrieked Gna Vanna with a blow of her clenched fist under her chin.

Scrambling out of her way and out of the way of the running water, Bastianu struck the box under the bed in which sat a hen open-beaked in the heat. With a squawk the fowl flapped out of the box and out of the room. Gna Vanna rose threateningly, but Bastianu had escaped with the hen.

Cumari Ciccia, the most good-natured woman on the street, had worked at the nuts until glances from Gna Vanna's eyes hinting that she ate too freely while shelling sent her to her own steps just opposite. From that point she could still talk with us, and now she came back with a pan of greens to pick over for minestra, saying, "I can tell Vossia another story."

The Old Man and the Bells

"Once upon a time an old man was digging in a vineyard when there appeared to him a young man who said, 'You must go to the church of the Madonna di la Catina to ring the bell.'

"The old man answered, 'It is far. I have not strength for the climb.'

"Then the young man, who was the Lord Jesus, replied, 'You have the strength and you have to go.'

" 'But,' said the old man, 'the church is shut.'

" 'The church is open,' said the young man.

"The old man carried his zappa to the straw hut where he had left his coat. Then he climbed the mountain side to the church where no one ever goes except in September to the great festa. Vossia has been to the festa? She knows the church, high up above Mongiuffi? The church was open. The old man went in, and began to climb the stairs of the campanile, when there appeared a woman who said, 'Good old man, where are you going?'

" 'To ring the bell. A young man told me I must come to the church to ring the bell. He said the church would be open, and it is open.'

"The woman was the Madonna. She said to the old man, 'What was the young man like?'

"The old man told her, and she said, 'It was my son, who wants to sink the world. Go away! Don't ring the bell.'

"The old man went down the belfry steps and back to the vineyard. He had just picked up his zappa and was going to work again when the young man appeared a second time, and said, 'Did you ring the bell? I did not hear it.'

" 'I met a woman who told me not to ring.'

"Then the Lord Jesus said, 'My mother! Must you break my heart again, troubling my plans?' At once he disappeared.

"If the old man had rung the bell, the world would have gone down in ruins."

Donna Ciccia retreated as soon as she had finished, for Gna Vanna took revenge for the almonds by nibbling the tenderest greens. Zu Vincenzu had come back from his corner, and now he suggested, "Vossia, when you go to your own country, you must make known to the learned what we tell you here. I myself must——" But Gna Vanna and the others interrupted the blind old man.

The idea of a benevolent power and a power for destruction crops out in many directions. Only a few days after the almond-shelling party there came a partial eclipse of the sun. An hour or two after the excitement was over Gna Vanna was snapping green beans when I passed her door, Zu Vincenzu helping by shelling beans out of the larger pods. When he had finished a handful he reached them out uncertainly in her direction.

"Signurinedda, did you see it?" Gna Vanna called to me, patting the back of an inviting chair.

Donna Ciccia, Cumari Lucia, who is Gna Vanna's goddaughter, and others of the cronies, dropped their work to come to the doorstep rendezvous. Donna Ciccia's nose and forehead were still blackened from gazing through smoked glass. "All the better it is passed," she said, her dark eyes twinkling good-humoredly.

Gna Vanna threw the refuse of the beans on a heap of wool flocks inside the door, her thin animated old face brightening at the prospect of an audience. "Yes," she repeated; "the less harm that it is over, for an eclipse always brings fear."

"Why?" I queried.

"Because the sun and the moon are angry with each other; they quarrel, and if the moon should win, it would destroy the world."

"But the sun always wins," I suggested.

"Yes," agreed Gna Vanna. "The sun is more powerful. The sun is the Madonna; the moon is her son, the Lord Jesus; you know that."

"How do I know that? I don't understand," I said.

"Certainly Vossia knows that. 'God is sun and God is moon.' You remember?"

JESUS AS DESTROYER

I remembered a couplet I had often heard her use in spells against the evil eye. So I quoted:

> [10] God is moon and God is sun;
> Work you ill there can no one.

"That is what you mean?" I questioned.

"Of course!" she returned triumphantly. "Vossia is convinced? The moon is the young master, the sun is the Madonna. The moon would like to burn the world, but the sun does not permit. To-day the sun, in order not to quarrel with the moon, hid behind the clouds. Instead of doing harm, the sun did good, because there came a little rain. The Madonna is always kind. She hides us beneath her mantle."

The neighbors did not contradict her identifications. More or less openly they call her a witch, openly and secretly they have, some more, some less, faith in her knowledge and powers. Cumare Lucia ventured a wish that the Madonna would send rain enough to do some good before the olives dropped off the trees.

The women drifted away to their own doorstones, and Gna Vanna began to fry peppers for supper. As I rose to go she paused in front of me, fork in hand, to say, "It can't rain; the rain is bound."

Her pale blue, bright eyes regarding alternately me and the peppers, she told me that certain masters

> [o] Ddiu è suli e Ddiu è luna;
> Supra di vui nun ci po persuna.

in charge of work that had been in progress for some months on the railway below us at Giardini had taken steps before beginning the job to insure good working weather. They had made, she said, five wooden figures of the size of one's hand and had wound them with cords, each cord tied with three, seven, or nine knots. With each knot they pronounced the words, "No rain! No rain! No rain! Always good weather!" These five pupi they buried on five mountain tops overlooking the town; on Monte Croce, at the Castle of Taormina, at the Castle of Mola, on Monte Ziretto and on Monte Veneretta. Until these pupi were dug up and the knots untied there could be no rain within the magic circle. Whenever clouds gathered instead of rain there came an evil wind, Farauni, and not more than a few drops fell.

I do not know into what depths of demonology and magic we might have plunged, if at this minute Cumari Pancrazia, Gna Vanna's daughter-in-law, had not come to show us a photograph she was about to send to her husband, who is in New York. Gna Vanna never talks magic when her daughter-in-law is in the room. She says that Tidda does not understand such matters.

The group picture which Tidda had brought included likenesses of herself, little Vanna, her daughter, and the two boys, Vincenzinu and Bastianu, all painfully clean and fine. She showed me gleefully how she had pulled down her short dress under her apron to make it long enough to cover her feet, and called on us to admire the boys' curls. The poor things had not had their heads shaved for the entire summer for the sake of growing those locks.

"He'll eat it!" she exclaimed, anticipating her husband's pleasure.

Gna Vanna's face expressed cold disapproval. She said the photographer charged too much. She said that Tidda, who in the picture was shown sitting in a high-backed carved chair, looked like San Pancrazio, the black patron saint of the town, in his throne seat above the altar. She said a number of other things which Tidda did not mind in the least, and so we forgot all about the weather and the peppers.

PART II

FAIRS AND FESTIVALS

CHAPTER I

Christmas

[11] Grande Virgo, Mater Christi,
Quae per aurem concepisti,
Gabriele nuncio.
Gaude quia Deo plena
Peperisti sine pena
Cum pudoris lilio.
—*S. Bonaventura's Hymn.*

"Rain! Rain!" said Carmela, beckoning from her doorway with that gesture of invitation which to the non-Italian means good-by. The rain, in fact, was coming down so hard that great drops jumped up from the pavement making "campanelli"—little bells.

Carmela lives in the Cuseni quarter of Taormina, where the streets are so narrow that its Corpus Domini procession is called "the Lord in a hole." I was bringing Christmas cakes to her smallest brother, so I took shelter hurriedly in the windowless room where three women huddled around the

---

[11] Great Virgin, Mother of Christ, thou who by the ear didst conceive, Gabriel bearing the message! Rejoice because, pregnant with God, thou gavest birth without pain, with the lily of modesty.

"conca" drew their chairs closer together to make room for a fourth pair of feet on its wooden rim.

"What a storm!" I exclaimed, shivering.

Even Ninu, Cicciu and Micciu, babies of eight days, six months and sixteen months, who lay on their mothers' knees with the passivity of Sicilian infants accustomed from birth to the click of knitting-needles, were heavily shawled.

"But no, Signurinedda!" protested Carmela, putting fresh charcoal on the white ashes of the conca. "It's not bad weather. It is only a little passion of the heart; and He is right, because He has made enough of splendor. For ten days what a feast of sunshine!"

"Yes, but to-day——"

"Signurinedda!" insisted Carmela, her big serious eyes continuing to reprove me. "One must not speak ill of the weather, otherwise He gets annoyed. And the sun, too; the sun buries himself deeper behind the clouds, because He is discouraged."

Carmela's sister Angelina, looking like a brown, anxious Madonna—in fact like the Madonna Panicottu pictured at Catania—was feeding Micciu with bread soaked in hot water. "Where is Babbu?" she demanded of the swaddled youngster, poking and tickling among his interstices, when I inquired for her husband.

"Babbu is in America; in America, figghiu beddu! Tell the Signurinedda Babbu is in America. When is Babbu coming home to Micciu? In two years,

Micciu, tell the Signurinedda. If Babbu makes a little money, in two years Babbu will come home from America. Will Daddy be glad to see his baby? Yes; Daddy has never seen Micciu at all, but he is very affectionate towards his little pet. Ask the Signurinedda, Micciu, if she sees your presepio most beautiful."

At mention of a presepio I glanced about the room whose smoke-darkened walls were hung with prints of the royal family of Italy, "coni"—icons— of various saints, and a high-colored poster advertising Rhode Island rubber boots. In one corner stood a table whose oilcloth cover was patterned with a big black Brooklyn Bridge and bordered with heads of Roosevelt and Washington.

The design of the Bridge, which is common in homes from which Sicilians have emigrated, was almost hidden by a presepio so elaborate that Angelina was right to be proud of it. Bits of lava, cork cut into ingenious shapes, sand, lichens and green moss had been laid out with the help of a little paint in a miniature landscape, where wandered shepherds with their sheep and herdsmen guarding cattle.

"If my Christian were here," said Angelina, interrupting the lullaby she was singing to Micciu, "he would have made a fountain and a river—Ninna, ninna, ninna, ninna——"

Against the wall at the back was a grotto of lava stones arched with ivy, twigs of orange and lemon trees in fruit and branches of the sacred thorn, a buckthorn, of which Christ's crown was woven. In the grotto, for lack of the traditional wax baby in a manger, had been placed a small colored picture of a Madonna and Child together with terracotta figures of Joseph and Mary, an ox, an ass and some goats and chickens. At the mouth of the cave were figures of the Magi and shepherds bringing gifts, all colored in time-hallowed tints of red, dull blue, yellow and gray. In front of the presepio were set offerings of oranges and lemons, nine snailshells and two toy automobiles loaded with dry pennyroyal.

For the automobiles Carmela apologized. One knows they are not appropriate to the presepio; but how does one do? Little Saru, her brother, insisted on using his toys. "He would even have put in a white porcelain pig!" she protested. "A rabbit, now, one might endure, but a pig at the manger!"

Carmela had freighted the machines with pennyroyal because the herb would blossom fresh at midnight of Christmas Eve, at the very moment when the Babe is born; provided, of course, she had succeeded in gathering it precisely at midnight of St. John's Eve. The snailshells were nine tiny oil lights for the nine days of the novena, lamps as old as the automobile is new.

At this point of her explanation entered small Saru himself, and at an ill-timed word about pigs cast himself on his stomach writhing. When I had produced "natalizi," which are twisted Christmas

THE PIPER

cakes pockmarked with hazelnuts baked in their shells, he discoursed to me tearfully between bites about the terracotta shepherds, pointing out the one that carried a sheep over his shoulder, the one who was offering a basket of curds and the old woman who was bringing chickens, naming one by one traditional figures which have not varied for who knows how many generations of time. He had just reached "chiddu chi suona 'a ciaramedda," he who pipes, when the drone of bagpipes came in at the open door.

"Gagini," said everyone in the room.

Presently there appeared in the doorway the old piper who has played the novena in Taormina for thirty years. From morning till night of the nine days before Christmas, Gagini trudges the ill-paved ways between the rows of tiled roofs gray and tumbled, sounding before every one of the fifty or more presepie his shrill pastorale. He brings lentils and figs which smell of the smoky fires of the mountains, and receives at the end a few soldi here, a few lire there, to which those good people who are able add macaroni and sausage.

Gagini is a goatherd. When his brown-black wards patter through the Corso at sunset and sunrise, and one begs for the milker's last good-measure squeeze into the foaming cup, then he is just a good humored old fellow whom the boys call "hair-feet," because he wears hide sandals; but at Christmas, when he fingers the stops and sends out the humming notes of the old pastorale, then comes Gagini's hour of dignity. His father and his father's father played the bagpipes. His son has gone to Argentina; but, he says, when he dies, someone will rise up to succeed him, for the shepherds played at the birth of Christ, and so long as the world shall last there must always be those who pay this devotion.

When the old piper had taken his stand in front of the snail-shells, and was blowing out his cheeks to begin the droning wail of the first motif, I slipped out of the house; for if one listens, it is to the very end, and then there are the colored leather tassels of the pipes to look at and the four pipes themselves, basso, falsetto, tenore and quarto. The sheepskin of Gagini's bag has darkened till it is almost black. The pipes, too, are dark and old, fashioned of some tough wood like heather.

But I did not stay, because this was the morning when Gna Angela had promised to tell me a tale of the birth of the Bambineddu as she had heard it from her "antichi." More than once Gna Angela had begun the story for me, but always there had come some woman anxious about the life or health of son or husband in America, for news of whom she must repeat the paternoster of San Giuliano; or we had been interrupted by some shopkeeper begging to have her shop rid of the damage to business caused by the evil eye of an envious rival. Gna Angela's repute as one who deals with mysterious powers is such that my friends seldom mention her except as "that one"; but they keep her so busy that I rejoiced in a rainy morning in the hope of finding her at liberty.

"That one" lives in the upper, under-the-castle quarter of Taormina, and the walk was windy. By the time I had climbed one of the long flights of steps that connect the upper streets with the Corso, the gale had grown worse. The persistent Sicilian sun shone fitfully, painting the water green, yellow and blue; but puffs of wind, falling perpendicularly from the mountains, drove into the sea to such a depth that spray rose high like jets from a fountain. Looking over the wall in front of the hospice, I saw far out at sea troops of little white waterspouts, like dancing storm spirits, driven towards shore by the wind that came scudding up the coast from Catania. Another minute and it looked as if a wall of water were advancing into the bay of Taormina.

Gna Angela's bent, tremulous husband stood at his door. The squall carried away his words, but I could see him muttering, "Evil spirits are in the air." Since the Messina earthquake one knows that the spirits of those killed before their time range abroad, seeking entrance into human bodies to complete their period of earthly habitation. It is they who bring us bad weather.

"Vossia!" stammered Zu Paolu, turning towards

me, "a tile might fall on your head; it's not safe to be out when such a wind is blowing."

Indoors was Gna Angela, bent as always over the "sciabica" she was netting. Yards of its fine mesh hung over a broken chair. At her side was a "conca," its wooden shell partly burned, its mortar bed holding nothing but ashes. "You here, daughter! I was not looking for you!" was her surprised greeting. Before kissing hands she wiped her lips carefully.

While I was shaking off raindrops the church bells and the bells of the clock tower began ringing to drive away storm demons, or, as one says nowadays, to call the people to prayer against them.

"Daughter, do you hear?" asked Gna Angela.

"The bells are tolling 'a penitenza.'"

"For the greater grief; there is fear in the town," said Zu Paolu.

The walls of Gna Angela's room are so grimed with soot that the saints of the many "coni" show but dimly. The battered chest, the bed, the rack holding bottles and a few bowls, the portable stove made of a square Standard Oil tin—every item of furniture had seen long usage.

The black fury of the storm which awed the two old people made the squalid place more desolate. Gna Angela sat hunched forward in her chair, her lean sinewy figure huddling under its gray shawl. Her lower jaw dropped, showing two or three yellow fangs. Her gray hair and wrinkled forehead retreated under her faded kerchief; even her watery eyes withdrew deeper into their cavernous sockets.

When I spoke of Micciu's presepio she plucked up heart to show me her own, which was nothing more than an arch of ivy and myrtle trained over an icon of the Madonna, a little shelf in front being covered with flowers with an orange or two as offerings.

Then she said, "If one talks it is more better," and haltingly, with many pauses to listen to the rattle of the hail, she began a story of Mary which "my grandmother told me," she said with a wan smile, "when I who now have four twenties and three was a beautiful young girl."

The tale must have been handed down in rhyme, I think, though Gna Angela gave it to me confusedly in verse and prose. There are many like it current in Sicily, woven in part, perhaps, out of old monkish versions of the ante-Nicene Gospels, modified by each generation of tellers and listeners; for a legend changes, but is never lost, say my old friends.

When "Mariolina" (dear little scamp of a Maria) was a child, she said, and went to school, the mistress one afternoon asked all the boys and girls to remember their dreams that night so as to tell them to her next day. In the morning, as soon as the children were assembled, she asked, "Alfieddu, what did you dream?" Alfieddu related his dream. Then the teacher asked the same question of Grazia and Carmellinu and Pippinu, and one by one all the boys and girls told her what they had dreamed. Maria's turn came last. When the mistress asked her, "Mariolina, what did you dream?" Maria answered:

"I dreamed of a ray of sunshine that entered my right ear and by my left ear came out again."

Gna Angela turned towards me, and lifted a gnarled yellow finger touching first the right side of her head and then tracing a course down through her body and up again on the left side to her left ear. "Like this," she said; "this was the course the sunray had taken."

The mistress was impressed by this dream. She told the children it presaged something strange and important. She said:

> These things are clear; it is no jest;
> All my books I'll burn; this way is best.

The mistress made a great fire, and called upon the children to give up their books also. Something so new and portentous was about to happen that books of the old wisdom she had taught them had become useless. Except Maria, all the boys and girls gave her their books. The teacher asked Mariolina among the others if she had burned hers. The little girl was a clever little rogue; and she answered with a play upon words, "c'haiu"; which might mean, "I have them" or "I have." The mistress supposed she had obeyed; but Mariolina kept her book. She hid it under her shawl, in her armpit.

The teacher told Maria that the dream was a prophecy that she would give birth to a prince or a king; and in fact before long the Bambineddu could be seen in the girl's body, lying visible as it were through the sides of a crystal box.

About this time Maria's parents and the highpriest and the judicial authorities married her to Giuseppe, a good old man who had a long white beard. Giuseppe had lands and houses in Egypt, and after the marriage he said he must go to his own country to prepare for his wife. He went away and after six months came back again. When the Madonnuzza saw him she said:

> [12] You are welcome,
> Royal husband;
> So long it is that I've not seen you.
> I cannot think whatever mean you.

Giuseppe looked at her with all his eyes; he saw she had grown big, and he said with a frown, "Make up my bundle." He had decided to leave her.

"Why are you going away?" asked the Madonuzza.

"Because you have betrayed me."

> [12] Si' bomminutu,
> Me spusu riari;
> E tantu tiempu ca nun hain virutu;
> Supra di vui nun sacciu chi pinsari.

(This is like the Protevangelium of James: "And she was in her sixth month; and, behold, Joseph came back from his building, and entering into his house, he discovered that she was big with child. And he smote his face and threw himself on the ground and wept bitterly.")

> He answered her in hostile wrath,
> "I go this day to my own hearth;
> To Egypt's land this hour I'm bound.
> All my houses I'll raze to the ground."

But at this point there descended an angel, and said: "Giuseppi,

> Of the mistress have no fear;
> See, your stick has blossomed here."

"Understand, daughter?" asked the old woman, speaking as eloquently with long lean hands and gestures of the shoulders and turns of the corded neck as with words. "Giuseppi stamped with his stick, and it flowered in his hand."

Giuseppe saw the miracle, and he exclaimed:

> "Now that I know all, how much and why,
> I go me not: I stay thee by;
> Ever I stay beneath thy cloak,
> Till unto life Messiah is woke."

So Giuseppe remained with Maria, and to while away the hours of waiting he took her to green places. She saw dates hanging from the branches of a tree, and she begged, "Climb up, dear husband, and get me some." Giuseppi answered:

> "Oh, woe is me! I'm grown too old!"
> The sacred palm bowed to the mould;
> Marie plucked the fruit of the tree;
> San Giuseppe saw the prodigy.

Gna Angela's tale went on and on, while her gray old husband, who is, he says, confused in his mind, interrupted and corrected, and now and then opened the door wide enough to let in a wet hen and a gust of rain. At last we came to the point where Maria said:

> "Let us climb up under yonder wall;
> There is a grotto with a stall.
> Let us enter, husband dear."
> The Madonnuzza's time was near.

San Giuseppe would have swept out the place for Maria, but there was not time; flights of angels descended and swept it for him. After the birth the Madonna was afraid, because there were animals in the grotto, and she called to Sant' Anastasia, who happened to pass:

> "Come in! Come in! Anastasia dear.
> Seest thou this mule? Ah, how I fear!
> Take this my son; keep him thee near."

Sant' Anastasia had no hands, but she stretched out the stumps of her arms, and when the Madonna laid the Bambino upon them, at once hands appeared. She gave the baby to her blind father, who was with her, and when he touched his forehead to the Child's forehead he saw.

"Understand?" asked Gna Angela again. "The Bambino made hands for Sant' Anastasia and eyes for her father. All day I sit quite alone and say over to myself these things of God."

But at this point Zu Paolu announced, "The weather is tired."

Tired weather is resting, preparatory to fresh activities, so I hurried away in the lull, as confused in mind as he between dim recollections which ranged from the old Egyptian faith that the crocodile, sacred to our Lady Isis, conceived by the ear when it brought forth Logos, the word; and from that other faith that Buddha's mother was a virgin impregnated by the sun, down to the Sicilian fairy tale in which a king's daughter shut up in a dark tower because a seer had foretold that she should conceive by light, scraped a hole in the wall with a bone, and bore a child to the bright beam that shot through the crevice.

When I reached home I heard the padrona calling, "Three castles and you want more?" So I knew that Mariuccia and Vanni were playing games with hazelnuts. In Sicily nuts take the place of marbles. One uses hazelnuts at Christmas and almonds in August, and the games are the same that were played in ancient Rome and that are played in America. Four nuts heaped pyramidally make a castle; at this one pitches a fifth nut, and he who knocks it down wins.

Luncheon was not ready, so we took a tile out of the dining-room floor, making a ditch to play "a fossetta." For this game you throw eight nuts at once. If an even number go into the ditch, you win and have the right to snap in the others with thumb and finger. If an odd number, you lose and the other player snaps in his nuts.

There had come for me a box from Palermo, a huge Christmas cake topped with a sugar image of the Bambino surrounded by spiky rays of gold and silver tinsel. After luncheon Vanni earned his share of it by rehearsing the piece he was to speak in church after the midnight mass Christmas morning, explaining the church presepio. He had not yet learned it glibly; but "rough cave," "squalid manger" and "Babe that wept for lack of comforts" came out effectively.

I had picked up somewhere a little old hand loom, shaped like a gridiron, and the good-natured padrona tried to teach me to weave braid, while we wore away the hours of a storm Sicilian in its beauty as in violence. Overhead there drifted a gray transparent veil of cloud borne by the wind, and spilling as it flew great hailstones that tore the first white blossoms from the almond trees in the garden and rolled them in drifts on the terrace. The sun burnt hot on the sea, streaking it silver and dark blue, except where the waters of the swollen Alcantara made splashes of gold, brown and gray. Towards mid-afternoon the gale increased, and the bells tolled once more their spell.

The padrona has almost as many old tales at her tongue's end as has Gna Angela. "Do you know," she asked smiling at my interest, "that three animals on three mountain tops announced the birth of the Bambineddu? First the ox lowed, 'E nasciutu lu Redinturi di lu mu-u-u-u-u-nnu! There is born the Redeemer of the world!'" She prolonged the Italian "u" to imitate the bellow of an ox. "Then the ass brayed from his hill, 'Un-n-n-n-n-'e? Where is he?' and from the third mountain the goat bleated, 'A Be-e-e-e-e-tlem.'"

"Then these animals are blessed?" I suggested, considering the reward of well-doing.

"But, no, Signora," she returned in surprise; "the ox, yes; because in the grotto it warmed with its sweet breath the Child's napkins. But the ass ate the Child's straw out from under him. And the goat also had no respect for the Child; it walked over him, and for this the goat is accursed; but some say only from the knees down."

So the day faded and at night Etna wore an aureole of gold. Next morning the streets were littered with broken tiles, but sea and sky had resumed their festival of sunshine. It was the twenty-fourth of December. Over the casino where gathers the "Civil Club" the knotted old bougainvillea vine was in glorious blossom. Hedges of red geraniums warmed the air, and the fields were full of wild iris.

Towards night a blind ballad-singer, led by his wife, plodded up the old road from Giardini. Up and down the Corso and into the narrowest side streets he wandered, singing to his squeaky violin a Christmas song that is common on the lips of the older cantastorie. In the evening when the Christmas fire was lighted in front of the church of Santa Caterina, he was still there, wailing in a cracked voice:

> On the eve of the Birth
> There's rejoicing on earth;
> For the dear Babe was born,
> To sound of drum and horn.
> S. Joseph, the little old man,
> To walk he began;
> With good staff in hand
> A hundred miles he walked the land
> Till a cavern he found,
> Where he swept the ground,
> For snow and rain had fallen there.
> So when came her hour to bear,
> A great lady bore her son,
> Bore a beautiful little one.
> He who passed her did adore;
> What beautiful fruit 't was Mary bore!

Just before midnight, when the long evening had been whiled away with nuts and cards, the starlit streets were filled with dark figures converging at the Duomo, where before the hour for mass the old red marble bench, once the throne of Taormina's Senate, now the rendezvous of unattached boys, resounded to swinging heels.

Mass over and a naked doll Jesus revealed on the altar by the lifting of a napkin, the flood of people streamed towards the Carmine, where a presepio with life-size figures and real hay filled one of the chapels. Vanni's discourse was not audible, for outside the church, as soon as the second mass was finished, red, green and blue lights flared, rockets fizzed, and preparatory to the street procession two brass bands began to flare. The crowd which had come almost to blows with uplifted chairs in its struggle to get in was even more anxious to get out again. At my side the peasant who had turned the wheel of bells to punctuate the mass, scrambled hastily across benches to get his banner, shaking over his head the while the white processional sack of his confraternity.

Presently through the dark Corso passed the image of the baby Jesus carried by the arciprete and lighted by flaring torches. Before it marched the "concerti musicali," and behind it three men played bag-pipes. Then came men costumed as Magi and shepherds, and after these the people of Taormina, a black mass of muffled figures, cloaked and shawled as if the mercury had said zero, instead of perhaps fifty-five degrees.

After the masses and the procession, when the fast of the vigilia is over, is the time to eat one's cake, with more substantial food, unless sleep seems preferable.

It is at Caltagirone that one should really pass Christmas, where the Bambino cult requires a living Bambineddu. The little Jesus is chosen by lot from among poor boys about three years old, presented for alms by their parents; but the lot never falls, I am told, on any except a beautiful blond. After the midnight mass Giuseppe and Maria lead the blond Jesus between them from the sacristy to the altar, where the naked mite, sometimes whimpering with cold, is exposed for perhaps half an hour.

CHAPTER II

Troina Fair

From Messina Roger advanced by Rametta and Centorbi to Troina, a hill-town raised high above the level of the sea within view of the solemn blue-black pyramid of Etna. There he planted a garrison in 1062, two years after his first incursion into the island.—*J. A. Symonds, "Sketches and Studies in Southern Europe."*

Before dawn I peered from my window in Randazzo at the impending mountain. Above a huddle of black old houses Etna loomed dark and clear and calm, a breath of smoke drifting from its vaguely white summit. It would be a good day.

Coffee had been promised for three o'clock, but when I had groped my way down stairs nothing in the disorderly inn seemed astir except swarms of flies that, disturbed by my candle flame, crawled sluggishly over wine-stained tablecloths, and then were still again. Stumbling over broken floor-tiles, I prowled in search of a bell. The eating-room was windowless, but as the light flickered along the walls from garish saints to steamship posters it touched a key hanging beside the street door. Despairing of breakfast, I fumbled with bolts and stepped uncertainly into the open air.

The stars had hardly begun to pale. The old lava-black city perched high on the Northern slopes of Etna was still asleep; dreaming, perhaps, of days when beneath its gates Greek and Saracen and Norman bloodied the waters of the Simeto and Alcantara. Behind Randazzo's walls in Roman times the slave Salvius gathered 40,000 slaves to fight for freedom. Past the church of Santa Maria that rose somber at my right marched Peter of Aragon's bowmen in the days when the Vespers rang the knell of the French in Sicily. Through the dim Corso winding left, Charles the Fifth, Emperor of the World, flaunted his bronzed captains and his laurels won in Africa.

As I shrank into the doorway out of the path of ghostly processions a voice said, "Signura?"

A muffled figure detached itself from the house-wall.

"Silvestro?" I ventured.

"Signura, it is late. Shall we go?"

"Let us go!" I answered, trying to recognize the driver with whom I had covenanted for a three days' trip to Troina, the first Sicilian capital of the Great Count Roger the Norman.

Two horses attached to a carrozzela shifted their feet sleepily. Silvestro, his long wispy mustache and faded eyes peering at me from under the shawls that wrapped his head and drooping shoulders, picked up my bag. I climbed to a seat. The whip cracked and our wheels were rattling when behind us there rose a clamor.

"Silvistru! The coffee of the Signura!" In the inn doorway, half-clad, shrieked the fat padrona, madly waving a candle. "Blessed little Madonna! Wait! Sil-vis-tru!"

"Silvistru! A gut-twisting colic to you!" bawled Pietro, son of the house, shaking back his lock of tow-colored hair as he tilted towards us on grotesquely tall heels.

"By the souls of my dead!" sputtered the old padrone, limping to the carriage-side with coffee pot and drinking bowl.

In spite of Silvestro's muttered "Accidinti! It is late!" I swallowed a scalding mouthful. Then after hasty farewells we clattered through the tortuous Corso flanked by grim mediæval houses—a stronghold in itself where in troublous times men might bar themselves against all enemies. Suddenly wheeling to the right, we plunged into a black passage. Straining my eyes towards the arches that linked the walls overhead, I was surprised by the stopping of the horses.

Alighting at a murky doorway, Silvestro picked from the skirts of a woman who came to meet us a mite of a girl whom he lifted to my side.

"Aita," he ordered, "put on your hat. Aita, blow your nose."

Silvestro has suggested to me earlier that his wife, who, like himself, came from the Alpine rock oi Troina, would like to see again the great yearly fair which was my excuse for the expedition. A mention of three bimbi too small to stay behind had restrained me from hospitality; but here was one child, and Silvestro had gone indoors. Must I transport the family?

"Her name is Agata?" I asked dubiously.

"Si, Signora; Aita," returned the mother, trying to adjust a flower-wreathed hat which the child pushed fretfully away from her light stringy hair.

Before I could question further the lank driver reappeared, cuddling something under his shawls.

"Let the Signura look!" he swaggered. He held up in the circle of his long arms two almost naked babies. "Let her see how blond they are!"

"Especially the boy?" I hazarded, glancing fearfully at the scant yellow hair of the wriggling twins.

"Gia! Turriddu is blond as honey. Daddy's big boy!"

"Turriddu is, in fact, the handsomer," beamed the mother; "but to-day he is ill, he eats nothing. The Signura will excuse that I do not take him, ugly with crying, to Troina? Aita will keep the Signura company."

Effusively I took leave of the small pale diplomat who had let me off with one baby. "Buon divirtimentu!" she called as the horses started. "Be good, Aita."

"Aita, put on your hat!" repeated Silvestro. "It

is late." But the five-year-old snuggled down in the coat I put about her, teasing sleepily, "Papa, buy me a doll?"

As we passed West out of Randazzo, Mongibello rose South of us, green and black against the whitening sky, the snow that still streaked its shoulders contrasting harshly with sooty fingers of lava. In the East filaments of dawn clouds floated; and, while I watched, the mountain top blushed saffron. In an instant the fairy glow had vanished; and, shut away from us by rugged heights, the sun had risen from the Calabrian hills.

We were following up the Alcantara between Etna and a scrap of rock that dropped abruptly to the river, beyond whose high valley we looked North to the foothills of the Peloritan mountains, mottled dark with oaks and the vivid green of wheat. Behind us Randazzo on its seat of ancient lava overhung the cliff, the Norman tower of San Martino thrusting up above the black houses.

Along the lonely road we passed now and again dark hooded figures hunched over slow-stepping mules. Huddled in a rough cappotto worn like a burnoose, its hood pulled over the forehead, its sleeves hanging empty, gun on his shoulder or slung at his back, man after man turned towards us a lean, leathery face with high cheekbones and keen, suspicious eyes.

Leaving the river, we held Southwest across a wilderness of lava that lay as grim in the early light as when centuries ago it crunched and hissed down from a spent crater above our heads, one of the two hundred "sons" that sprout from the sides of Etna. Hardly had we entered this waste, sardonically gay with flame-colored lichens, when the air was filled with bleatings. Bunched beside the road in an amazing hamlet we came upon black pens roughly piled of slag and clinkers. Of the shepherds' huts beside these grimy folds a few were roofed with new red tiles but the most were caves supplied by bubbles in the lava.

"Licotta!" lisped Aita, struggling to a sitting position.

"Ricotta? Sure! What says the Signora?" asked Silvestro, twisting his bent shoulders towards me. "Zu Puddu!" he shouted, as in a yard where steaming kettles spoke of cheese-making there started up a dwarfish old man.

"Don Silvistru!" returned the other.

Agile as a lizard the shepherd came towards us, his little black eyes lively with curiosity. Behind him raced swart children and from a hovel peeped a bare-legged woman. "Ricotta?" she echoed. "I myself strained the milk through fern leaves and stirred it with wild olive twigs." Her great earrings shook as she trotted to the carriage-side, fetching a wooden bowl full of curds made from "recooked" whey.

While we ate Zu Puddu questioned, "Is it true that in the land of the Signura they do not know ricotta?" His face puckered with wonder. "When the cheese is made the 'Murricani throw away the whey?"

After breakfast our road forked, one branch veering South towards Bronte, home of the thunder god, and the other, which we followed, West across the mountain-surrounded valley from which issue both the Simeto and the Alcantara. Running seaward, one West and South of Etna, the other North of it, the rivers enclose the mountain, opening highways which Sicanians, Siculians, Phœnicians, Greeks, Carthagenians—every race that has known Sicily—has followed between the coast and the interior of the island.

The land was blotched with lava. On its Northern face Mongibello's black glaciers sprawl until they strike the Peloritan rocks and the hills of Cesarò and Centorbi backed against the Nebrodeans. One minute we were passing green waves of wheat or fave, the mouth-filling broad bean; the next we were crossing an old lava flow, whose slowly crumbling substance lay here in hummocks and there in pools wrinkled like molasses. Here molten stone had tossed in inky surf and there it had broken over some obstacle in mud-colored rapids of coke and clinkers.

From crevices of the rock grew mullein stalks and sunburnt weeds. Dwarfed and twisted cactus wrestled for existence. Over the road hovered sulphur-yellow butterflies. Once or twice we started quail. We met a begging friar riding a mule whose saddle-bags bulged.

"Beetle!" spat Silvestro, making the sign of the horns.

The enormous straw hat above the brown habit did not turn. The fingering of the rosary went on as mechanically as the plodding of the mule.

It was the first day of June and the sunrays began to prick. A light scirocco was stirring, the cloudless sky looked pale. Etna had hidden his oaks and chestnuts, his yellow splashes of genestra and his stretching lava fingers behind blue aerial veils. Quivering in the distances ahead of us blue and white dream castles seemed to float on clouds. Silvestro named them—Agira, where Diodorus Siculus was born, though Silvestro knew him not, and where S. Filippo cast out devils; Centuripe on its hundred rocks and lofty Troina.

"It makes hot," fretted Aita.

She twisted herself out of her wraps and disclosed an odd little figure in a soiled blue dress. Red strings tied up greenish stockings.

"Put it on, Aita!" bade Silvestro; but the mite, instead of complying, dropped at her feet the distasteful hat.

"Aita is wild," pursued Silvestro. "Not that I hold with hats; chinicchi-nacchi!" he added. "But let one woman bring home fantastic gear from America, every skirt in town goes mad for it." He shrugged his shoulders, exposing patched, sun-faded raiment, far from fantastic. "Aita, blow your nose!"

We had crossed the dry bed of the Flascio and had come to a succession of no-trespassing signs that read, "Duca di Bronte; Private Street." "Duca di Bronte; Hunting Forbidden." North of us lay the vast feud, once of the Abbots of Maniace, which Ferdinand IV gave to Nelson, rewarding with a dukedom the Admiral's betrayal of the Republic of Naples.

The strawberry-leaved notices marked more than the "too fine compliment." "La Nave," the lava stream that flooded the valley, lay desert as far as our road, but across it on the Duke's side shimmered waist-high wheat. As we drew under the wooden ridges that shut the valley to the North Silvestro prattled of the Duke's rich lands, of his olives, his vines and his strange machines. So we reached the crossways where the road from Bronte, traversing the "Ship," cuts the highway before climbing to the nook in the hills where lies Nelson's castle.

The plain of the "sconfitta," Silvestro to my delight called the region; for after a thousand years daily speech still records the rout to which in 1040 Georges Maniaces here put 60,000 Saracens. The Greek was besieging Moslem Siracusa when Abd Allah's hosts poured down from beyond Etna to our plain, not yet blackened by La Nave, whence he could reach the sea. Taken thus behind, Maniaces led his Norse and his Russians, his Asiatics, his

TROINA FAIR

Italians and his Norman knights up by the Simeto. He camped near wood and water, and the spot has never lost his name. Abd Allah sowed the ground with caltrops, but Maniaces attacked with a wind that drove with him and, despite the iron barbs his cavalry "reaped" the Saracens.

We crossed the Simeto and began to crawl up the interminable windings of the hills down which came Abd Allah and, later, a greater than his conqueror —Roger, son of Tancred, who added Sicily to the domains of the Normans.

It was a confusion of mountains that we entered, mountains that rode one another's backs. Aside from the red-painted stations of the road-menders, there were few houses, fewer trees. The sun was blinding on the white ribbon of the road. The baked soil opened in drought fissures.

As we climbed past thirsty wheat and fave, the horses, gray with white feet, like those Goethe saw in Sicily, stopped to breathe; and from a close above the roadway limped down a gray man wrinkled like a baked apple. Eyeing us curiously, he piled my lap with scalora, refusing payment with head and hands as well as voice that squeaked, "The owner, it is I!" But when Silvestro priced artichokes, fearing Troina's high cost of festa, our owner, turning merchant, turned miser. Ten minutes he haggled before the horses' water basin was heaped with them.

As we crept up zigzag after zigzag Aita nibbled

the straight green lettuce. High above us Cesarò showed at moments, a gray mass above a gray mountain. In the hot sky to the left quivered Troina. Silvestro bargained with a gunner for a quail to make broth "for Turriddu, who eats nothing."

After we had broken fast on bread and eggs at a roadside locanda, wayfaring in the noonday heat grew slower. The sun beat on lonely pasture country where the silence was broken only by the wailing song of laborers stacking scant hay. On rocky hillslopes stretched sheepfolds defended by the thorny spina santa. Conical thatched huts rose near them, the shepherds' shelters.

At last the road twisted downward, grazing precipices, looping over ridges, dipping into hollows. Below us lay the valley of the Troina River, a green streak in a gray desert. Under naked banks cattle cooled their feet in the trickle of water. Beyond the river we crept for an hour up dizzy shelves of the mountainside, catching glimpses now of the depths below, now of the eagles' perch above. The gray tufa blocks of which it is built mortised squarely into its tufa cliffs, house above house, street above street, Roger's city sits its mountain ridge as if astride a saw.

Reaching wearily the tumble-down Cenobio of S. Basilio, we skirted the slope where the greatest animal fair of Sicily would open at gunfire, and wound along under the far side of the town; for no road attacks the ancient citadel except cautiously, from behind. Was it to this same gate, I wondered, that Roger led his freebooters when, plundering Sicily twenty-two years after Maniaces, he threatened Greek Troina; and its Christian people, still free from the Moslem on their rock in the wild Val Demone, opened to the blond Norman horse thief and welcomed him with crosses and swinging censers as a protector against the Saracens.

Inside the gate Silvestro pulled up at a squalid locanda provided, he assured me, with "all the conveniences of English usage. Put on your hat, spoiled child!" he railed cheerfully at Aita as a knot of acquaintances started towards him.

The Stella's fat little asthmatic padrone led me into a dark passage that ran through the inn and opened one of a procession of low doors.

"What pleases you?" he panted amiably. "Shall Silvistru unharness?"

The grimy walls once whitewashed and the dirty floor to which I was introduced did not please me twenty francs' worth, that being the room's price per night; but, explained my host, in June God gives Troina the providence of the fair. When Uncle January should send snow to stop travel, my excellency might stay the night for a lira. Besides, his wife was giving me her own room.

His wife had already fetched a petroleum tin full of water, drops of which made mud on the bricks. Mumbling that the servant creature was out, she produced soap and a broken comb. She uncurled a mountainous roll of mattress at the foot of a bed, spreading it on boards that rested on iron horses. From a deep chest she took homespun linen and a blue spread figured with red, trumpet-blowing angels.

While she examined my hat and dusty clothing, fingered my watch and flattered as "blond" my tanned skin, I tripped over everything I tried to say, fascinated by the erratic motions of my hostess' one tooth and by her straining eyebrows, dragged up from the yellow parchment of her face by a sinfully tight knot of hair.

Before I had detailed, as in duty bound, my personal history and excused the absence of other members of my family, Silvestro returned alone, having shifted to a sister the job of getting Aita's hat on. With him as guide I abandoned my "English comforts" for the narrow street, where pushcarts and benches, ropes of sparta grass and forks for thrashing, sickles and "ingeneri," which are wooden angles for holding grain in reaping, awaited the opening of the fair.

A foxskin hung beside a door, hinting at wild country; but as we climbed the Corso Ruggiero I saw little, aside from crumbling walls bare of windows and balconies and grimly eloquent of winter, of such individuality as marks Castrogiovanni and other mountain strongholds.

At the top of the town, 5,600 feet above the sea,

we came to Roger's cathedral, built beside his castle by masons whom the Great Count brought from "all parts soever." Rebuilt except its belfry, it covers now the castle ruins. Above its high altar sat enthroned, not Mary, patron saint of the devout marauder, but S. Silvestro, a monk who worked marvels in Troina in Roger's day, and who for centuries has been Troina's patron. His festa it was that the great fair honored.

I had barely a glimpse of his silvery robes and the silver vara on which he takes his outings, and of the brown old pictures in the sacristy of Roger and his brother-in-law Robert, first Norman bishop of Troina; for it was four o'clock, the hour of gunfire. Down a narrow way on the east side of the town Silvestro rushed me to a rock shelf defended by a parapet directly above the uneven stretch of rolling hillside called the "plain" of the fair.

Seldom has fairground a more grandiose setting. Over a world of mountains our isolated peak stood guard, watching the passes in the valleys. Far below us the Troina River joined the Simeto. Beyond Cesarò rose naked hills, ridge above ridge; sunburnt lands of wheat and pasture. Almost in front, under a rain of light and shadow dropped by the sun through motionless clouds, dimly visible through the scirocco, loomed Etna, and beyond it something hinted the sea.

A shot rang out and the empty plain was black

with cattle. From everywhere and from nowhere trampling droves covered the hillslope; rushing from this side, that side, meeting, passing, losing themselves in swirling maelstroms, each stream of horns or tossing heads driving hard towards its own goal.

"What a sight!" shouted Silvestro. "They shoot, and gone is the grass!"

The grass had vanished under the hoofs of horses and mules, bulls and cows which milled so thick "one could not drop a grain of wheat between them!" And this, Silvestro boasted, was only the prelude! A fine show, yes, but nothing to the fair next day.

"From as far away as Calabria," he gloated, "come beasts to Troina!"

After the confusion of harried animals had subsided I scrambled down to the plain. Men and beasts were settling themselves on hummocks and in hollows; the herdsmen in taciturn groups leaning on goadsticks—black as Moors they were, with high cheekbones and wild, not unkindly faces; the cattle snuffing the grass that had grown three months uncut to give them forage. A path was already trodden to a fountain behind the Stella, and boys all patches and beady eyes were fetching water.

As I ventured among the horses, few of which were hobbled or tethered, I caught gloomy phrases about a "cold fair." With its bustle and its hugeness the fair looked far from "cold"; but perhaps neither the booted and spurred signori who cantered their mounts up and down, inspecting the better nags, nor their retinues of velveteen-clad guards, whose guns slapped about on their backs as they slid to the ground to lift a foot or wrench open a mouth, had warmed up to Silvestro's enthusiasm.

More attractive than the rather commonplace horses were the thousands of big sleek mules. With their handsome "basti," their gay long-tasseled saddle-cloths and saddle-bags decked with red wool and embroidered with scrolls and arabesques, saints and animals, the mules were the stars of the fair. The rough-coated colts and young mules, fifty or a hundred to the bunch, were too restless to visit; but the ugly, awkward little donkeys submitted to be looked at, as did the tall red cows with horns a yard long, the very cattle of Helios hunted by the companions of Ulysses. On the outskirts sulked huddles of sheep with noses to the ground; intruders they felt themselves in the great fair of the "pelle rosse"—red-skinned bovines and the horse kind.

The collars of the bell-cows, which I had come to see, proved sadly crude and uninteresting; though patience found me a few carved and painted in the old manner with saints and Madonnas, double-headed eagles, bandits, carabinieri and their train.

Two girls whose orange-colored kerchiefs and huge earrings caught my eye were tending a cow as big as an ox which at my approach turned its neck stiffly in a tight wooden yoke covered with figures. On one side St. George in red spiked a green dragon, on top was a crucifix and on the other side a swarm of beseeching Souls in Purgatory.

"How are you, Excellency?" asked the younger girl, adding in Mulberry Street English, "Wat-a you do 'ere?" Laughing, she hid her face in her apron.

We laughed together as a hot-air balloon in the shape of a horse drifted over the fairground from the heights of the city. There followed a swollen, unwieldy cow and a menagerie of other animals, some of which, taking fire, blazed merrily.

As the air grew dusk and I climbed towards the Stella, cloaked and hooded figures, silhouetted against the sky as they galloped along a rise of the hill, seemed to shift the scene to a camp of Bedouins.

"What would your Ladyship like for supper?" was my landlady's greeting.

"What is there?" I retorted.

"Bread, wine and sleep."

The humorous old padrone rested her head on her hand, feigning slumber.

"Bread and wine," I agreed; "but no sleep till after S. Silvestro's procession."

Doubling a sheet over a greasy pine table, she fetched in addition to bread some hard sausage, very salt, and a plate of faviana, green beans.

Before I had eaten, Aita was at the door with Silvestro; Aita washed and dressed in white and

HOTEL AT TROINA

"MOST BECOMING"

A HERDSMAN

GOING TO THE FAIR

wearing her flower-wreathed hat. She carried a doll, she was eating "torone" and Silvestro wanted money. He had a toothache, he said, and in fair-time no dentist would look at him for less than ten francs.

"Doll," teased Aita; "my doll." She twitched my skirt with sticky fingers, holding up the doll. Of course Silvestro needed money.

Going out into the warm darkness, we met Aita's aunt and cousins near the cathedral—the title lasts, though the Great Count himself who built it transferred the bishopric to Messina. With chairs which the party carried we sat blocking the street in comfort until in the distance rose frenzied "evvivas." From S. Silvestro's own church below the paese half of the city was upon us, following his relics to the cathedral.

With flare of rockets and deafening drumbeat there approached a host of torches lighting up the long white sacks and black mantles of a confraternità that followed. Candles flickered over bronzed faces that looked out from under turbans whose white flowing ends drooped to the shoulders and rolled behind the back into a queue. Other drums and a phalanx of torches led a second confraternità with red mantles, and then a riot of shouts heralded a third whose color was blue. Last of all passed priests and friars escorting the Eucharist and the silver image that holds a bone of the saint's skull. As the torches moved, flaming, up the high steps of the cathedral, rockets flashed skyward, and from stands above our heads there broke out crashing music.

Between blare and bang Aita fretted, and her aunt told shivery tales of S. Silvestro's tomb. Sunk below an altar of his church, it rises. "Half an inch," she said, "since last year. Something will happen!"

And something happened. Silvestro said that next day we should see neither an "Intrillazzata" nor a Cavalcade.

Though he is but a second class thaumaturge, with little more to boast than that he healed a king's son and rode his stick to Catania and back in a day, and that a falcon and a flame revealed his burial place, lost for centuries, S. Silvestro's festa has been honored by spectacles that might stir the jealous wrath of many a greater saint.

He had a miracle play; has it yet, sometimes; and against hope I had hoped to see black-robed Lucifer in his priest's hat and the angels and God himself who figure in the "sacra rappresentazione," now legend, now Bible story; for as time goes on and towns spend less and less on festas, Troina's miracle play, seldom put on paper—for peasant poets who cannot write give out their rhymes by word of mouth to peasant actors who cannot read —may soon become a memory.

If the Sindaco is generous or his own income permits, S. Silvestro holds a Cavalcata, when

Roger's knights spur shining steeds through Roger's Corso. In Scicli, for the Madonna of the Militia the Great Count still struggles, festa after festa, with the Saracen; and so at Aidone. But Troina, Norman capital, celebrates Norman victory.

In Troina Ruggiero stood that hungry siege when he and his newly wedded Eremberga shared a single cloak. Once his horse was killed under him when he had sallied from the gate; but, swinging his sword in gleaming circles, he dragged off bridle and saddle—so, grown old and garrulous, he used to boast to worshiping Malaterra—shouldered the harness and hewed a bloody way back to the walls. In the fight above Cerami St. George on a white charger scattered with his gold-tipped spear 50,000 paynim, and the Norman handful, triumphant, gloried in the miracle.

And so for S. Silvestro, who saw that fighting, his devotees, when there is money, don helm and spear like those of the warriors painted on the carts, and in guise of paladins they prance and curvet now rising in their stirrups, now leaning from the saddle, to divide to ladies at their windows and to the mob the flowers and confetti carried by their squires—spoils of the vanquished dogs of Mussulmans.

"Quintals of sweets it takes," explained Silvestro. "Not every year can we see a Cavalcade!"

"In the old days they gave chickens," sighed Aita's aunt.

That night when braying mules and trampling horses murdered sleep I vowed to ignore next year such modern things as miracle play or strife of Cross and Crescent, and to reach Troina a week before the festa to see an ancient function whose roots are deep so that it fails not—the bringing of the laurel.

When Apollo re-entered Delphi after he had killed Python he wore laurel plucked in Tempe to guard him from avenging ghosts. And every eighth year thereafter throughout the old years a Delphian lad burned a mimic dragon's den, and fled, blood-guilty, to Tempe and the purifying laurel, bringing branches home with pomp and music before the Pythian games to crown the victors.

And every spring to-day Troina men go out to fetch the laurel, wandering for days, for there is no Tempe near. On Sunday two weeks before the festa hundreds who went on foot return in procession, crowned with the sacred leaves. Seven days later the hundreds who went on horseback clatter home, firing guns as they approach to call Troina to the parapets. Gay with boughs and ribbon, the Cavalcata d'Addauru, spurring to the cathedral, casts sprigs of laurel at it, keeping the rest, blessed and blessing, throughout the year.

Next morning the "A-a-a-h! A-a-a-h!" of donkey boys waked me before sunrise. In the courtyard under my window horses were being put to an ante-diluvian stage named in tall letters "Automo-

TROINA FAIR

bile." Slipping out of doors behind pattering asses buried to the ears in hay, I followed to the fair ground.

The encampment on the plain looked chill and sluggish. The black masses of cattle chewed indifferently at the red-flowered sudda in their forage. The men stood in silent groups, rigid, motionless. Each had his "scappularu" buttoned across his chest, or one end of the long cape was flung over the opposite shoulder. Hoods were pulled forward over dark wild faces. Men of tougher fiber they looked than the people of towns.

Breakfast was in progress. Against heaps of saddles sat cowherds and horseboys, the skin sandals that covered their feet sticking out straight in front of them, hacking chunks of bread with their American knives from the round loaves which they pulled, together with cheese and onions, from their saddlebags, and drinking from wooden bottles hooped like casks.

I found one of my cowgirls of the day before muffled in a black shawl, an end of which was drawn across her mouth. An old woman had joined her, and the two, cushioned on mounds of clover, were munching bread. Presently the other sister appeared balancing a tin of water on her head, leading the big cow at the end of a rope and knitting.

The scene was as yesterday, the light brilliant upon the wonderful circle of mountains presaging heat. Boys were passing up and down with water flasks; animals drank at the great fountain. The women with cows wore enormous earrings and faded gowns of print. The sheep huddled together, faces toward the ground.

At eleven o'clock we lunch on bread, eggs and wine, and start. Aita's white dress is soiled, but she still has the medal. Silvestro, who has paid five lire to have his offending tooth drawn, is tired and cross. The fair in the street is now lively; sheep are roasting; unidentifiable meats are frying; there is noisy sale of small necessaries, sickles, sparta grass ropes, three-tined hay-forks, pots, pans and the like. A relative of Silvestro going down to Linguaglossa ambles beside us on muleback; later he is to leave his mule at home and ride with us. We are all sleepy, even the horses; but Silvestro's young relative scrutinizes every bunch of cows or flock of sheep we pass, and asks what they cost at the fair.

White, winding, shadeless road; browned fields; brown, bare mountain slopes, the farther hills in summer haze—down again to Fiume di Troina, which helps make the Simeto; it is nearly three o'clock when we make the beetling crag of Cesarò, our first goal, where we eat again bread, eggs and a handful of green fave, washed down with wine, and are off.

Near a country house the family—two boys, three or four girls and the mother—are furbishing up a "cona" of San Calógero for his festa, which is due at Cesarò, June 18, a great fair. The shrine is of the usual wayside sort, a miniature chapel with cross on top, figure of the saint in a niche and a little shelf for oil and flowers. The girls have whitewashed it inside and out, and are now putting on stenciled decorations. At each side of the front wall a girl has put a yellow flower pot with yellow plant; she is adding a large full-blown blue flower. Her stencil pattern is cut out of brown paper; she holds it with one hand against the white wall and dabs paint with the other. It takes her only a minute or two to blue-flower both walls. Silvestro asks if they light up the saint all the year round, and they reply, only at the time of the festa. He tells them that if they leave Calógero in the dark all the year except at festa they cannot expect him to do much for them.

We chat with the girls while the boys climb up into the fields above to cut artichokes for us. Silvestro haggles to get four for a soldo, but he has to give a trifle extra.

Looking back on the way to Randazzo, Troina's low black houses in the distance seem like nests of birds or the lair of beasts of prey. The men talk about animals while Aita sleeps, nodding when her father scolds her because she drops her sweets, or doesn't blow her nose often enough, or will not wear her hat. We pass a big plantation of fave and Silvestro says we can gather there, as it belongs to a cousin, and Aita wakes up to eat.

There is a fine view of Randazzo as we at last draw near, with Etna in the evening light vast and serene; and as we plunge into the streets of the town we find them gayer than is their wont, the long main street especially thronged for the procession of l'Annunziata, the balcony flower pots gay with Bermuda lilies, roses and bright geraniums. So, consoled for the gayeties we had cut short at Troina, we look for a little at the procession, the torches, the robes of the confraternità, the Madonna and the angel—a grim, dark face under a white head-cloth—until sleep has its will of the weary.

CHAPTER III

SAINT PHILIP THE BLACK

The expulsion of demons from the bodies of those unhappy persons whom they had been permitted to torment was considered as a signal though ordinary triumph of religion, and is repeatedly alleged by the ancient apologists as the most convincing proof of the truth of Christianity. The awful ceremony was usually performed in a public manner and in the presence of a great number of spectators.—*Gibbon's "Decline and Fall of the Roman Empire."*

CALATABIANO means "Citadel of Bian," and to this day the gray little town beside the Alcantara huddles under the ruins of the Arab chief's stronghold. High on the castle hill near the fort's outer wall stands the small mediæval church of Bian's successor in the protectorate of the neighborhood, San Filippo the Black, the great exorcist of Sicily.

As well ask who was the forgotten Bian as who was S. Philip the Black. His color tells nothing. San Pancrazio of Taormina, San Calógero of Girgenti and the Madonna of Tindaro are black. In Sicily, as in other Catholic regions of Europe, black Christs and black Virgins have succeeded to black Isis and the black Venus of Corinth.

In Calatabiano San Filippo is called "the Syrian."

Omodei, who lived in Castiglione on Etna in the sixteenth century, says that he came from Constantinople into Sicily in the reign of the Emperor Arcadius, and drove out the demons that infested the country. Agira, where he died, and Calatabiano have been centers of devotion to him for many hundreds of years; and in other towns of Eastern Sicily he is famed as a liberator of the "possessed" and for the frenzy of his processions.

It is not more than four or five years, for instance, since Sicilians in the United States sent money for a new statue of San Filippo to their home in the mountain village of Limina, where the old one had been broken by many falls. At Limina, when the saint goes out in yearly procession, the contadini who carry the beams at one end of his vara, acting not of their own will but as automatons under his control, push and pull so madly against the tradesmen who carry the beams at the other end that these battering rams are hurled against trees and walls, until not infrequently vara and saint go to the ground. If in the tug of war an outer stairway or a projecting balcony that encumbers the street is demolished, or the growing crops of an unpopular landlord are trampled, this was San Filippo's will; his bearers could not help themselves.

The new American statue remains discreetly in the church. It is still the scarred veteran that inspires the Dionisiac madness of the procession.

At Calatabiano the feature of San Filippo's procession is speed. The "traditional, most rapid, miraculous descent of the simulacrum of the saint from the castle hill in less than five minutes"—to quote from a notice posted annually in near-by villages—draws thousands of spectators.

Yet at noon of a hot, still eighteenth day of May Calatabiano was drowsing so heavily that if I had not seen a carter bargaining with a cobbler for four pairs of children's white shoes, I might have thought I had mistaken the date of the festa. It is true the descent was not to take place until six o'clock in the evening.

As I climbed the narrow way that leads between gray wasps' nests of houses plastered against the hill to the mountain path, four children picked themselves up from the powdery soil and followed. There was Nunziata, a tot in a dusty blue dress that came to her heels. From broken stone to broken stone of the precipitous ascent she struggled on, though at times a bobbing head tied up in an orange-colored kerchief was all that we saw of her. There were Saria and Cicciu, wiry creatures, yellow with malaria, who darted ahead in chase of lizards or for the cautious gathering of prickly wild artichokes. And there was half-blind Ninu, a waif and a beggar, who paused now and then at one of the rudely painted stations of the cross to pass his hands over the pike of a soldier or the nails in a basket carried by one of the Jews.

The way was deserted, except for the bees in the

yellow blossoms of the cacti, until half-way up we came to the solitary church of the Madonna del Carmine, where strong brown women were getting in the ecclesiastical hay. "Time of almonds," they said when I asked the date of the Madonna's festa; "in the time of ripe almonds." It seemed, that sleepy afternoon, a definite enough reply.

And so we came to San Filippo's mountain chapel. Here a couple of men were planting rough stone mortars beside the path, and digging out from them the refuse of old charges of powder. No one else was to be seen.

"Vossia, can you read?" asked Saria, as we turned to the gray little church balanced precariously on a shelf of the hillside.

Her tone was one of simple inquiry, but no sooner had I said "yes" than Ninu and Cicciu abandoned the mortar men, though these had arrived at the stage of loading in fresh charges, and cried out with her in chorus, "Can you read this?" pointing eager fingers towards a weather-beaten Greek inscription over the old Byzantine-Norman doorway.

Without waiting for an answer, they poured out the marvel with which they were bursting: Nobody could read that writing! "Not even the king!" said Cicciu. Saria giggled a little doubtfully at this assertion of the king's incapacity, but the children agreed that the letters made an incantation. If only I could understand it and we could come to the church again together on Christmas eve and repeat the charm aloud, at midnight precisely, three times without missing a word, the mountain would open and show us heaps and heaps of gold.

"We could take as much as we wanted," said Saria, cutting away the prickles with Ninu's broken knife from the artichoke she was eating.

But through the open doorway we caught sight of something more entrancing even than enchanted treasure. San Filippo's vara was in plain sight. The church was not empty. We hurried inside.

It was still early afternoon. Aside from a drooping woman who sat, coughing and exhausted, surrounded by two or three villagers, the sacristan and his helpers had the place to themselves. A dusty closet above the high altar was open and the half-length figure of the patron saint of Calatabiano had just been taken down.

San Filippo is not a pink-cheeked boy doll like Sant' Alfio. He is ebon black; his beard is forked and the whites of his fiery eyes give him such a fearsome look that Nunziata and even Saria shrank when they saw his halo unscrewed and the unwieldy wooden image brought towards the vara which had been placed opposite the door.

The conveyance on which a saint is taken out of his church in procession varies from a simple barrow to the towering car of Santa Rosalía of Palermo. San Filippo's vara is a substantial platform, standing on legs and covered by a standing top in tarnished gilding. It is carried on the shoulders of some thirty men by means of beams run through sockets below its floor, projecting in front and behind.

When San Filippo had been dusted and screwed to his pedestal under the canopy, the sacristan brought out his holiday vestments. San Filippo's toilet is not elaborate like that of a woman saint—Sant' Agata of Catania wears more jewels than did Isis—but the taking off of his rusty every-day chasuble and the putting on of another shining with gold embroidery, the changing of his stole and maniple and the refitting of his silver halo occupied some time.

Before the process was complete people had begun to arrive, bringing bunches of flowers and young wheat—first fruits—which were tied with red ribbons to the vara. One or two watches, a bracelet and some rings were hung to the saint's uplifted hand. A woman fastened a hen with red rags to a column, where it dropped as forlorn as the one goose Julian the Apostate saw offered to the Apollo of Daphne in place of hecatombs of fat oxen. The spikes that fenced the four sides of the vara began to blaze with candles. A weeping girl who had climbed the hill in stockinged feet brought a wax torch taller than herself.

Next to the vara the forlorn woman I had seen on entering the church was the center of interest. The villagers said she came from Messina, and that since the hour when she was taken from under the ruins of her house after the great earthquake she had been unable to speak until that day. Hour after hour in the bare little church she had mutely implored San Filippo, and at last had come the sign of liberation: All her clothes had fallen from her, so that "to see her was a scandal." She had brought new clothes in faith, and the by-standers had re-clothed her piously. Now she could speak. The dumb demon had been expelled. In gratitude for her healing she had licked crosses with her tongue upon the pavement three times across the floor.

In proof of this first miracle of the festa the people showed me hanging in a side chapel, the faded shawl and skirt and the broken shoes she had dedicated. Ghastly white, the poor soul affirmed, "It is true, Signura."

Men as well as women were coming up the path, among them young contadini in whose holiday attire red neckties flamed conspicuous. Two or three of the children were recognized as of those to be honored by carrying San Filippo.

We climbed to Bian's ruined castle. The children found the one piombatoio that remained above the arched entrance, and put it to its original use, hurling down stones. The nearer hill slopes were planted sparsely with olives and almonds and glowed with yellow broom. To the South heaved up the bulk of Etna, still snow-crowned, its lower slopes dreaming under blue veils of summer haze.

To the West lay the valley of the Alcantara, whose waters have been bloodied age after age by the struggles of race after race—Sicanians, Siculians, Greeks, Carthagenians, Mamertines, Byzantines, Arabs, Normans, Spaniards, French and Germans. To the North rose the mountains of Taormina, and to the East the blue and silver plains of the sea.

While we lingered in that rapture of light, Saria spied a movement below.

"Come on!" she cried. "Let us go!"

San Filippo must be making ready for his exit, for people were swarming out of the church and scurrying down the broken path to avoid the rush of his bearers. We scrambled down ourselves, and mid-way between church and village found half the countryside massed on the abrupt slopes above the dry torrent bed down which for half his course the wild black saint must come. It had taken us perhaps fifteen minutes to reach a place of vantage. Cicciu and Saria climbed a rock above the heads of the impatient throng and pulled the rest of us up beside them. Still there was no sign from above; but the wait was not long. At six o'clock exactly the mortars crashed their signal. "Now!" called eager voices. "Now!"

A minute later roared the multitude! "They're coming!"

The vara with its thirty bearers came lurching towards us, past us, down into the valley, reeling, rocking, hurling itself in flying leaps, seeming to hit the earth and rise again, a tremendous human projectile.

There was a gasping silence; then "Viva San Pilippu!" echoed from every rock of the mountain. Once again the "traditional, most rapid, miraculous descent" of the cannon-ball saint had been made in less than five minutes. At a guess, the precipitous descent is three-quarters of a mile.

"Fine! Eh, Vossia?" asked Cicciu. "Great! Wasn't it?"

"A miracle!" I answered. If they reach the foot alive, the greatest miracle San Filippo ever performed!

We hurried with the crowds to the bottom of the hill, where priests, banners and torches had awaited the vara. The triumphal progress of San Filippo through the village was made with slow pomp, with bands of music blowing horns and clashing cymbals, with children strewing the way with golden broom flowers and the red petals of geraniums, with confraternità in white sacks, with priests in golden vestments. The setting sun gilded the vara as it moved towards the Matrice, followed by the greater part of the population.

From the door of the mother church the vara sprang forward with great leaps to the altar and then back to a place in the rear, where the brown young peasants who had vindicated the saint's prowess and their own dropped into chairs, fingering bruised shoulders where the vara beams had rested, panting, wiping away the sweat that rolled from their foreheads. Five had fallen in midcourse. Broken ribs are not uncommon.

The vara meanwhile was taken by assault. Men clung to its columns kissing the saint with frenzy. Parents lifted children to kiss him. Women kissed their fingers that had touched his vestments. Cicciu and Saria swarmed up on to the platform and reached down towards Nunziata.

"Take me! Take me!" cried the baby, twitching my skirts and speaking for the first time that afternoon. I picked her up, but too late. Men were at work again, unscrewing San Filippo's halo.

From the vara the black saint was carried to the main altar and set high above us. Below him burned candles rank on rank. In the dim church gleamed and swayed tinsel hangings of many colors. At the chancel rail blazed huge wax torches.

Next morning Calatabiano awoke to the boom of cannon, the clangor of bells and the drums and brass of parading bands. Even before sunrise, on foot, muleback, in high two-wheeled carts, by early trains, the countryside flocked to the fair that accompanies every festa, until by nine o'clock the piazza in front of the Matrice and the narrow streets adjoining, the center of a village of less than 5000 inhabitants, were packed with many times that number of people.

The day proved hot, and the sellers of rainbow-hued ices rent the air with their calls: "Like snow! Like snow! One cent each! Cool as snow!"

From the copper pans where chick peas were popping came the return challenge of the ciceri men. "Hot! All hot! Hot peas here! Taste! Come and taste! He who has money let him eat! Hot! All hot!"

From the donkey fair beyond the bridge that crosses the Torrente Sincona rose the braying of asses whose mouths were wrenched open by prospective buyers and of mules galloped furiously to show their paces.

Gay carts were almost as numerous as at the festa of Sant' Alfio. Mule saddles stuffed with straw and covered with coarse linen were heaped in great piles, each bastu flaming with red flannel scrolls, figures of men and animals and signs against the evil eye.

Sickles, broad straw hats and stacks of rushes spoke of haying time, of the tying up of vines and of the nearness of the grain harvest.

In the church mass succeeded mass. At the beginning of each function the sacristan, armed with a drum, beat a tattoo at the door in competition with the horn that tooted at one side of the steps over a barrow-load of bright summer muslins—"Five cents a yard, women!"—and the shouts that rose at the other side over the game of feeding the dragon. The dragon was tall and stood on his tail. One tucked into his mouth a ball with flattened numbered sides; betting, as it squirmed down through his red and yellow contortions, on which face it would fall at the bottom.

The church when I entered was a sea of many-colored kerchiefs in tempest. San Filippo's empty vara, where yesterday's flowers were fading, stood forsaken, while men and women elbowed towards a recess at the right of the main altar from which came shrieks and shrill laughter. The hysteric and insane who had been brought to the saint for the casting out of the evil spirits that possessed them had been present in the church during the earlier masses; but now before high mass they were being removed.

When the sacristy door had shut behind them and quiet was restored I found sitting beside me two dainty little girls who radiated such bliss that I hinted how "simpatici" I thought their new blue dresses. They preened themselves, spreading out pink scarfs and turning up the toes of white shoes; and presently, while San Filippo glared in the candle light and the lean sacristan wormed his persistent way between close-set rows of chairs in quest of his lawful soldi, they began to chatter about "Babbu" who had sent the money for all these pretty things. Perhaps I had bought meat of Babbu, since I was " 'Murricana" and he a butcher in New York. Babbu had been gone seven years, but he never forgot new dresses or wax for the day of San Filippo.

They pointed out to me Mamma's wax torch among the many blazing at the rail. More than a meter tall it was, and trimmed with roses and red ribbons. After mass they would help her carry it home, to light in case of illness. The flowers, too, they would save to lay on the bed of a sick person. Next May, perhaps, Mamma would melt on more wax to the torch and lengthen it to offer again.

"Mamma," who sat beyond the children, looked so uneasy and the sacristy door remained so obstinately shut that I abandoned mass in quest of luncheon. The little shops turned for the day into eating-houses put out hard boiled eggs, sheep's-milk cheese and round brown loaves of bread on small stands as signs. The one table was occupied in the room down into which I ventured—its floor of broken bricks was below ground level; but the stout padrona, whose big hoops of earrings swung with the vigor of her movements, set a plate for me on the shelf of her American sewing machine.

At the other end of it seated himself an old "hairfoot" wearing the homespun and the hairy sandals of the mountains. Setting down his stick, engraved by a patient knife with men on horseback and stiff be-aproned ladies, he pulled out a lump of bread and called for two soldi worth of wine.

Service was rapid, for just inside the street door, not three steps from the table, stood the cookstove. Once it had been a petroleum tin; but wires run through its middle made a fire rack, a vent had been cut below; and, mounted on the box in which it had traveled from Texas, it seemed on terms of old friendship with the terra cotta cooking pot where simmered a stew of kid and peas.

At the other side of the door stood the family bed, the mattress of which, rolled up for the day, left half the length of three wide planks as a sideboard for bread, lettuce, plates and other necessaries.

The short brown men at the main table, who might have been itinerant venders—the gypsy folk who gather at every fair—had the squinting eyes, the deeply lined faces and the faded dust-gray clothes of men who live under a powerful sun. They ate fast and much, swallowing wine from the carafe and haggling over every soldo.

"Eat like Christians and pay like Christians!" admonished the padrona, not once but often; for when the first were gone there came others, and yet others like them, so that the padrona went to market, bringing back yards of white butcher's waste to follow the kid into the pot for a stew of tripe and entrails.

Luncheon over, exit from the shop was blocked for a time by the crowds that gathered about a strolling auctioneer who set goggles on the eyes of every purchaser to enable him the better to admire his bargain.

The streets were as gay as the shifting scenes of a kaleidoscope with the orange, blue, green and

SAINT PHILIP THE BLACK

red that blossomed together in the dresses of the dark, oval-faced women as naturally as flowers in gardens.

In the piazza "La Sonnambula" was heralded by the tooting horn and raucous voice of her exploiter as "Paula the privileged, born at midnight before the day of San Paulo! Paula who has a spider under her tongue! Paula who cannot mistake! Paula who sees your past, present and future!"

Paula, who was a girl just entering her teens, slept to order for two soldi wherever she happened to be standing.

On the steps of the church, blinder than the day before, blind Ninu was begging. Cicciu, who led him, interrupted his cry of "Blind! A poor blind boy! Charity for the dear sake of the Madonna!" to greet me with a gleeful, "What a crowd, Signura!"

In the dim cool church there were not a hundred people; but I had not sat long in the restful quiet before there came a stir at the door of the sacristy. The "spiritati," whom people oftener call "li spirdi," were coming back to San Filippo.

In other years, when the last mass had been said and the curious crowds were scattering, I have seen "li spirdi" and the old women who are, as in all time they have been, specialists in exorcism take possession of the church. I have seen the coaxings, the threatenings and the physical violence which are supposed to influence evil spirits, going forward in half a dozen places at once; before the altar, beside the vara, wherever the various groups of exorcists and their patients might find themselves. But this afternoon the manner was different.

Marshaled by priests and sacristan, a little procession moved decorously across the church, pausing to bend the knee before the altar, then continuing towards the recess which the "possessed" had occupied in the morning. Across the mouth of an open chapel a fence of benches had been drawn; but before the group had passed behind the barrier a disheveled woman, breaking away from her conductors, stumbled uncertainly through the church an instant, then ran toward the nearest door. There was a glimpse of a heavy, sullen face, of rough hair and a dirty white dress, then up came the sacristan and a hurrying swarm of people.

"Ugly devil!" shrieked the guardian old woman who retook the distracted creature in charge. "You will not kiss the saint? Birbante! You will not speak? You would run away?

"Kiss San Filippu!" she cajoled, changing tone. "Shout 'Viva San Filippu!' My joy! My jewel! My heart! Pray! Pray with all your soul! Kiss San Filippu!" she held up a penny icon.

To kiss the figura of the saint and to shout vivas are a *sine qua non* of exorcism.

The woman jerked away her head. She would not kiss the picture. She would not look at it. The crone became a fury. Taking the younger woman by the shoulders, she shook her, screeching, "Ugly devil! Kiss San Filippu! Cry 'Viva San Filippu!' Ugly one!"

The people swarmed close like bees, weeping aloud, begging the woman to kiss the saint, catching her by the arms, by the dress, imploring her to cry "Viva San Filippu!" The old woman continued to shake her, again pleading, "My love, my treasure, kiss San Filippu! Kiss the saint!"

The woman's hair tumbled over her shoulders and her shawl fell to the floor. She would not kiss the figura and she would not speak; but after a little she allowed herself to be led, scowling, back to the chapel.

Here, behind the row of benches, huddled five women. How often men are brought to San Filippo I do not know. I never have seen one. Two of the five, whom the people crowding in front of the barrier nicknamed "the twins," sat squeezed together, one short and dark, the other a big, round-faced blonde, neither far removed from idiocy.

The oldest of the five was a gray woman of more than fifty years. Her stringy hair pushed plainly back, her high cheekbones and brown channeled skin, her tight faded bodice and full gathered skirt were not unlike those of twenty other women in the building. Nor did anything in her manner mark her off from them, except an occasional smile made sinister by a lift of the upper lip at one side, showing a fang. Under the altar of San Giorgio she sat, smiling and malign. The gossiping crowd called her " 'a jatta," the cat.

There was another of whom the gossips spoke as "she of the lovely face." The loveliest thing about her was a mass of dark hair that fell nearly to the ground as she sat, veiling her worn and faded clothing—red skirt, blue apron, green bodice. Mechanically, her eyes fixed on vacancy, she rubbed a picture of the saint over her head without ceasing.

Backed into a corner, the poor creature who had run the gauntlet remained impassive, save for heavy defiant eyes that watched for another chance of escape. At her the people shuddered, whispering, "She would not kiss the saint!" They called her " 'a 'Murricana"—the American; and said she had in her the spirit of a wicked man who had been murdered. Her husband had brought her all the way from New York to San Filippo, but the American spirit did not understand Italian, and there was little chance of her liberation.

In popular opinion the spirits that invade the bodies of such unfortunates are mostly of the murdered and of those cut off before their time; souls that wander through the air causing storms and seeking homes in other human bodies because they cannot find rest until the appointed hour. Since the earthquake at Messina with its holocaust of victims the number of such errant demons has been fearfully multiplied.

Behind the barrier with the five possessed ones

were the priests who had officiated at high mass, the sacristan, the old woman who had recaptured " 'a 'Murricana"—a sinewy crone with scant white hair and a white kerchief open to her waist; and two other ancient dames, less active, whose kerchiefs were like flower gardens.

For a long time little happened. People who had rushed into the church at the reappearance of the possessed strolled out again. A plump middle-aged priest returned to the sacristy. Two others, thin young peasants, went and came aimlessly. The archpriest, a thick-set man of more than sixty, paced up and down before a great crucifix, a benevolent, white-haired figure, not too intelligent, bored apparently, awaiting like the rest of us the events of the afternoon.

A little boy found his way into the choir and threw himself on his knees, alternately kissing a picture of the saint and shrilling, "Viva San Filippu!" People said he might be trying to "stir up the saint."

And still the possessed women sat quiet. The two old women who seemed to be under-mistresses of ceremonies held icons before the lips of "the twins" without visible results, except that the wretched girls, moaning and babbling, wept their swollen faces yet more sodden.

The people in the church fretted audibly. Why was nothing done? Why were not the possessed made to call upon the saint? Were the evil spirits so much at ease in San Filippo's presence that they did not even stamp? Why were not the women shaken? Spirits do not issue for an "if you please."

While matters were thus at a standstill, the thin, grasshopper sacristan leaped over the benches, the ribbons of his black tie streaming, his arms flung above his head as if he himself were bewitched. Storming at a group of on-lookers, he drove them out at the church door. Relatives of one of the poor creatures, said the people. San Filippo is powerless in presence of a spiritata's—suppliant's—family. What wonder nothing had been accomplished!

And now, indeed, "she of the beautiful face" stopped rubbing the saint's picture over her hair. Starting from her seat and thrusting aside the old women, she began to whirl up and down the space behind the barrier, slowly at first, then spinning like a dancing dervish. With every round her shrieks grew louder and her pace became more dizzy until at last she dropped to the floor.

The archpriest calmly brought water. Two of the old women lifted her and helped her to a chair. The head old woman incited her with wild gesticulations. Almost at once she was on her feet again, stretching her arms towards the black saint above the altar and screaming, "Viva San Filippu!"

"Louder! Louder!" exhorted the old women and the sacristan. She began to beat the floor with her feet, stamping rhythmically to the shouted words, "Vi-va! Vi-va! Vi-va San Filip-pu!"

SAINT PHILIP THE BLACK

It was for this the people had been waiting. "She stamps!" they said delightedly. "The stamping begins!" At last the demon in the woman felt the saint's power. All day in church it must have been uneasy. It had made her dance, and now it was stamping. "She is freed!" flew from mouth to mouth. No one had been liberated for the whole day, but now at last the work was beginning. Men and women came running into the church. They pushed and thrust to reach the barrier. They elbowed and kicked. They climbed on chairs. They began to shout with "the pretty one," "Vi-va! Vi-va! Vi-va San Filip-pu!"

The cry that began uncertainly with three or four voices was taken up by hundreds; and presently the sacristan, springing again on one of the benches that fenced the chapel from the rest of the church, began waving his long, windmill arms at us and shouting like a cheer-leader at a football game. "Now then, boys, all together—Vì-va! Vì-va! Vì-va Sàn Filìp-pu!"

Swinging half around towards the woman, he urged her, "Stronger! Stronger!—Vì-va! Vì-va! Vì-va Sàn Filìp-pu!"

And so, marking time with his lean black rocking body, he led the excited crowd in a chant the beat of which became ever more pronounced until the roof shook.

The paroxysm did not cease until the woman once more fell heavily. The three witches lifted her and the archpriest brought wine. There was a period of consultation, and then Catina—as eager voices began to say that "she of the beautiful face" was named—was urged to try again. She rose to her feet, and the sacristan, still acting as cheerleader, inciting her with waving arms and "Force! Force!" as she beat the floor, and us with "Shout, boys! Louder!" recommenced his measured cry more frantically than before.

Of a sudden he interrupted himself. "Get down from the chairs, boys! Stop breaking the chairs!"

He wriggled through the crowd, pulling people from the cane seats of the church property, to which at once they climbed back again. In the confusion the archpriest cuffed the nearest boys. Two "carabinieri" who had been in the church throughout the afternoon forced people back from the line of benches which had become as crooked as a worm fence.

After a minute the archpriest sprayed Catina with holy water, and the three old women took places beside and behind her, shouting with the sacristan now returned from his excursion, "Vi-va! Vì-va! Vì-va Sàn Filìppu!"

At length Catina sank into her chair, where she fell to weeping and to rubbing the picture again over her hair.

This scene had been repeated perhaps three or four times when I left the church for a breath of air. Half an hour later on my return the heat was more stifling and the sweltering mob more closely packed than before. It was not possible again to approach the freed ones; but an old acquaintance who haunts the fairs of Eastern Sicily, little Lucia, a beggar child without hands, beckoned me to a perch beside her on the high base of a column.

"The Signura will be crushed," she said, smiling at me like a hostess, "down there among the 'popolazione'."

Catina sat drooping in her chair. The archpriest had taken off his purple stole, and was holding the embroidered cross to her lips. He put the stole upon her shoulders. He seemed to speak encouragingly. Then the old women led her forward and the rhythmic pounding and shouting recommenced.

Of a sudden Catina stopped in her chant. Starting from her place between the old women, she staggered towards the barrier, lifting her arms and livid face towards the gleaming eyes and forked beard above the altar.

"Do it now, San Filippu!" she implored as if her tormented demons were speaking through her. "Do it quickly! We are ready! Show thy mercy!"

She opened her mouth and spat violently.

The crowd was hushed. Excitement touched hysteria.

"Quick, San Filippu!" she repeated. "We are ready! Grant us this grace!" Again she spat, shuddering and swaying; writhing as if she would cast out her very soul.

"Out with it!" squeaked the head witch. "Spit it out! Out of her, Satan, in the name of San Filippu!"

"They go!" groaned Catina, spitting convulsively. "They are going!"

"They are gone!" Gasping, she dropped into the arms of the old women.

"Liberata!" It was not a word, it was a vast sigh of relief that went up from the church. Like the Messalians of old who spat and blew their noses without ceasing, to rid themselves of the devils that filled them, so Catina had cast out her devils at her mouth; and more than one of the spectators snapped his own shut, not to afford them refuge. The old women stroked and patted her, helping her to a seat, adjusting her dress and smoothing her tangled hair.

Yet something like a chill seemed to damp the audience. Catina's clothing had not fallen. If the spirits really had been cast out, why had they not, in leaving, torn off her clothes? She should have been left naked! Was there not a sheet in readiness on the altar of San Giorgio? Spirits do not go out so decently. So the people reasoned, doubting the miracle. They were hardly persuaded even when the sacristan, climbing up behind the altar, hung to the saint's hand a thank-offering of two fine old earrings.

Catina was a widow, little Lucia told me; she

had three children, and could spare little except her earrings in return for liberation.

After some minutes she came out alone from the chapel, walking unsteadily to the chancel gate. Her long hair had been bound up, and a red ribbon—"the measure of the saint"—hung about her neck. She knelt on the altar steps and repeated aloud a formula of thanks to San Filippo. Then she passed wearily on to the sacristy.

All the spring was gone out of the tired sacristan. Half-heartedly he helped the old women conduct the sullen one and "the American" in front of the main altar. One smiled at the saint her malignant smile, the other refused to look at him, and presently both were taken away together with "the twins." The crowds were dispersing.

"Signura, I go," said Lucia, putting up the stump of an arm to brush away a lock of her bright, pretty hair.

"I, too, am going," I answered.

I left Lucia at work on the steps of the church, where Ninu and Cicciu still clamored, "Help the blind!" There were to be fireworks that evening and a band concert. For Ninu and for Lucia festival days are days of harvest.

CHAPTER IV

The Miracles of Sant' Alfio

(Paul had) shorn his head in Cenchrea, for he had a vow.—Acts XVIII.
To some of these deities the Egyptians give thanks for recovering their children from sickness, as by shaving their heads and weighing the hair with the like weight of gold or silver; and then giving the money to them that have the care of the beasts.—*Diodorus Siculus*.

Alfio, Filadelfo and Cirino were Christian brothers persecuted under Decian and Valerian. Persisting in their faith, they were set to carry from Taormina to Lentini a heavy beam fastened across their shoulders. Near the hamlet now called Sant' Alfio, above Giarre, a whirlwind caught away the beam into midair. The soldiers of the escort stopped with their prisoners at Trecastagne to rest and recover from fear. Arrived at Lentini, the three brothers were martyred by Tertullus, commander of the garrison. Alfio suffered the pulling out of his tongue; Filadelfo was broiled on a gridiron; Cirino boiled in a caldron of pitch.

The martyrs were taken as patrons by the towns of Sant' Alfio, Trecastagne and Lentini, each of

THE MIRACLES OF SANT' ALFIO

which celebrates a festa in their honor for three days, beginning with the tenth of May. The festa at Trecastagne, the largest spring festival in Eastern Sicily, is mainly in honor of Sant' Alfio, the only miracle-worker of the three.

Sant' Alfio stood up under the beam, while his brothers crouched. Thus he became ruptured, and acquired the power to heal rupture. He lost his tongue, and gives speech to the dumb. With Sant' Agata of Catania he protects the mountain villages from Etna; and, as do many saints, he watches over emigrants at sea.

Like Demeter "of the big loaf"—of the full dinner pail—a modern saint who influences weather and crops, or who heals the sick, is sure of votaries. "He is too miraculous," say my friends who fear Sant' Alfio. "It is a pain to see his miracles. He is a saint who makes himself respected for sure."

Agatina's grandmother did not approve of the levity with which Agatina and I prepared for our trip to Trecastagne. Agatina's nonna is a dignified old woman who, like the saint, makes herself respected. She had been buying "ox-eyes" of a passing fisherman, choosing those best speckled with red, and still sat in the doorway of the antiquities shop, the little shining fishes in a plate on her lap, while she glanced up and down the Corso observing the news of the morning.

Near her house in Catania there lived fifteen years ago, she told us, a man who was paralyzed.

On the eve of the festa of Sant' Alfio, as this man lay in his bed praying, there appeared to him a stranger clothed in white, who asked what ailed him, and who rubbed him with an ointment, after which the paralytic got up and walked. The stranger was Sant' Alfio.

"In the days of to-day the saints no longer appear to men, because there is no faith; we others are not worthy," she concluded, re-tying the knot of her purple and white head-kerchief, and rising heavily to carry the fish indoors. "We are not children of the saints, like our ancients."

The old woman's disapproval checked our light-mindedness. I had been teasing Agatina for putting on her pretty gray spring dress with its lace blouse and the plumed hat that framed her delicate face so becomingly. "There will be more than 30,000 people," I said; "why try to make a figure? Sant' Alfio won't see your finery."

Agatina declared mysteriously that she was a practical woman.

That evening, when we reached the house of Agatina's parents in Catania, her stout, child-burdened, good-humored mother, after scattering her family to Catania's great fish-market to buy our supper, to the bed-rooms to turn down our beds, to the dining-room and the kitchen, found time, as she tied on her work-apron, to disapprove of our trip even more thoroughly than had the grandmother.

"Capers and clover!" she exclaimed. That two

women should start for Trecastagne at two o'clock in the morning along with the riff-raff who would be swarming up the long road in the darkness, how was Pippinu thinking?

She cuffed Alfieddu, the sticky-fingered three-year-old who clung to her skirts, instead of cuffing me; ejaculating as he screamed, "Mary Mother, what torment! He drives me into hysterics!"

"Listen," laughed Agatina; "how Mamma is jesting!"

Agatina had telegraphed Pippinu, her husband, for permission to come with me to the festa; but from the depths of Calabria, where he had gone with a gun for quail and bad Christians and an eye for old furniture to sell to tourists, Pippinu had not answered. This lack we concealed.

On his return from the fish market, Agatina's sensible, middle-aged father brought, in addition to our supper, the driver he had chosen for our carriage; and while the red meaty slices of tunny fish were cooking, he instructed Santu not to race his horse, and not to bring us back next day by the highway, where the traditional "return of the drunkards" would be in full swing. We were to take a quiet side road, and we were to have as escort Agatina's seventeen-year-old brother, Michellinu.

At this Michellinu looked bored. Later, while one sister was brushing Agatina's long hair, and another was censoring my Sicilian, my friend excused her brother. "È appassionatu," she said; "he's very much in love. We others are live flames." We Sicilians, that is to say.

"He doesn't look it," said the younger sister. "Signora, say 'tri'; ah, you can't do it; no one but a Sicilian born can pronounce Sicilian! Signora, try again; say 'tri!'"

At two o'clock in the morning, when the sound of horses' hoofs roused us from brief rest, Michellinu did not look a live flame; even a boy of seventeen cannot, when he is sleepy.

Below in the darkness our carrozzella was waiting. Somewhere in the distance sounded revolver shots. "The gallants," volunteered Santu; "the young bloods are starting up their horses."

As we moved towards Catania's main street, shouts and the rapid fire of crackers became louder. Once on the Via Stesicoro Etnea, the jingle of bells, the snapping of whips, the rattle of tambourines, even the gun fire, were merged in the confused roar of thousands of people. Half Catania was keeping vigil. The broad street was packed with carts and carriages three and four abreast, all moving in one direction, straight towards Etna. It was a dark stream of which one could not see the end.

The carriages were overloaded with people able to hire them. Two-wheeled carretti carried ten or a dozen each of "little people," men, women, children and babies, laughing, beating drums and shaking tambourines, waving flaring torches, discharging pistols close to the horses' ears. The sidewalks were jammed with other thousands jostling forward, shouting.

"Viva Sant' Aaaaarfiu!" was the bellow that imposed itself through the din.

Catania had gone mad, as it does every year on the evening of the tenth of May. Santu turned cautiously into the torrent.

"There will be a horse dance all the way"; had said Agatina's wise old father; and indeed the play of whips as each driver lashed his crazed team to force it ahead of the one in front threatened something worse than a dance of horses. The hospitals are busy after the race to the shrine of Sant' Alfio.

Beyond the city and its suburbs, on the long straight course into the foothills, the scene was wild. Though the stars were bright, it was dark between the high walls that shut away vineyards and lemon gardens; all the darker for the yellow glare of cane torches that flamed on straining horses and black, swaying figures as the galloping procession, carriage after carriage, cart by cart, lurched past us.

"May your horse drop dead, cold as a pear!" growled Michellinu, rousing himself. "Can't he go?"

"He is l'Allegru, the Lively," said Santu stolidly. "Forty lire were offered me to let a young fellow race him to-night; but I'm too fond of him. He'll be in at the finish, without dripping blood like these others. Shall we bet on it?"

Michellinu wound a shawl about his head and lapsed into gloom.

We were climbing steadily. It was cold. Agatina had left in Catania her fine frock, and was wearing the common one her practical mind had hidden under it. A black head scarf and heavy black shawl had turned her into a brilliantly pretty contadina.

"Michellinu is cross," she answered Santu; "because he didn't want to come. But—here comes another caravan of the nudes!"

At every stiff grade where we slowed to a walk, groups of "nudi" passed us at a trot. They were not moving in great bands, as I have seen them at the festa of San Sebastiano at Melilli; but by tens or twenties. Except for a red or white loin sash, some were literally naked, as was David when he danced before the Lord girded with a linen ephod; or as were the Bedouins when they made the sacred circle of the Ca'aba in the days before Mahomet. Some added to the red sash short white cotton breeches. Some wore a sleeveless shirt, as well as drawers and streaming ribbons. A few wore their ordinary clothing with the red band draped from one shoulder under the opposite arm. Almost all were barefooted. When the head was not bare, it was covered by a white kerchief knotted like a turban.

Each was making his pilgrimage as he had vowed it; "dressed nude" as the phrase is, or simply bare-

THE MIRACLES OF SANT' ALFIO

footed. Each carried his monstrous candle, trimmed with flowers and broad red ribbons.

Each group moved past us at a lunging run, looking neither to the right nor the left, panting with dry throats, "Viva Sant' Aaaaarfiu!" Their breath came in gasps. They pumped out the words. One man was a mute who moaned grotesque, inarticulate cries. One man limped; he had hurt his foot, yet not for that did he give over the vow he had sworn—eight miles, involving more than 1,800 feet of ascent, without slackening pace to Trecastagne.

One of the "nudes" was not running; he walked beside his wife, a small woman in black whose hair streamed loose over her shoulders. He carried a torcia decked with red rosettes, she a red-rosetted baby.

There were many women who walked, like Petronius's Roman matrons when they prayed Jove for water, "up the hill in their stoles with bare feet and loosened hair." But the greater number of these Catanese matrons, even when they let down their dark braids and made their pilgrimage with disordered hair, removed from the feet their shoes only, and walked in stockings.

Horses continued to pound past at a furious pace, the flags and tall pheasants' plumes that rose from their heads wig-wagging, their fly-nets, covered with red, white and yellow artificial flowers, slapping madly. L'Allegru was not so fine; Santu had put no holiday touches to his harness beyond his gay little bells.

It was the mules and horses drawing the painted Sicilian carts whose trappings put us most sadly to shame. Not a harness showed a hint of leather. Many a man had spent the savings of months on the mirrored panaches of vari-colored plumage that towered from back and head piece, and on caparisons that made the carter's mule as gorgeous as the steeds of Rinaldo and Charlemagne, whose knightly exploits were pictured on his cart. In tinsel and spangles, flashing with mirrors and vivid with isinglass, were wrought scrolls, arabesques, double-headed eagles, knights' heads and cherubs that glittered with every toss of head or lift of hoof, and housed the animals till they looked weighed down by their own splendor.

We reached a low black village crouching in the lavas of Etna. There were lights in the doorways, where people had gathered to see us pass. "The first stage," said Agatina, as we came to a wine shop the door of which was wreathed with ivy and fresh lemon boughs. Over the door were hung round loaves of bread. In front were tables set with coffee cups. Many a man threw himself exhausted on the ground to rest while eating.

At the watering trough was a mix-up of horses' heads and legs in the dance to approach. "Some dispute might arise," said Santu, as, to Michellinu's disgust, he kept l'Allegru still in the rear.

THE MIRACLES OF SANT' ALFIO

Up and up the dark, narrow road we climbed. The scent of lemon and orange flowers no longer drifted over the walls. We had reached the vineyards of the terre forti, Sicily's strong lands. The "nudi" overtook us on every rise; on every descent we left them behind. They had no breath left. Painfully they wheezed, "Sa-ant' A-a-rfiu!"

Imperceptibly the sky paled. In the East there came a faint red streak under the waning, just-risen moon. Overhead the heavens were blanching to white. The West sulked blacker than before. From the moment of the start Mungibeddu (Etna) had loomed across our path, a ghostly shape; now it appeared a sharp-cut silhouette against the sky. There came a cold dawn light over the snows of the mountain and in the blue air. The procession of carts and carriages looked interminable. The red streak in the sky widened. Below us the quiet sea was the color of steel.

We began to see more clearly the villages we passed, with here and there a fondaco lighted for the sale of bread, wine, bran and hay. We met beggars, the one-armed and one-legged, the blind and the dumb, who swarm at every festa. A cripple who had vowed to the saint a wax leg if he should be healed carried on a tray his "miracle" while he begged money to pay for it.

The "nudi" quickened their pace. Their shirts were gray with dust. Their eyes stuck out bloodshot.

Trecastagne was just ahead. We could see the jagged skyline of its houses and church spires. On each side of the way were now "sons of Etna," as the human sons of the volcano call the many eruptive cones it has flung out upon its sides. Those near us, dead for ages, seemed alive once more, shining with the green flame of wheat.

It was well before sun-up when we reached the foot of the steep incline at the entrance to the village. Here in the old days the racers tied the fore legs of their horses before beginning the last frantic dash to greet Sant' Alfio. That custom is gone, but the mad race continues.

Horse after horse struggled past us, sobbing for breath, streaked with bloody lather; the driver on his feet, swaying, swinging the lash and screaming. Just in front a nervous white horse, fretted by his housings, and his two towering panaches, balked, blocking the way. The whip rained cuts on his bleeding flanks, and he bolted. Behind us the moment's halt had brought up half a hundred vehicles with their babel of bells, cracking whips, shouts and gunfire.

To this point l'Allegru had come sleek and cool. Now for the first time Santu's whip sang in air, and he bent forward, calling softly, "Let's be going!" L'Allegru took the hill at the head of the mob.

Michellinu's head poked out from under the folds of the gray shawl. Casting it from him, he scrambled upon his seat, holding to Santu's shoulders and shrieking to the horse, "Ah ccàa! Ah ccàa! Carriccà! Ah, ccàa!" At every team we passed his fingers made the derisive sign of the horns.

"Get down, Michellinu!" called his sister; but to me she said proudly, "A live flame, isn't he?"

And so we entered Trecastagne, scattering holiday crowds, endangering the street stands of hawkers, rocking from side to side, galloping to the very church door.

"Is your Lordship satisfied?" asked Santu yet more softly, stroking l'Allegru's nose.

"He can go," grunted Michellinu, falling back into indifference.

Early as it was, the piazza could not hold its swarming multitudes. The place was like a great camp of gypsies waking to the business of the morning. Fortune tellers, merry-go-rounds and gambling games were in full swing. A moving picture show was hanging out Tripoli war posters. We stopped to look at nothing, but went at once to the church of Sant' Alfio.

The building was of some size, though of no architectural pretensions. From the doorway it looked as if entrance would be impossible. Thousands of people had left their homes in distant villages at sunset of the previous evening, and had been kneeling before the high altar since the church opened at midnight. The press to reach the altar rail was suffocating. The church was hot, and echoed with the confused noise of men and women moving about, weeping, praying aloud. The air was heavy with candle reek and incense.

We could see but little. Columns and walls were hung with the gaudy paraments of tinseled paper which in days of festa degrade the decent white plaster of Sicilian village churches. These were the usual heavy draperies in elemental colors—red, blue, yellow and green, spangled and gilt-bordered, gleaming darkly in the shadows where the flame of the great altar candles did not penetrate.

Near the door by which we stood the walls were covered with votive pictures, perhaps like those which Juvenal had in mind when he said that Roman painters got their living out of Isis. All were small, some dim with age, some fresh with colors not six months old. Here, painted on tin or wood, were sick men spitting blood or dying with cholera; here were a soldier wounded at Misurata in a Tripoli campaign; a man saved from the Messina earthquake; a house saved from Etna; a ship saved from wreck near New Orleans. Each scene was sketched with the crudest realism, and bore name, date and description of the miracle.

Above and beside the pictures hung wax ex-voti, models of legs and arms, throats and stomachs, gruesome with red marks of wounds or pits of disease; "the price and pay for those cures which the god hath wrought," says Livy of just such objects that hung in the temples of Esculapius. Behind the ears of a wax head clung wax leeches.

THE MIRACLES OF SANT' ALFIO 241

A column near us was hung with children's clothing; straw hats and caps, little breeches and petticoats, offered to Sant' Alfio for the healing of the infants, as to San Sebastiano of Melilli, San Calógero of Girgenti and many other saints of Sicily. Beside the column stood a table where two priests were selling penny pictures of the saints. From the high altar to the main doorway ran a railway for the processional exit of the "vara," the saints' car.

Little by little we edged our way towards the front of the church where flowers, flung over the chancel rail by almost everyone who entered, lay in heaps at the foot of the altar. Beside a table to the left of the chancel stood a stout sacristan receiving offerings. As we approached he held up a watch with dangling chains, and the church shook with vivas.

Next came a ruptured baby. The sacristan took it in his arms, laid it on the floor among the flowers, and then held it up, bare legs kicking, to show that the flesh had closed and the rupture was no longer visible.

A mother placed on the table her little girl, and stripped off green skirt, pink waist and yellow kerchief until the mite stood before us naked. The sacristan, expressionless as a sheep, received the bundle, while the mother reclothed in a fresh dress the little one, now free, according to tradition, of all trouble.

At my side a woman held a red-frocked baby. "An idiot," said another neighbor in my ear; she asked the mother, "Was the miracle made?"

"Not yet," came the sighing answer.

Two mutes were flinging up their arms and writhing in frenzied struggle to call upon the saint, the expected sign of liberation being the power to speak his name. Tears rolled down their cheeks. Their inarticulate cries rose above every other noise; an agonized "uh, uh, uh, uh!"

Beside one of them, a man seemed to stretch with his whole body towards the great golden doors above the high altar, behind which in their niche the saints were still hidden. He was thin and worn-looking, shabbily dressed. Clasping his hands high in air, he moaned without ceasing. "Sant' Arfiu! Do me the miracle! Liberate my son! Sant' Arfiu!"

Our neighbors said that one of the mutes was his only child.

There was a sudden stir in the church. We were flung back with a violent wave movement as the throng gave place before the entrance of a group of "nudi." Shouting they ran, their candles flaring as they swopped past us to the altar, where their yells of "Sant' Arfiu! Viva Sant' Arfiu!" made the roof ring. Their brown faces lined and haggard, shirts dripping sweat, their quivering bodies painted with the red of their sashes they stood triumphant, casting down flowers, holding up huge torches to the sacristan.

THE MIRACLES OF SANT' ALFIO

I wondered then, I wonder now, how Columbus dressed when he carried his "wax taper of five pounds" to St. Mary of Guadaloupe after his escape from shipwreck returning from the discovery of America.

As the men disappeared in the admiring care of relatives, a blue-clad girl of eight or nine was lifted over the rail, struggling and holding out her arms to be taken back again. Her father bade her kneel, and she did as she was bidden, looking about wildly for a familiar face, her plump cheeks streaked with dirt where her fingers continued to rub away tears. Women sobbed as loud as she, saying one to another, "She has no speech, poor little thing."

The girl's mother fought past us with frantic feet and elbows, shrieking, "My child is frightened! Let me pass! Let me pass! My child is afraid!"

She dropped on her knees at the chancel rail, but we did not see what happened, for there came another wave of excited movement in the church.

"They are making the vow of the tongue!" said Agatina, dragging me with her toward the rails laid for the wheels of the processional car.

Up the track constructed for the vara from the doorway to the altar there came a man who walked slowly backward, flicking with a handkerchief the pavement grimed with the tread of thousands. Behind him crawled one of the "nudes" on hands and knees, painfully licking crosses on the floor. His movement from doorway to altar was blind and wavering. After each slow forward grope there came a pause; one wondered if he would have strength to proceed.

The people pressed close to the track crying hysterically, "Bravu, son! Courage! Courage! Another little and we are there!"

"Back! Back!" called others. "Don't you see he is suffocating?"

Inch by inch the man lapped his way towards the chancel. Behind him came a second and a third. There were seven in line. Earlier in the morning at one time there had been ten. One or two were supported by a knotted kerchief passed under the neck and held by a friend.

Staggering dizzily to his feet at the altar rail, the first man tottered a minute, staring about him, stammering thickly, "Viva Sant' Arfiu!" The building echoed and re-echoed with the answering shout. Then, wiping with a handkerchief his swollen tongue, he lurched to one side and disappeared.

When all seven had passed there came a gray haired woman in black, who looked nearer sixty than fifty years of age. So slowly that it seemed as if she could never finish, wandering from the track in spite of the guiding rails, trembling from exhaustion, she fulfilled her vow. Her mouth was full of blood as friendly hands lifted her.

Agatina had turned very white; she whispered, "Shall we go?"

Not far behind us a woman had begun to flourish scissors. A younger woman at her side had taken off her white head kerchief, and was fumbling with hairpins. Down fell two long dark braids. A minute later the scissors were laboring close to the younger woman's head. The hair was thick; we could hear the grinding of the blades. Presently there came away one of the tresses. Its owner coiled and pinned what hair remained, and hid her disfigurement under the kerchief. Then she tied the severed braid with a red ribbon and gave it to the sacristan, who held it up for exhibiton.

There had appeared at the altar a young, red-cheeked priest in golden vestments who gave communion to kneeling devotees. One such brought a candle so heavy that only with great effort could he lift it. It was fully two meters long and thicker than a man's leg. Its owner was taken over the rail with it. "Any more? Is there any other?" the priest was calling, holding up his wafer, as, clinging together, we reached the open air.

It was not seven o'clock. We had been in the church only two hours, yet we have gone back to the times when Julius Cæsar crawled on hands and knees up the steps of the Capital to appease Nemesis.

In the piazza the crowd had become so dense that it was almost as hard to move about as indoors. The square was of some size, surrounded by the small gray-plaster houses of a Sicilian village. It was given over to hawkers and hucksters, for the festa presents the same medley of religion, trade, athletics and amusement that constituted the Olympian games.

At one end were piled tons of garlic. Beyond were pottery, glass, copper, tin and iron ware; saddles and donkey-harness; straw hats and caps displayed on the ground. Push carts and improvised tables were heaped with nespoli, cherries, sides of bacon, fishes in oil. Long lines of booths were devoted to high-colored sweets, toys, kerchiefs and scarfs and many sorts of small wares.

In a dirty inn we drank a dark, muddy, sweet fluid that had all the vices and none of the virtues of Turkish coffee. The owner of the shop had nailed up a rough shelf outside the door and hung a balance. He brought out in his hands a roasted sheep, smoking hot; and, after haggling with a customer, hacked it with a cleaver. The buyer received a quarter on a kerchief, knotted opposing corners and so carried away his portion.

Two or three doors away a rival dealer brandished the head of a ram impaled on a pointed stock, its dead eyes glaring, its horns ready for battle. The two barkers shouted in competition. "Roast sheep! Roast sheep! Better than sweets! Roast sheep! Better than sweets!"

On the other side of the narrow way there ballyhooed three or four vendors of roasted "ciceri," the chick-peas of Cicero's family name, and squash seeds, peanuts, dried chestnuts and roasted beans.

THE MIRACLES OF SANT' ALFIO

One of them was crying: "Hot, all hot; red hot the ciceri! Here I have them all hot! Red hot the ciceri!"

To which another responded: "'Murricani! 'Murricani! Who wants to eat American nuts? Peanuts! Peanuts!"

The peanuts were small and poor; they lay about in sacks marked "Portland cement."

The brown, seamed face of the woman who roasted the ciceri fascinated me. Her orange headkerchief was knotted at the back of her head, showing earrings that touched her shoulders. Her black dress was tucked up, leaving her petticoats protected by a huge blue apron. On a circle of lava stones rested a deep iron pan over a fire of vine cuttings. In the pan was sand, which she stirred with a wooden shovel till it came to the right heat; then she turned in her peas, stirred briskly till they began to pop, and then with bundles of rags lifted the pan—it was patched, for I counted, with nine pieces of iron nailed on—and turned the sand through a sieve into another big pan, delivering the hot peas to her husband, who acted as salesman.

"A-li! A-li! A-li!" drivers shouted to their mules. Carts and carriages were still coming up the hill, plumes waving, harness glittering. Champions were giving exhibitions of whip-snapping.

Fishsellers arrived almost as exhausted as the "nudi." Like these, they had run all the way from Catania, bringing fish taken during the night. In the flat baskets on their heads eels were still wriggling.

Some distance up a steep side street Santu had unharnessed L'Allegru. With him we found Michellinu, who had slipped away from us while we were in church, and who could not be brought to cheerfulness even by Agatina's promise of a share of her "falsamagru" at luncheon. Wearily he came with us to look at the carretti.

Every writer on Sicily talks of the painted carts of Palermo; but he who has not seen the festa at Trecastagne has missed one of the great cart sights of the island. Over a large part of Eastern Sicily every carter who affords himself a new cart or has an old one repainted times the work to have it fresh and shining for Sant' Alfio.

Among the carretti parked in Santu's neighborhood were one or two decorated in the older style which Pitrè says was general down to 1860, having the panels of the drab or yellow box painted with fruit or flowers. But the rest of these vehicles, whose mission in life it is to carry charcoal, sulphur, stones, sand, oil, bricks or any other merchandise, were vivacious as a moving picture show. The two panels of each side and the three panels of the back were covered with figures, and each figure, in a style sincere, vivid and mediæval, got action.

Against a background of dragons' blood red the paladins of Carlo Magno tilted in the lists, crusaders fought Saracens, San Giorgio slew the dragon, or

The "American" Cart, and Detail Showing Lincoln

Sant' Agata worked miracles. Columbus discovered America and Ruggiero repeated all his real and legendary Sicilian victories. One or two of the Catania cart painters had departed from tradition, and made to live again such recent happenings as the assassination of King Umberto, King Vittorio Emanuele watching an aviation display, the Messina earthquake and battles in Tripoli.

"Look; the starry flag!" said Michellinu, pointing out a cart which showed the Stars and Stripes wreathed with the Italian tricolor as framed to its pictured panels.

The paint was shining new. Stepping closer, we saw that the cart bore the date May 1, 1913. On one side was blazoned a rendition of Washington Crossing the Delaware, flanked by Lincoln Receiving a Group of Freed Slaves. On the other side were Washington's Farewell to His Troops and Washington's Farewell to Lafayette. On the tailpiece was the Assumption of the Virgin with at one side Envy, green and scowling, and on the other Fortune, in yellow with streaming banner.

The owner of the cart came forward to enjoy our interest in his horse's brilliant caparisons. He was called Bernardo Pappalardo, and he said he had worked four years in the woolen mills of Taunton, Massachusetts. He had saved a little "pile," and had come home with it a year earlier to Catania. Needing a cart, he had sent to Boston for picture postcards to help in its decoration.

Proudly he called attention to the carved Turks' heads that finished the key bar under the box and to the two mottoes set into the lacelike iron-work below the portrait of Garibaldi:

"*Se nemico sei, guardami con invidia; se amico sei, con piacere,*" ran the first: "If thou art an enemy, regard me with envy; if a friend, with pleasure." The second said, "This cart is thus elegant to give an answer to the ignorant."

We ate early the chicken that Agatina had brought, and her "falsamagru," which was rolled like a jelly cake with chopped meat, eggs and good black olives inside. From a huckster's cart we got wild artichokes and scalora, a variety of endive.

High mass was beginning. Its progress was marked by the clangor of bells and the explosion of mortars. At a certain point we knew by the roar of cannon from the hill that the golden doors above the altar had opened, and the three saints were disclosed to adoration.

When we tried to push our way back to the church, it was twelve o'clock, almost time for the saints' triumphal procession through the village. The piazza was all but impassable. The vendors of tin ware, the men with copper pots and braziers and brass lamps, the men with pottery, the men with strips of hide for shoes, the men with saddles and donkey harness, were gathering up their goods from the ground.

The tin especially interested me. Out of empty

cans the smiths had contrived graters, cups, lamps, lanterns, sauce-pans, utensils of many sorts still bearing the manufacturers' labels of canned sardines, tomato conserve or biscuits.

The oil jars, the mixing-bowls, the plates and the basins of glazed earthenware shone in brilliant greens, yellows and blues. The water jars were of uncolored red terra cotta. We watched an old shepherd from the mountains squat, choose a "quartara" and test it carefully by sound for any imperfection in the baking.

In the morning a great stretch of ground had been covered with spreading hats of dwarf palm; now these were hung against the walls of houses. An energetic woman stood over a quantity of cheap German cloth caps trying one after another on the head of a loutish boy who drooped in the sun as his mother critically surveyed him.

The mountains of garlic had diminished. Every other man and every mule wore a rope of garlic as a necklace.

Small gambling games did a lively trade. On a table under a big red umbrella little nickel horses, legs and tails in air, raced round and round, ridden by knights in red, green, yellow and black, whose colors corresponded with those of other little horses painted in the many narrow radiating segments that divided the circle of the table.

At the next stand was a fishing game. Your hook caught an envelope which held a ticket which gave the number of the trinket you won. The fisherman's invitation, punctured by his jangling bell, ran, "Come in, fellows, let's go fishing! To the miraculous fishing, come on!"

Swarms of flies settled over the cherries and the sweets. Every hawker had thrust into his goods a split stick carrying a picture of the saints, and had wound his balance with roses.

Little terra cotta whistles crudely colored to represent saints were among the toy-dealers' best sellers. Michellinu chose one that stood for the risen Christ; Agatina took the Madonna Addolorata; I chose Sant' Alfio.

The people who, like ourselves, were struggling for viewpoints near the church were mostly of city types unlike the mountain gnomes one sees at Randazzo or Bronte, higher on the slope of the volcano. Some mountaineers there were, small, dark people, their eyes squinting at the sun; the men wearing short pendent caps, the women heavy antique earrings. But more numerous were handsome, white-skinned girls of Catania with soft, rounded faces, black hair and big dark eyes half-hidden under black shawls.

There were many brides, marked by shining dove-colored silk dresses and shawls. In the old days it often happened that a Catania bridegroom bound himself in his marriage contract to take his bride to the festa of Sant' Alfio. Perhaps it happens sometimes to-day.

THE MIRACLES OF SANT' ALFIO

Near the main doors of the church a brass band worked so industriously that I did not hear when Carmela spoke to me, nor did I see the hands that she and her sister and her mother stretched to draw us into their position of advantage. Carmela had told me only two days earlier that she should not dare to come to the festa because she had not yet the money to buy a wax stomach; yet here she was; to help her sister, she told us.

Carmela had vowed a stomach to Sant' Alfio something more than two years earlier on recovery from an illness; but when his festa came around she had not saved money enough to present more than a rotolo of wax, about a pound and three-quarters. The next year, still unable to spend sixteen lire for the stomach, she offered a candle weighing two rotoli. This year she had feared the saint would look bored if she presented herself for the third time stomachless; but her sister's great candle had to be brought, and the sister could not bring it alone.

The wife's husband, who had just emigrated, had written from New York that during a storm at sea he had vowed a candle of five kilos if the ship should come safely to land. "He said," continued Carmela, "that his wife must fulfill his promise."

Carmela and her sister are dark, wholesome girls with high cheekbones and the regular features of Arabs. Their mother still has a red glow in her olive cheeks, but most of her teeth are gone, and her forehead is puckered from the effects of strong sunlight. Carrying by turns the eleven-pound candle, the three had walked in stockings the twenty miles or more from Taormina, arriving at Trecastagne the evening before.

They had been in the church since midnight, and could tell us the gossip of the festa. The woman whom we had seen sacrifice her hair had done so because of a grace given to her a few minutes before our arrival. She had brought in her arms from Catania a seven-year-old daughter who, after a long illness, had become lame. The mother implored Sant' Alfio to liberate the child, but nothing happened. At last the two sat down in the church, the mother sobbing. But of a sudden, said Carmela, "The little one jumped up, walked and shouted, 'Viva Sant' Alfiu!'" The mother fainted for joy, and when she recovered she caused her hair to be cut in gratitude for the miracle.

Our friends said that most of the men who had licked the pavement had done so because during the eruption of Etna six months earlier Sant' Alfio had caused the lava to spare their vineyards.

But, before the women had time to tell us more, with a clamor of brass and tumult of bells the gilded "vara" appeared on the threshold of the church, and Sant' Alfio, San Filadelfo and San Cirino, three seated wooden figures painted in green, gold and red, were before us, receiving the salute of 40,000 frenzied people.

THE MIRACLES OF SANT' ALFIO 255

Hot air balloons went up. "VIVA SANT' ALFIO," written in huge letters across the facade of the church, flashed out in sputtering fireworks. The bells in the campanile crashed an ear-splitting gloria. The air was thick with powder smoke. The ground shook with the explosion of mortars and cannon.

Meanwhile on the golden car sat the three brothers side by side, each impassive on his chair of state, a full moon halo shining at his back; each dressed in brilliant vestments and hung with jewels and flower garlands.

The struggle to approach the vara was appalling. Men carrying babies kicked, shoved and cursed their way towards salvation for their infants. Sant' Alfio is criticised, Carmela told us, because it is mostly men who obtain the miracles; but this is not his fault; it is only because women cannot get at him.

Across the middle of the flat car ran a gilded fence, behind which, under the canopy of the saints, stood the priest and sacristan we had seen in the morning. Outside the bar on the front platform, immobile, expressionless as the statues, stood two carabinieri. Clinging wildly to the sides and front were shrieking men, holding up watches, money, children. Some were mutes, some possessed with evil spirits; some merely distracted fathers.

Some of the gifts received by priests and sacristan went into the box over which the policemen stood guard; some were pinned to Sant' Alfio's clothing, which presently was a-flutter with paper money. I recognized numbers of American bills. One man reached up a kicking kid which the priest laid over his shoulder. Another offered a live hen, gay with red ribbons.

Now and then the priest, reaching down, took a child from its father, laid it on the platform of the vara, and after a minute, picking it up again, held it high in sight of the shouting mob, or gave it back to the father without showing. A few favored children, placed on the floor of the car before it issued from the church, remained there throughout the procession.

After a long wait the sacristan tinkled a bell and the car started forward a few paces, running on low wheels and pushed by every hand that could reach its long side bars. Behind it blared the band; in front walked hundreds of people carrying great candles. After a minute it stopped again, facing us. There was a fresh outburst of gunfire.

This time we could see more distinctly the resplendent painted images, each bearing the palm of martyrdom. Sant' Alfio sat between his brothers, so bedizened that earrings, bracelets, watches and golden chains combined to make for him a glittering barbaric garment. Men and women who could put a finger to his chair or to that of either of his brothers kissed the finger devoutly.

"How he is beautiful!" murmured Carmela's mother. "He looks as if he were going to speak."

At this moment a three-year-old boy in a conspicuous green skirt was passed up to the priest, mother as well as father stretching after him eloquent gesticulating arms. After a little while man and woman struggled back in our direction sobbing.

"He didn't!" wailed the father; "He didn't do it; the saint didn't do it! Poor son; poor little son of mine; Poor broken baby!"

They passed out of our sight. Later I saw the green skirt on the vara a second, and then a third time.

"Look, Vossia," said Carmela at my ear; "the saint does look out of sorts; I ought not to have come."

"Out of sorts? How can you tell?"

"I know," returned Carmela; "without the stomach I ought not to be here."

Carmela's trepidation, or fatigue, was so genuine that we withdrew with her and her people to the balcony of a house that overlooked the route of the procession. From this vantage point we watched for another hour the offering of gifts and the prayers for assistance. Next day we heard that in money, jewelry, loads of wheat, wine, carts, and horses Sant' Alfio received nearly $5,000. He is very rich indeed.

After the procession had passed the side street where we had left Santu, we returned to the carriage. Preparations were in progress for fireworks and other spectacles in the evening; but the mass of holidaymakers were already tying bunches of garlic and pictures of the saints to the panaches of the mules, and beating drums and tambourines as they climbed into carts, or mounted their women folks behind them on asses, ready for the occasion.

A blind tale-singer recited to the notes of a squeaky violin:

> [13] When San Filadelfu was druggist,
> And San Cirinu was the doctor,
> With Sant' Alfiu the surgeon,
> They made pass every pain.

With eleventh hour desperation the hucksters thrust small wares into women's hands, shouting, "What fine goods, women! It's a piggish shame to leave them."

It was good to turn away from the noise and the shouting for the quiet Mascaluccio road which Agatina's father had recommended for our return. We took Carmela into the carriage, since she refused to rest for the night with her mother and sister at Trecastagne.

"Sant' Alfiu always smiles at sight of the people at his festa," she said mournfully; "but to-day—he did look out of sorts."

> [13] E San Filadelfu era speziali,
> E San Cirinu era lu dutturi,
> E Sant' Alfiu chirugo magari
> Facevunu passari ogni duluri.

THE MIRACLES OF SANT' ALFIO

The Mascaluccio road is not beautiful, but its grades are so stiff that few carts followed us. Carmela and Santu told tales of miracles as we jogged homeward through old fields of lava, where the tree like genestra of Etna blossomed fragrant and yellow, though we were too tired to listen. It was still mid-afternoon, but even l'Allegru, the Lively, was subdued. Michellinu had deserted us for the cart of a friend.

Down through the region of vineyards and of lemon gardens we came to the suburbs of Catania, where thousands of people had come out to watch the annual spectacle of the return, which is not in any Northern sense of the word a descent of the "drunken." For a Sicilian a little meat and a miracle are an orgy. Through the long Via Stesicoro Etnea we rattled as we had done the night before, in a hubbub of bells, cracking whips and tambourines.

Agatina's mother had prepared a great dinner equal to that of the last day of Carnival; but we did not stay to eat it. Tinuzza and Turriddu, Agatina's children, were expecting us in Taormina.

From the doorstep of the antiquities shop they shouted as the old post wagon came willingly to a stop: "A fairing! A fairing! You promised us a fairing! The ciceri?"

We gave them saintly whistles and tambourines; but the ciceri were saved for the morning.

When the children had whistled and drummed

themselves away, Agatina's nonna explained why Sant' Alfio cannot grant a miracle to everyone who asks it. "Not a leaf moves without the will of God." And then one must comply with conditions.

Once a mother asked her three-year-old child who was dumb, "What will you give Sant' Alfio if he liberates you?" This is custom. One asks a child, and it holds up perhaps the bread it is eating, perhaps a toy; the first thing it sees. The offering must be just that. The three-year-old held up a bean. To the mother a bean seemed too mean a thing to be accepted by the saint, and she had it copied in silver.

"The child was not liberated," concluded the dignified old woman.

"Before next year I must buy that stomach," said Carmela, shaking her head forebodingly.

I left Agatina telling her grandmother about that live flame, Michellinu.

CHAPTER V

THE CAR OF MARY AT RANDAZZO

The heap of old houses blackened by the sun and beaten by the winds, on the edge of cliffs under which runs the Alcantara—who looks at the merlature of its walls and its gates, the Gothic windows of Santa Maria and of San Martino, cannot resist a sort of fascination, almost an hallucination: It seems that the city's barons are on the alert.—
Italia Artistica.

AT four in the morning the Bagnoli Croce is awake. It is still dark, but there are lights in the houses, and I hear voices. Going down to Giardini, I meet mules coming up, laden with barrels of water and wine. A muleteer warns me, "Carefully, Signura; the road is bad." It is dawn before I reach the marina; twenty-five or thirty men are hauling a net. The Alcantara is reduced to a thread of water. Etna looks very near and very brown. At Giarre men are loading into a freight car great bales of snow from its upper slopes, protected by thick layers of broom and oak leaves.

The garden behind the Circum-Etna station at Giarre shows what can be done with irrigation. It it a riot of roses, hibiscus, geraniums and oleanders. The vineyards on the lower slopes of Etna are heavy with purple clusters. Knotty, rheumatic-looking vines, closely pruned, from which half the leaves have fallen, carry grape bunches that must weigh several pounds. At frequent intervals we pass a straw hut, newly built or put in repair, the sheepskins on its raised floor showing that the watchman is not far distant. Every palm of ground is cultivated. The "sorbi" are turning red. Pear trees overladen are propped by long canes.

As we climb higher, the tall genestra of the Etna slopes still shows a few fragrant yellow blossoms. Near Castiglione the plantations of hazel nuts, planted as regularly as the hills of a cornfield, show themselves heavy with fruit.

Some stations before reaching Randazzo our third-class car becomes overfull. Women carry big pasteboard boxes that hold their gala clothes. The guard jests with a group of boys. "To the festa? Yes? Bravo! Then take care of this half of your ticket. You'll need it coming home. Do you understand?" A little girl clutches in her sweaty hand the claws of a frightened sparrow. She doesn't know she is cruel. She tries to feed the bird.

From Giarre one goes up and up among terraces and vineyards, flourishing in lava which has become rich soil. As one passes them one sees the lava not yet reduced to cultivable powder piled into the walls of terraces or into heaps. What infinite labor to reclaim even these patches of fruitful soil!

There are wonderful views of the sea where the

A STRAW HUT

THE CAR OF MARY AT RANDAZZO

Alcantara comes down, a streak of yellow and white, becoming green, and melting into the blue of the sea. The clouds throw shadows that lie on the mountains, deep blue at some hours, towards sunset red. The transparency of the air is such that to name a color is almost impossible. Deep, deep blue predominates. As one rises higher one comes to scattered pines and passes through miles of hazel woods and birches. Before and after the hazel groves one passes pine groves of enormous extent, but the trees are all apparently young.

Beyond Solicchiata one passes lava ejected in 1879, a dead country; the lava assumes grotesque forms of giants and dwarfs, animals and sea waves, at the caprice of nature. Where a teaspoonful of soil has accumulated springs a brilliant yellow flower. Here and there the lava is piled into terraces to give place to a spot of cultivated ground. The black lava stones are in color a murky, brownish black, dead, without character or shape; amorphous.

It is hard to explain the existence of the villages that one sees lost among the mountains. What brought anyone here to live? Castiglione is three and one-half miles from the railway, yet it looks prosperous and populous.

Randazzo itself, stern and black looking in its lava dress, and with successive waves of lava flows of the past scarring the country about it, is spelled in terms of power. Even to-day the strategic importance of the valley of the Alcantara is recognized by the Italian government; the valley dug out by nature, between Etna and the Nettuniani mountains, is a great way of travel between the Eastern coast and the island centers; who holds Randazzo is master, commanding the roads to Messina, Milazzo and Patti. So Peter of Aragon must have reasoned, who came here after the Sicilian Vespers, and his crowning in Palermo in 1252, to liberate Messina beseiged by d'Angio. So perhaps thought Federico, Frederick II of Aragon, who chose it as his summer home.

L'Arezzo, il Riccioli and others may be right who insist that Randazzo was inhabited by the Romans, and by the Greeks before them; they must be right, considering its commanding site; but its historic fame is slight before those spacious times when Robert Guiscard came into the land, "in stature taller than the tallest," as Anna Comnena describes him; "of a ruddy hue and fair haired; he was broad-shouldered and his eyes sparkled with fire; the perfect proportion of all his limbs made him a model of beauty from head to heel." Bloody battles were fought in its neighborhood by the Byzantines and the Normans against the Saracens, and the city was taken now by one party, now by another; after nine centuries the plain where Georges Maniaces gave battle to the Paynims still bears the title "della Sconfitta"; of the Defeat; eight centuries ago, only, Roger sent hither Greek slaves from the islands of the archipelago who established the silk trade—an infant industry, quite, in these old lands!

From Randazzo the hard mountain slopes look even more bleak than in winter; all brown, lacking the cool contrast of green and snow. But no one has eyes to spare from nearer scenes. The tree-shaded space at the entrance to the town is the scene, as usual, of the fair that accompanies the festa. There are mountains of green melons, baskets of figs and of fichi d'India, apricots, grapes, pears. There are heaps of terra cotta wares, tin, glass. Under the trees at each side of the way are tables for the "little horses," targets for shooting at the mark, rough benches for luncheon, the usual merry-go-round and band stand.

A band from Riposto, followed by all the population, parades the streets. They are brilliant with devices to call attention, vocal with cries of vendors, fortune-tellers, showmen and all the traveling chasers of coin whose calendars are marked with the dates of island festivals. And from the country about the peasants have poured in. Under the fluttering flags, going towards the Matrice, I notice just ahead an elderly man with an elf-lock, sticking out from among the short grizzled hair on the back of his head. The younger men wear sprigs of basil in their buttonholes; older people dress as in winter; the women in white wool mantles, the men wearing stocking caps. The great vases hooped into their iron rings on every balcony are gay with brilliant blue morning-glories, petunias, fuschias, carnations, roses, basil and kitchen greens. A cantastorie is singing and selling songs of "The Great European Conflict." A word or two comes to the ear in passing.

"Every poor mother afflicted, whose dear sons have departed, prays from her heart the hand divine to send them back in safety. Every mother weeps, evening and morning; sad have become the poor, the rich and every sort of people; peace is ours no more, we are anxious."

Men of hard brown faces stop, listen, shake their heads and pass on. Children gather about a lame, bright-eyed old fellow who is selling whistles made in the form of small, rude terra cotta images of saints, painted in primary colors. Any member of the heavenly choir, from St. Michael, the Archangel, to the Madonna Addolorata, can be had for a soldo. But to me the price is four soldi. "Why? Because I am Sicilian, and sell according to the customers. You, a lady, are able to pay four soldi; the boys are not. What are you doing, kid?" And he hobbled off swearing at an urchin who was fingering the basket load of saints.

"The risen Christ? All right; bravo!" The boy goes off, shrilling on his penny whistle.

In the Matrice, or Mother Church, men and women are kneeling before the chapel where lies a life size image of the dead Madonna on a lace-covered bier. Long hair flows about her shoulders.

She wears a blue mantle and a pink silk robe tied with a flowered sash. Marble feet in leather sandals peep from beneath her skirts; her head rests on a silver halo. At her head and feet watch papier-maché angels. Over her body is thrown a veil of tulle. Tall candles droop in the heat; as do the basil and flowers that stand in great jars behind the chapel rail.

At my side kneels a woman hidden, except forehead and eyebrows, under her white wool mantellina. She is praying in an undertone loud enough to catch the ear: "Beautiful Mother, I entreat you that my son be not called as a soldier." Not many of us that day were in festival mood!

From the moment of my entrance into town I have seen the framework of the tall car backed up against the wall of the sacristy of the Matrice, and the throng of people drawn to the town's chief pride, superintending the operation of preparing it for the procession. This car deserves a detailed description, for it is the vehicle of a strang rite, suggesting atavistic survivals from very old days.

The entire car has a height of fifteen or sixteen yards, about a yard higher than in recent years. It consists of a low, heavy base car from which rises a mast of wood bound with iron, to which the various "fantasies" are fixed. This mast is made to turn by four men who sit on supports arranged under the floor of the car, which rolls on wheels.

The "fantasies" are arranged in eight tiers. From

the floor of the car the tomb of Mary, a great sarcophagus in anything but mourning colors, gleams with red, yellow, green, pink and blue, and carries a huge M on one side. Above this comes what is meant to be a mass of fleecy clouds among which peep the heads of cherubs. The clouds are done in yellow picked out with black.

Above the clouds comes a great triple wheel in red, gold, green and pink, set vertically. Then two ranks more of clouds; then a second wheel not so large as the first, but rayed like a sun with spokes of many colors; then a third wheel in blue and gold. Above these a crown in red and gold supports a blue globe, which in its turn bears a tall gold cross and banner.

The base of the car is adorned with a balustrade of columns in gold and white paper. All the decorations are flimsy paper and cardboard on a framework of cane.

The twenty-five boys who sing the verses, the "praises of the Madonna," bound to this structure, are kept nearly fasting as a precaution against nausea and dizziness. They get a little dry food, biscuits and cheese, but no fluids, for a whole day previous to the procession. They look as if they were twelve or thirteen years old. They are required to confess and take communion before putting on their gala clothes. In former days many accidents are said to have taken place, but now the car is better built, or possibly Maria is more vigilant. The boys mount to their places by ladders set against the church wall, and are well fastened.

"It is a most ancient tradition," said a man who seemed to have in charge the ornamentation of the car. "Give her a turn or two, and let the lady see how it works," he called to the men who were busy tacking paper jars of flowers in place.

Obedient to the command, the men dropped their tasks and turned the levers that made the tall mast revolve in its socket, carrying around and around the tomb, the clouds and the great wheels. The fantasies are bedecked with much isinglass which sparkles as it turns.

The car is backed up against the sacristy next the apse of the Matrice between two scaffolds, with ladders at the sides. The work of trimming it is going on busily when I arrive; a crowd of people are watching. The head mechanician takes me inside the enclosure to show me the works, assuring me there is no danger, though when the wind blows and the tall mast sways it may look perilous. The boys, he says, are well tied. For them it is *un giuoco*. They enjoy it, and they get a lira for their pains.

"Another turn or two;" and the mast groans and creaks and revolves experimentally; revolves vertically as it swings in its circle, and the mechanician looks on proud of his job. There is nothing like it, he says, anywhere else in the world.

The base cart or box is heavily framed of wood

and iron; it runs on low, small wheels, and from the floor descends a well, in which stands the iron-bound mast. Under the floor on their cramped seats crouch the four men who push the iron handles that spring from the iron ring encircling the mast, and make it turn.

As the hour for the procession approaches the boys scramble up the ladders and one by one are fastened into their places. On the great triple wheel each lad is tied into an iron belt, while his feet are bound to iron footholds. Most of them look like caricatures of mediæval knights, with helmets, slashed doublets and hose; marionette figures copied out of the "Reali di Francia," but without the armor of fighting men. Their colors are as gay as the isinglass paper—pink, green, blue, yellow, etc. Their pink fleshings, doublets and cloaks have seen service and do not fit; but the boys make up in enthusiasm for all deficiencies.

The scene at the finish is a riot of enthusiasm, as the boys scramble up the ladders. Tying them in takes time. Clouds are gathering, but the people say it cannot rain; the Madonna will not permit. Everyone is explaining to his neighbor all about the carro. One says the figures on the car in the procession at Messina before the earthquake were nothing but papier-maché. In Naples they make a procession with a car in the form of a ship, but it has not the significance of this, which sets forth the Ascension of Maria into Heaven.

THE CAR OF MARY AT RANDAZZO

At the very top is the boy Maria in a blue robe by the side of the Padre Eterno, who wears a beard and carries a cross. Two or three angels are in attendance. On the wheels are boy angels in the attitude of flight. Below among the clouds are cherubs and groups figuring scenes from the Bible. The archangel Michael, with his sword, is dressed in red. Guarding the tomb are Roman soldiers.

There is intense excitement as the last touch is given. At a signal from the attendant priests the boys begin to sing—

> Bedda Signura, Matri Maria,
> Evviva la Vara, ...

What follows of the lodi is lost in the wild cheers that go up from the crowd. Little cannon explode. The mast sways in the wind as it begins to revolve, groaning and squeaking. The great triple wheel turns slowly, then faster, as the car swings out from its place between the scaffolds, and is pulled and pushed by hundreds of hands towards the main street, the Corso Umberto.

It is an amazing sight—the shining car, the gay tomb of the Madonna supported by the angels, by tall vases of gelatine paper flowers; the three revolving wheels, the second of which swings higher than the roofs of the low houses, the singing boys whirling perilously in air, the isinglass and tinsel glittering as the dazzling procession takes up its march in the sunset light through the length of the town. People lean from balconies and roofs delirious with excitement.

The whole population of the town follows the glittering car towards the dazzle of the sunset, the gloria rung by the bells of each church, as it approaches, heralding its passage. At the west end of the town, under the Norman campanile of San Martino, the car halts and turns; its return must be accomplished before the passing of the summer twilight, for the electric light wires have been removed to give room for its passage.

Once again at a stand in the open space behind the apse of Santa Maria, there begins a frenzied work of spoliation. "They grab off all the fantasies," says the lame man at my side; and indeed the boy angels are casting themselves upon every bit of ornamentation within reach, pulling in pieces the yellow clouds, wrenching away the cardboard cherubs, stripping from the wheels the gaudy sun-rays and casting them to the crowd, which fights for the scraps to be preserved as charms for an entire year, until there are other rags of another festa to be fought for.

The angels, as is meet, keep for themselves the best. At the top of the mast little boy blue Maria is scuffling with the Eternal Father for pink pasteboard cherubs. The two attendant angels watch their chance to rob both, but Maria gets the better of all three and remains triumphant with his arms full of chubby heads and spreading wings.

TYING THE BOYS IN PLACE, AND DETAIL OF THE CAR

When the mast has been rifled, it is pushed back between the scaffolds against the wall of the sagrestia, and the work of untying the boys begins. Each, as he is released from his iron belt, stands a moment, cramped and stiff, then slowly clambers down.

"Were you pleased with the festa?" asks Saitta, proud, happy, sure of my answer, limping enthusiastically at my side as we hurry to the convent of the Cappucini to get a closer look at the boys before they have time to strip off their angel robes. Tired, sweaty, dirty, the band of angels lies on the grass in what was once the garden of the cloisters. "Tired? Yes, Signura; very tired."

And frightened? Maria laughs at the idea. Maria is never afraid of anything! "Disconcerted?" Well, a little nauseated, just at first.

Maria is a chunky boy, as blond as a Swede, with yellow hair and colorless white skin. In the scuffle for the cherubs his blue mantle has been twitched to one side, the golden halo is awry, his pale blue eyes still gleam with berserker battle light as he hugs the torn and ragged prizes.

The riches of Santa Maria, which pay for these religious rites, were inherited from the Catanese baroness Giovanella de Quattro, who died in 1506, leaving her entire property to this church. The boys come together in the morning of every August 15th at San Domenico, where in one of the rooms of the antique convent they put on the robes kept for the purpose.

The spectacle of this car, painted with a thousand colors, from which hang those clusters of little whirling creatures, is something which recalls not so much the Middle Ages as the customs of more distant places and barbaric times. It is a sort of car of Moloch and of Vishnu which, if it does not reek with human blood, yet costs a sacrifice. Those angels, those miniature warriors, are kept fasting from the previous day; they undergo hunger, nausea and fear gladly for the honor and the fame.

The vara of Messina, which Randazzo scorns, dates from the sixteenth century or earlier; in "Feste Patronali," Pitrè says much earlier than 1535. When the Imperatore Carlo V entered Messina in triumph after the Tunis enterprise one of the cars that came out to meet him was an Assumption car, with Charles and Victory substituted for Maria and the Eternal Father. In 1571 the August festa with the car was repeated in November in honor of Don John of Austria, victor at Lepanto.

Pitrè illustrates the car as seen and sketched by the French artist Huel before 1784. It shows certain differences from the car of recent times. The great wheels have sun faces with rays as spokes; the angels stand on clouds; Maria is held in the hand of the Eternal Father. There are only two banks of clouds.

Pitrè also illustrates the car as it was in the first

THE CAR OF MARY AT RANDAZZO

half of the nineteenth century, with clouds and sun faces. He speaks of the moon and earth; and the earth is obvious. There are apostles, angels, archangels, cherubim. The Padre Eterno is represented by a man with a beard, cross in hand. The children are attached at the ends of the principal rays of the sun; they rise and fall in such a manner as always to remain erect, like those on the wheel of fortune. The angels are enjoying the triumph of the Virgin.

The basic ideas of the car may be confused: Mary ascending into Heaven mixed up in naïve incongruity with old wheel festivals that typify the sun and his fructifying magic. The earth and the clouds, the sun and moon, the angels and "the souls in their degree," all are in place. No one can fall, since the city and the festival are under the protection of Mary. On that day, at least, no malignant spirit can walk abroad, seeking to do mischiefs.

Well, it is over for the year! Randazzo turns to its daily problems of war and work.

From the window of my room in the primitive hotel I look over the red tiled roofs of the city towards Etna. To my right is a palace with a fine double window; two dark arches of lava in a dark facade; beyond is the refreshing green of the oaks of the town; still beyond, the great mass of Etna, broad of base as seen from here.

The streets are gay with catch-penny games. Half a dozen men have set up marks for shooting. The barker nearest me has a wooden box which he hangs to an acacia tree; inside are crudely painted figures of Turks or Arabs, reminding me that some of the streets of the town have been re-named for the Tripoli war—Ain-Zara, etc. The weapon is a rude cross-bow, shooting stones. Another man has a "miraculous fish" game. You pay a soldo for an envelope containing the number of your catch.

At another pitch are tables for playing the ponies —gorgeous nickel-plated ponies gaily caparisoned, their tails in air, their legs prancing. They race under belled arches round and round, one horse carrying a tri-color banner. The hard-faced woman who acts as starter has a little switch to keep too importunate customers in order. She is not barking, but presently her place is taken by a man who barks in competition with the other ponies under the next tree. The ponies are yellow, green, red and black. The bannered horse carries a marker that ticks the slate of the barrier fence. The circle of the table is divided into segments of the four colors, each segment marked by radiating lines into little segments, where painted horses, from 1 to 10 in number, gallop briskly. You bet on your color and win as many soldi as there are horses of your color in the little segments where the banner stops. The barker cries: "Green, color of hope; yellow, color of gold; the Red Cavalier gains! The Black Cavalier wins!"

It is hard to get anything to eat at the little hotel; at night they seemed to think I had had enough at noon. At noon they had refused me chicken, though

I could see fowl upon the tables. The guests had brought their own. At last an old man reluctantly pokes his head out of the kitchen and offers me asparagus omelet, bread and nespoli.

While I eat, the daughter of the house tells me that the women in nun-like dress I have noticed are "monache di casa," home-staying nuns, of different orders. For l'Immaculata the dress is celeste with a white girdle and a long white wool shawl or scarf, with a white band across the forehead. The Carmelite dress is coffee-colored, with a black shawl. These nuns call one another sister, and help one another. They live at home but occupy themselves with their devotion, much as if in a convent. Not many women now become home-nuns, but always some; "there is always religion." The old monasteries and convents of Randazzo have now been turned into schools; one is a factory; one the post office.

I rose early to take a carriage for Maniaca, a matter not to be arranged without difficulty. Finally I start with Pietro, the waiter, on foot. He has missed his morning coffee and is ill-natured. But the way is beautiful, Etna in deep blue.

To the right as we climb out of the paese rises a chain of mountains. The Mountain of the Wood of Maria belongs to the church of Santa Maria, the church of the car, which Pietro says is enormously rich; it has an income of 700 lire per day—which must be a mistake—and thus is able to celebrate its great festa every year. Beyond is the Monte Flascio. We pass a desolate lava tract where it is hard to understand why anybody should live; but there is almost a village. It is "for the convenience," Pietro says. There are several new houses going up; houses built of the lava itself, sometimes in large part excavated in the black lava rock, their roofs of red tile very little above the ground level. A party of men on muleback overtake us, and without ceremony, offer us a mount. We ask them about the way to Maniaca; it is obviously impossible to walk there and catch my afternoon train, so we turn off toward Maletto on the hill to our left.

Our new way leads for three or four kilos along a rough track up a lava flow; but before this is a strip of clayey soil, wet in winter, split by cracks in summer, poor land. The lava is old and rough, almost as desert as it is twenty years after an eruption. The path is worn into hollows by the feet of mules, yet lonely as it is desolate. In an hour's tramp we see two men. There are ring markings on the lava as if it had stiffened in waves while cooling. Where bubbles of lava broke are grottoes sometimes big enough for sheep pens. Now and then a few square meters of soil have softened enough to permit of a patch of culture.

Not far from Maletto is a wee trickle of water to our left where women are washing linen and spreading it to bleach. The village itself is of perhaps 4000 souls, dominated by the ruins of an old

THE CAR OF MARY AT RANDAZZO

castle. Some of its streets are arched, making passages like those in Berne. The conspicuous church is that of the patron, Sant' Antonino.

People gaze as we wander, looking for something to eat. We go at last into a clean looking house where the woman conducts us from the shop into a back room, and sends out a boy to buy us provisions. He comes back with a bit of meat, and her husband cooks it for us over a portable stove that stands outside on the balcony, overlooking another narrow street. The woman spreads a sheet over a small table and brings out bread, cheese, sausage and scalora.

I bargain with a carrettiere to take us back to Randazzo. Pietro has given out. Stefano, the carter, ties two chairs in his cart and harnesses a white mule, Concettina, very slow and sedate, who is said to have a very beautiful harness, but it is used on days of festa only.

Stefano is middle-aged, brown and wholesome looking. He comes from Adernò, but has been sixteen years at Maletto, and does not want to go to America; he has his cart, his mule and his wife; what more could a man want? He believes in the miracles of Sant' Alfio; has seen a dumb girl made to speak after three pilgrimages made in three successive years.

Pietro goes to sleep. The sun comes out, making the day glorious. Stefano urges me to get out of the chair and make myself more comfortable on the sheepskin rug on the floor of the cart, which bumps and jars over stones and rough places.

At times Stefano sings; at times we talk of Etna, always in plain view, and its terrors. We talk of bandits; there are said to be few, though many men in the lonely country carry rifles. Pietro thinks they have learned that in order to eat it is necessary to work. We talk of the Duke of Bronte, Admiral Nelson's English heir and successor in that vast estate. The Duke's men never leave him and are mostly old. His service is well liked. The gardens of the estate are very beautiful, and everything is well administered. And, so talking, we jog along back to the little albergo just in time to pay my bill and catch my train.

If I had listened to Stefano I should have had to stay another night in Randazzo; he had suggested that I get down from the cart as we approached the town, thinking I might not like to enter in so rural a vehicle.

Considering the inn, that would have been to pay dearly for sinful pride!

CHAPTER VI

"Red Pelts" at Castrogiovanni

At the end of May I have seen the men wrapped up in a mantle which hides their faces and rises above their heads like a cap; and the women, like the men, . . . swathe themselves in a mantle which they clutch with one hand under the chin.—*Gaston Vuillier.*

CASTROGIOVANNI is a little over 3,000 feet up in the air, and I have never seen it really warm. Past the middle of May, the time of which Vuillier writes, a season elsewhere of bare brown earth and sun-baked herbage, I once more found the mountain much of the time bathed in fog; why do they hold the greatest animal fair in Sicily high in the clouds?

Possibly because it is the center of the earth—Enna of the ancients, Kasr Jani of the Arabs, halfway house between East and West, the famous fighting ground for men from both sides. It is a city in the shape of a horse-shoe, a rocky nest, with a steep valley in the middle. One sees old palaces here and there, relics of former strength, huge fortress-like structures of squared stone blocks with few windows, more like the mediæval palaces of Florence than the plaster ones of Catania. These fortresses and the imposing churches contrast with streets that are not streets, but narrow ways among the rocks, worn by the men, the mules and the carts that have passed there hundreds, thousands of years—for no one knows when the first men came.

The people are the most interesting I have seen in Sicily; the men darker and leaner than those of the lowlands, clad in dark blue hoods and coats; the women with pure oval faces, olive complexions and red cheeks, and with black hair; of the Greek type, perhaps; in any case, beautiful. There is also a type almost African in tint and feature, with skin extremely dark and hair kinky as well as black, black! They wear a black mantellina or a heavy black shawl, and they crowd about the doorways to look at us. Visitors are not many.

Yesterday I saw a wedding procession. Walking in front was the bride with her two sisters, all in handsome dresses of dove-colored brocade, rich and heavy, with black silk embroidered shawls hung with long, rich fringe. Their heads were bare. Behind the bride came her female relatives and friends, all in peasant dress, with black headkerchiefs and dark clothes. Behind these was the procession of the men, led by the bridegroom between two friends, two or three dozen others following. Paper confetti were thrown from the doors.

"There they are marrying a bride," said the boy who guided us, in his imperfect Italian.

Stupidly I asked which was the bride, and the sisters, hearing, pointed out the pretty girl in the middle whose eyes were red from weeping. Peasants never wear orange blossoms or put on white for weddings. The gray brocade is a gala dress for a lifetime, and the embroidered shawl the most treasured of possessions.

There are here in Castrogiovanni the usual Madonna legends; one is of an image found drifting in the sea and towed to land by sailors. It was put on an ox-cart, when the oxen without guidance brought it to Castrogiovanni. At her festa in July men dressed as reapers with shirt outside the trousers carry this Madonna from the Mother Church to the convent, where it remains for thirteen to fifteen days—every day a festa—and people come from far to pay their devotions.

A kindly old woman told us that here in Castrogiovanni is the belief that some day the Madonna must appear in person at the Franceschini church —la Madonna della Visitazione. Her church in Rome has been shaken by an earthquake, a sign that she must leave it and come here; the Pope must come also, with all the devout of earth, and so Castrogiovanni will become once more Enna, the center of civilization. In the church, of a usual bare plaster type, a sacristan showed us the body of Angelo Musico, a frate of Caltagirone who died two centuries ago, whose relics have worked miracles and who some day may become a saint. The corpse, that of a toothless man of seventy-two years, a wierd spectacle, is preserved in the habit of the order, with cord and staff.

Beyond the garden of the convent one looks out over a prospect second only to that of the Castello; over an endless succession of hills blue in the azure shadows of the scirocco; blue, blue hills without end. Never a road, but hills, hills, hills—and nestling among them the lake of Pergusa, fishless for its sins.

This Lago Pergusa is the spot from which Pluto bore away Persephone. Legend says it was once full of fish; good ones. Two rotoli of fish were vowed every year to the Saviour by the men who leased the fishing, but they were not paid, so the lake was caused to yield only tiny fish not worth taking. And so, shamed and accursed, it remains.

At sunset, from the old Castello, now a prison, there is a view of the snows of Etna and of the Madonni mountains, also snow-capped; a view of the lower lying Salascibetta; views of interminable wastes of wheat and fave, dark green and light green, spaced by black cypress trees in groups of two like carabinieri. Near the town a few fruit trees, pears and cherries and quince, with now and then an apple tree, are seen. But for the most part wheat and fave alone speak of culture and give the tone to the landscape. Sterile and deserted the land looks, sand showing between the grain; there are few roads and no signs of life on them; everybody lives in the town and homes early these long days.

A strange town it is—60,000 people with one weekly journal, less a newspaper than a Socialist circular; with one kiosque where out-of-town papers are sold; with a decent public library, not large— and a gun shop in every block. Small boys on the steps of blacksmith shops finish off bullets moulded in the old fashion, and trim away with nippers the strips of lead in which they are imbedded.

I do not know whether to be more disturbed by the Bowery manners of these Sicilians who have been in America or the excessive politeness of older people who have stayed at home. In the street yesterday a girl saluted me with, "Say, mister, how do?" I asked if she could not use better English and she explained, "I no speaka much. I back three years." She had lived four years in Brooklyn, near Coney Island, and would like to go again, but Babbo "no want, because he got store now." Father's store, set up with Brooklyn money, is a hole in the wall where tobacco, wine and flour are sold, with spaghetti and other indispensables.

On the other hand, there was the old woman who was picking up manure in her hands for her grandchildren's garden. She looked eighty years old, dodging about the heels of the donkeys. But when I made her acquaintance her pity was for me, not herself. She smiled and said, "Give me your blessing!" the common salutation to a superior, sometimes improved to "Your Excellency, bless me!" And she went on: "Are you quite alone, Your Ladyship?" A bystander helped her lift the basket of manure to her head and she walked with me toward the church, a stately model of courtesy toward a stranger.

Better excuse for keeping long awake who could ask than the unceasing song of the nightingale? This morning there was Etna, white with mist half way to the top; then a band of blue, and then the pearl-white snow and the deep shadows of the summit, almost more beautiful, more dream-like, than from Taormina. And beyond Etna the sea.

But for morning sounds, to ears that had hearkened over-long to Philomel, there came a sudden clamor of bells, jingled by cows, oxen, asses, mules and horses climbing up from below in procession. I did not know there were in Sicily so many animals. The plain of the mountain was black with them. It is strange how black the "red beasts" can be when massed together with fog blurring their outlines at a distance, as at intervals it did in the early morning.

From the church of Monte Salvo down and up the hills and beyond on each side were these black masses of cattle, tethered, hobbled, free. I never reached the limits of them; I don't know how many acres there were; always more black masses in view. Where do all the animals go at night?—some are sheltered in the ground floors of houses; many

"RED PELTS" AT CASTROGIOVANNI

must stay at the Inn of the Beautiful Stars. The forage, largely clover in flower, is brought on the backs of asses.

For the men, there are two or three barracks of poles covered with canvas, sheltering tables and portable stoves. Most of the guests pull from their pockets bread and a bit of cheese. There is not yet such an abundance of trinkets for sale as at a festa; no dried chick-peas or sweets; a man's affair it is, and strictly business. Two or three men are selling knives—which here may be necessaries. Each carries a stout piece of cane into which the knives are stuck, the handles pointing up. "American knives," they call; "genuine American knives."

Not that relaxation is wholly lacking. A young fellow has a fortune-telling stand; in a column of water little figures sink and rise; one comes to the surface and brings your fortune in a slip of paper. An old man brought me his, asking me to read it. It said he had had many misfortunes, had suffered much but should not despair. His distant friend was well and would come home. He must not trust all who would speak smooth words to him; he had false friends. But things were coming his way and he would live to be seventy-four years old. The brown, lean old fellow asked eagerly if all this was true. Could he trust it? Voscenza would know. He thanked me gratefully.

The bargaining is most animated. There is much opening of animals' mouths to read the record of the teeth; much lifting of saddles for possible galls to show; much heated argument. When a price dispute becomes acute the seller will swear that he will give away the animal—here a magnificent gesture!—but sell below his price, that he will not, bear witness the old gods!

There are splendid big mules with handsome trappings and saddle-cloths; a few fine horses; rough-coated young mules, fifty in a bunch. The bands of color on the saddle-bags are strips of red wool with applied embroidery of set designs, scrolls and arabesques in green and yellow and white wool stitched down with crewel. The broad tail-piece is decorated similarly. The ornamentation covers one end of the saddle-cloth and the lower ends of the pack-saddle. At each side is a strip of red. Sometimes the pack-saddle has gay red wool corners; sheepskins are often used as saddle-cloths. A horse fully loaded with basto, saddle-cloths and saddle-bags is "caricato."

Men with the air of masters, attended by guards and foremen, look over the animals. Most of them are dark, lean and sinewy, with high cheekbones, foreheads lined, eyes keen and alert, squinting from the sun. The noses are straight or aquiline, the brows straight and heavy. Every man carries a staff or goad stick, and the guards have double-barreled guns on their shoulders or, if mounted, carried in front on the saddle. In "making proof" of an animal the herdsmen ride like Arabs or like cowboys. A group of them silhouetted on the skyline moving at a gallop is a wild picture.

Women appear and set up shop for the hungry. One has loaded a lemon basket with her wares. Another balances on her head a great water-jar. A third has a heavy cooking pot full of onions. Bargaining is as keen as the hunger. Curiously, the onions come from the shore; they say it is too cold for them to thrive on these heights.

There is a stir in the crowd. A donkey in gay harness clatters wildly towards us. Someone is trying out a donkey before accepting him. The donkey bumps into a mountain of onions and scatters them; he stampedes a bunch of sheep that have drawn together in a huddle, their patient noses to the ground.

"Holy Patience!" says my photographer companion; "One of St. Joseph's!" A "St. Joseph's donkey" is a special breed, small, strong and bad-tempered, mouse-colored and marked with two black lines that form a cross, one stroke down the spine, the other crossing the shoulders. Later in the day I came across this beast and his purchaser. The animal cost twenty dollars and was bought for speedy reselling.

You need a special lingo to chaffer at a fair. It is an art.

You glance at an animal, refraining from showing deep interest.

"Suit you?" asks the seller with equal unconcern, but politely.

You answer with a little grimace, and pass on, paying attention to other animals. After a time, wandering back into the neighborhood, you carelessly ask the price.

"One hundred lire."

"Blood of Christ," is a mild oath at a fair. Up go your hands in amazement. You hardly trouble to add: "Now if you had said fifty, we might talk." The other, knowing his ground, is indifferent to your scorn.

You turn as if to go away; but at the moment up saunters friend Pietro, a judge of animals; in fact, an agent. He also glances at the beast and makes some slighting remark. Follows the agent of the owner, a poet in praise of the animal. Discourse becomes animated. What looks like and sometimes is a quarrel may result, as when a would-be buyer tries to force earnest money, to bind the bargain, on the seller against his will.

In one group we watched the chaffering over two young cows and a restless young bull, plunging and tossing his rope, I noted four old peasants, the shawls over their shoulders in stripes of black and white wool. These are mountain men, with brown, lined faces, skin shoes and an air of coming from wide spaces, a sharp contrast to the more ordinary types from the shore. I gather that they are from Limina. Their middleman is not tactful; he disparages the judgment of the other agent in such fashion that the seller stalks away, angry. The herdsman himself strides after him, the trouble is patched up, earnest money taken and the red bull led away.

It is hot now. A couple of girls who have pigs in charge have thrown themselves on the ground for an early siesta, each pillowed on a pig. A boy threads his way in and out, calling pictures of the Madonna of the Chain for two cents. A blind ballad singer sets up a broad sheet of canvas painted with scenes of tortures inflicted by Arabs on Italians in Tripoli. The colors are greens, blues, yellows and reds; the sketching crude but spirited, especially the sweep from heaven of the rescuing spirit, one of the "souls of the beheaded." The singer points to each tableau as he sings of the episode it pictures, then offers printed copies.

It is eleven o'clock now, and the meat ovens are being drawn. Inside each oven one sees a brown, sizzling stack of flesh and bones, with rich perfume escaping. The meat is sold in half an hour. Beside each oven stands a crier, a long form in his hand and on the trident a sheep's head. He is hoarsely calling: "Roast sheep! Roast sheep! Better than sweets!" Men stand in line to buy. A quarter is the usual purchase, for the sheep are small and a quarter may not be many pounds. Each customer takes his portion in a big handkerchief which he knots and carries off, perhaps to one of the luncheon booths that have sprung up in the shade of the lemon trees by the dry stream bed. These are roofed and sided, like the dry goods pavilions, with flowering branches of oleander or screens of split and plaited cane. They are furnished with rough tables and benches, and the keepers sell little but the necessaries of life—wine, peasant bread, raw onions, garlic, Sicilian cheese; but it is understood that the patrons will for the most part bring roast sheep and will buy only bread and wine to complete the Homeric feast. How they eat meat, these Sicilians, when they do eat it, as if storing up flesh food for months when they do not see it!

Our party was not large—the photographer, his cousin, Sambastiano, a friend from Limina, a man who had come to attend a flock of goats a cousin was selling, Mastro Peppino, two children and myself; but when Mastro Peppino failed to get more than what seemed half a sheep, distress was obvious. We carried our baskets out of the crowd toward a spring at the stream, some distance from the fair, but the picnic ground we had known in winter was sadly changed. For lack of rain the crops had failed, only yellow stalks sticking up out of the ground.

We sought the shade and Sambastiano broke up the hot meat. "Excuse my hands," he said; "if we send to buy forks the meat will get cold." There was bread from wheat grown on Sambastiano's land, and ground by his mother in a hand-mill.

Gossips at Castrogiovanni
The Laundry

"White Wings"
A Pig Pillow

There was no butter, but "ricotta," buttermilk curd dried in the sun and baked, food for Sicilian gods. There were fresh figs, bought at the fair; the early summer figs, sweeter and bigger than later cullings. There was wine pressed from Sambastiano's grapes, not more than a year old, pure and delicious.

While we ate and drank, Don Vincenzo told stories. Don Vincenzo is the Sindaco of Limina. Short, dark, fresh-complexioned, plump, bright-eyed and good-humored, he has been in America and come home well-to-do. He is so pronounced a radical that he has caused this inscription to be picked out in pebbles on the front of his house: "Here lives Vincenzo ——, Socialist." Yet he directs the yearly festa of San Filippo, whose miracles are the marvel of Sicily. In short, Don Vincenzo is a man of the world and a good picnic companion.

After we had eaten, the horses were put to, and we set off down the break-neck slope with, as presently appeared, a broken rein, but a whip in excellent state, along with carts, mules, donkeys and a stream of home-going people, personally conducting the goats, pigs and sheep they had bought.

The washing place below the town is not enclosed from rain and cold, and we stopped to commiserate with the washer-women there. But they would have none of it. What would you? It is known that one must work! Below is a watering place for animals, busy beyond its wont with the needs of the newly purchased beasts. A water carrier there told us he had worked in America, in mines near "Pittisborgo" where he earned ten lire a day; in Castrogiovanni he can get but three, and not always that. But his wife and children are here. And thereabouts came to us also one Lina Potenza, who had been four years in America, and hopes to return when her father is able to travel. She has a brother a barber in New York, a dressmaker sister and another who is a featherworker. She has herself, though even now but fourteen, earned six dollars a week working after school on feathers in New York.

Also, I regret to say, there were boy beggars. I had earlier written in my notes that no beggars accosted us in Castrogiovanni. It was not, in fact, then or now the begging season; few tourists ever saw the fair of the red pelts.

But news of our strange taste in sights must have got abroad; for down into the plains, amid the lowing and whinnying and mooing of the boughten beasts, and the twittering of the sparrows keeping pace above them; down past the miraculous crucifix, a steep way with a never-ending procession of women and donkeys carrying water; down through fields of asphodel, and small red Adonis; down the white ribbon of road we could see winding for miles ahead of us, we were followed, quite in the fashion of the "Milordi" travelers of tradition, by "Gimme a penny! Give me a little soldo!"

So were the proprieties tardily preserved.

PART III

ISLAND YESTERDAYS

CHAPTER I

ETNA IN ANGER

Etna, that proud and lofty head of Sicily.—*Seneca.*
"Madre Mia" becomes an actual personality, terrible or beautiful, and silently worshiped. The Sicilian peasants are pagans at heart in their regard for Mount Etna.—*William Sharp: Three Travel Sketches.*

Terrible or beautiful," the "actual personality" of Etna stirred in his sleep, waking the countryside to apprehension. There had been in September a lava flow, that "unapproachable river of purple fire"; and still in January the mountain grumbled. As N—— and I drove with Salvatore as coachman to Castiglione—perched on its rock, facing that side of Etna from which the lava came down—the flow of four months earlier still smoked blue and wierd against the snow, and it was hard to believe it was not still moving.

The people told us of two brothers who had great wealth. One, when the lava approached his vineyards and thickets of filberts, refused to let the poor gather wood or help themselves to what could be carried off, saying that if the lava came it would come—that was fate—but meanwhile what was his was his. He lost all he had, buried a thousand years deep. The other vowed his year's harvest to the Madonna del Carmine if his yield was spared. The lava went around his farm; nothing was touched—and now he is selling his crops to provide money for the restoration of the church.

Some little girls took me up to the church of the Madonna who worked this miracle, and told us a tale that is repeated of half the saints of Sicily. When she sees that her people are in danger and wishes to come out in procession to save them, the heavy marble statue makes itself so light that it can be moved almost at finger-touch. When she knows there is no danger she makes herself so heavy she cannot be budged. She came out against the earthquake of Messina, and Castiglione did not suffer. She refused to come out when Etna threatened, and the lava did not touch the town.

We had been too hasty; Etna bides his time; but two months later the eruptions suddenly assumed terrible proportions. And from Palermo I came hastening back to Catania for another ascent to the devouring streams of fire.

The houses you pass on the way to Nicolosi are black and ugly, built all of lava blocks, but they look comfortable and I saw quantities of meat for sale, and abundant bread. The region produces, on the slopes of age-old eruptions, the best wine in Sicily; broom plants, almost like young pine or larch, border the way and there was the mocking green of young vegetation just on the edge of all that horror above, of which, here, there was as yet little hint.

We reached Nicolosi at six o'clock, left the carriage and set out, on foot or by muleback, two hours to the lava—so near to it that my face was scorched. In the black night the river of fire was hideous and fascinating. At the point I reached, the lava was two kilometers wide and nearly forty feet deep, spluttering stones that came tumbling with a grumbling, thundering sound down the menacing front of the red lava stream that pushed them on. Sometimes they split, showing the dull glow of the heat within; and the vast mass moved implacably onward, so that you must gradually draw back before its advance.

Another crater had opened that day and the lava was moving faster. As this blasting flood reached a tree or shrub it flamed like matches; poor little peach trees, just in trembling spring flower, or glorious great chestnuts with spreading branches alike must yield, shrivel and fall. When the mass touched a house the walls, as Papalia says, bent in a curious, wavering fashion, then came tumbling down. Sometimes they sturdily stood against the pressure. It was the same in the end. The lava covered all.

The processions of peasants, on foot and on mules, going to the lava and returning from it, with despair in their faces, the children crying, the women praying—it was a terrible sight! I cried myself as bitterly as any of them. I talked with one man who had lost 30,000 vines; with others whose poor bits of land were covered and would yield nothing for three hundred years. Priests were going with candles to bless the lava and beg it to turn aside from threatened villages.

I stood more than two hours unable to turn away. Two parties came up, each with an image of the Madonna. They arranged little altars and threw themselves flat on the ground at the feet of the Virgin.

If you can imagine a cataract of fire dropping hundreds of feet, and rolling down with it huge blocks of half-molten stone, you may know what I saw. The night was so cold that we sat on half-hot lava to keep from freezing. The sulphur gases blew in our faces and when the wind cleared away the vapor a little we were covered with snow. Finally we went into the mountain climber's refuge, a little hut occupied by twenty persons. One of our party fainted and the rest were not much better off. At six in the morning we began the descent and did not reach Nicolosi until nearly noon. Thirty hours of the inferno!

Still the mountain spouted lava! Still it covered little farms, depopulated villages; gulped down trees in blossom. So once again we made our usual trip to Nicolosi. Once more we called for mules. We got one with an excellent side-saddle, and another with something that had been a side-saddle but was broken out of all resemblance to its family.

I said I could ride it astride, so I arranged a blanket over the mule's back and begged rope to make stirrups. They brought me bits of cord so slight that I did not dare put my weight on them, and we started on the most toilsome trip I ever made. The usual path over the flow of 1886, where it swept down through these valleys between many extinct cones, was so completely blocked by new lava that we had to pick our way diagonally through a lava stream where I do not suppose twenty people had ever been before us. The lava, mostly of 1886, entirely surrounding a hill green with young blades of grain at our left, was grotesque. In places it was as if the waves of a storm at sea had suddenly been petrified—as if stone surf were plunging toward you; sea waves arrested just as they were breaking, white and savage. In others there were wierd shapes of men and animals; sometimes the flow was covered with white lichen.

The mules picked their way so slowly that we were nearly three hours crossing the flow diagonally. At last we came upon beautiful fertile slopes, green with wheat and planted with chestnut trees. We were high enough to get a broad view of the upper slopes of Etna, streaked and scarred with black lava streams, some new, some old, running down through the valleys according to the tilt of the land, now dividing to leave a green hill untouched, now uniting again, spreading like the fingers of a grasping hand.

On our left was a moving stream of the new lava thirty feet high, winding down like a serpent, burying vineyards and engulfing or pushing over great nut trees that seemed to suffer death agonies at the shriveling touch.

We climbed up beside it for another hour, watching the peasants cutting trees and loading mules with the trunks to save at least the wood. These processions of mules coming down with their melancholy loads were saddening to see. In some places charcoal burners had put up huts to utilize the wood.

As we got still higher we passed the timber line and reached a country covered with patches of coarse, prickly grass, where sometimes the snow lay, blackened with cinder and ashes. We were close to three new cones, and all about were those of previous convulsions. The muleteer told us the name and age of each little mountain, but I could not listen. I was tracing the black streams of death of all ages and all widths that have run like rivers down the dreadful mountain, leaving here and there below us a green spot of a few acres where one could see a house and picture the effort at tillage, the isolation—and again spreading over miles of country.

It was intensely cold, with a bitter wind, and when we reached the shelter hut after five hours of riding, I could scarcely stand. We were told it would be useless to try to go to the top, since the central cone was sending out no lava, and so we started on foot to visit the highest craters we could reach. The trip was not unlike the previous one, except that we went much higher and were able to approach two craters closely because they were not throwing out pumice or stones. The ground was everywhere covered with blocks of pumice, yellow with sulphur, which the craters had vomited. But as we neared the highest vents the lava flowed rapidly and silently. When the sulphur fumes allowed, we could go within a few feet of one crater and watch the violet and orange lights, the play of colors in the cavern. Our faces, and my dress, were burned and we were nearly choked. It was an awesome thing to see this river of fire pouring down hill, red, like molten metal.

As the darkness came on we could trace its course, winding among the hills for a distance that our muleteer said was several miles. We were close to two craters; one, higher than the other, was pouring lava over its lip; the lower one had built itself something like a well-head, and the lava had tunneled below and was coming out from a long cavern. The two streams gradually approached, ran side by side, leaving a great ridge of cold lava between, and finally became one river, pouring together through a high gate they had built, and down to desolate the country. The nearer brook was about thirty feet wide, the other much the same. The only sound was like the soft lapping of a stony surf, as the lava poured itself along.

Back at the hut we were shaken by two little earthquakes. The ground quaked everywhere; it was like walking on jelly; but there were no severe shocks. I wanted to stay overnight to get more photographs, but the weather was too threatening to urge anyone to sit in a chair all night in a tiny room packed with twenty men, so we mounted our mules to return. If you can imagine the sensation of sharp descents over jagged rock in pitchy darkness without stirrups, you will believe that I did not greatly enjoy this return. We reached Nicolosi about midnight, and N—— said she had been afraid of the ghostly rocks. I had been afraid of nothing except going over the mule's head, but very much afraid of that. I tried at one time to have the man lead the mule, but he had to let the animal's head down so much that the poor beast kept stumbling worse than before. The muleteer had one small lantern, but the oil gave out just as we reached the old lava flow. When they lifted me off the mule I was so near fainting that N—— got me wine, while the good woman in the hotel made hot coffee. There was no room; the place was crowded with newspaper men and tourists. We swallowed an incredible number of eggs and started by carriage for Catania. At five o'clock in the morning, not having gone to bed, we took train for Taormina, reaching there at 7:30.

Late in April—for this was a drama of months; a mockery of spring; a daily visible tragedy seen

DRIVEN BY THE LAVA   FRUIT TREES FOR FUEL
            RUINED BY ETNA

afar from the fairest scenes of earth, by people who had little heart to enjoy the beauty about them—late in April N—— and I went again to the lava. Our fourth visit to Hell followed the now familiar route to Nicolosi, which we reached about noon, eating luncheon in the carriage driving up from Catania, so that we were ready to start at once for the new craters; but the lava had spread so terribly that all the nearer ways were blocked, and we were told that to reach the nearest crater—there were seven in eruption—would take five hours on muleback and four for the return. We could get no beds at Nicolosi, so we contented ourselves with going to the main lava stream and climbing beside it as far as time allowed. We had an appalling view of the fire from three of the craters, getting near them as the crow flies, though to reach them we must have made a detour of more than ten miles.

Then we came down to the head of the lava, the advancing wave of the main stream. It was moving about fifty feet per hour and in places was more than one hundred feet high, in others perhaps fifty. The advance of the horrible thing brings the tears into your eyes. Upon the previous visit, in the evening, the rivers of fire were like dreams of the inferno. But by daylight I was even more impressed. The sky cloudless; everywhere the beautiful, smiling spring; peach trees in delicate pink blossoms, the vines putting out their first juicy little leaves, the almond trees all a tender green. The Sicilian spring is an enchantment. I never tire of the rich green of the wheat, the blue of the flax, the red of the poppy fields—and down into this smiling country was moving black desolation!

N—— and I sat on a low wall in front of a beautiful chestnut tree. To our right were young olives, a few apple trees with their blossoms just opening, one or two pear and cherry trees and a clump of fig trees. All around us was the richest imaginable soil, fine as powder, black and immensely fertile, planted with American vines, like most of the vineyards in Sicily. The best table wine of the island came from these slopes; much like the Vesuvian brands about Naples.

The crowd of onlookers was as interesting as the lava—perhaps six or eight tourists, the rest peasants from the villages threatened with destruction. One of the visitors was the pretty royal Princess of Nomatterwhat, who laughed heartily at the spectacle of the peasants hastily cutting trees to save the firewood and carrying away even the smallest branches of the olives. They were doing this with frantic haste, because until the last minute they could not bear to touch the precious nut trees which, almost as much as the vines, mean their livelihood.

When this blonde Princess laughed, a poor old woman spoke to me, as I was trying to take a photograph, and asked, "Why do you outlanders come here to mock our misery and take our pictures?"

I told her that I would throw my camera into

the fire if that would do any good, and that I certainly was not laughing. Then I said that perhaps my pictures might some time show other people how Sicily was suffering, and asked if she would not like to see some of them. I had received in the morning, just as I was starting, half a dozen that I had taken with a borrowed camera on my other visit—taken with a slight time exposure before it got really dark. She looked at the first of these, recognized her son in the foreground and was delighted. I gave her the copy, and she began to talk faster than I could follow the Sicilian.

It was a pitiful story of years of sweat and toil to buy the ground over which the lava was advancing; a little bit of ground, I fancy, for in this region there are both very large and very small properties. But she and her husband had given their lives to but their tiny plot, and plant it with American vines and bring these into bearing. They were splendid vines, with big stalks; she had tears in her eyes as she bent to show me the knobs or shoulders of the old vines in full vigor. Little shoots of green were starting from the big knobs, and the woman touched them as if they had been her children. She said all this work had been for the son whose picture I had taken. He had been in school in Belpasso and was to have gone to a higher school, but now all was over. The vines were being buried; her son—she did not care for herself; she was old and must soon die; but her boy——

"All yesterday," she said, "I lay flat at the feet of the Madonna and begged her to spare the fruit of blood and sweat; but the fire has covered half the vines already, and before night it will cover the rest. And there is nothing we can do."

It would have been mockery to say anything encouraging; I answered only: "It is true; there is no hope but in the good God." I do not know why I said such a thing in the face of cruel nature, except that the faith of these people is so simple that one must bow to it.

The effect it produced was astounding, even to one who knows Sicily.

"Do you pray to the good God?" said the woman. "Then you must be much better than we. We pray to our Saints and to the Beautiful Mothers because they are nearer and may perhaps hear us. We are not good enough to pray to the far-off God."

N—— came up with two Englishmen from Taormina and the woman saluted them respectfully with "Bless you, Sirs!" but when it came my turn she hesitated a minute and then threw her arms around my neck and kissed me, begging me to pray for her to the good God. I had no great faith in prayer, with the fire rolling down at our very feet, so I went to the carabinieri who were policing the place, and inquired about the woman. She had told me a true story, and I went back and gave her a few lire. She said that if they could after a year or so save a little money by working in other vineyards the son would—come to America! That is the dream of half Sicily.

I wish it were possible to picture the sight. The blue shadows on the hills, the laughing flowers, the throng of sad people watching, nearly all holding rough alpenstocks which until yesterday were supports for the doomed vines—pulled up out of the earth because no longer needed. The stream of lava moving toward us, one formed of many streams, was here probably three hundred meters wide. Under the sun it was blackish, except when a great piece fell away from the high front and rolled down at our feet, red and emitting sparks. There was a continuous fall of small stones and powdery material, with the occasional descent of a great mass, so that we saw our beautiful chestnut tree buried almost to its top and the olives and fig trees one after another uprooted and covered. This wider river moved with greater noise and tumult than the smaller rivulets of lava we had seen farther up the mountain; many such must have united to make its thousand feet of menacing width.

It is a piteous sight to see a little peach tree all in flower shriveling before the fire. Back and back we moved, for the lava scorched our faces. The hundreds of people in mountain capes and hoods, the women with yellow and white kerchiefs on their heads, were very quiet. They had come to expect the worst. For the most part, they said nothing. Only now and then when seemingly half a mountain fell with thunderous noise, someone would cry out, "Oh, Madonna Mia, we are ruined!"

As night came on, it was as if we saw cataracts of flame. The activity of the lava increased, or seemed to do so, and one saw nothing but running fire, fluid streams of fire, pouring from the lava mountain wall that slowly pushed its way downward. Now and then great caverns of fire opened and tons and tons of molten lava came down with a crash, breaking tree trunks and knocking down walls. People were moving about with flaming torches and lanterns. It needed only a group of tourists to dance upon partly cooled lava, as some are said to have done with strange bravura, to finish a study of the inferno in action.

And so once more, and for the last time, we came away, reeling with fatigue, sick with horror, ready with sympathy, able to do nothing in the face of the appalling disaster.

The beauty of this cruel region is incredible. Throughout the earlier days of the eruption Taormina was in a fog of smoke and mist, the wind much of the time a terrible scirocco. The terrace was always strewn with ashes, and Etna lowered through slate-colored clouds, a threatening monster, a perpetual menace. Now and then tremendous clouds of smoke were visible from the terrace, whirlwinds of smoke, and at night gorgeous spectacles of fire.

Then the sky cleared. After a belated snowfall

How the Lava Advances

A Useless Vigil

there were glorious sunrises. Etna with new snow whitening its sides was beautiful as a vision, with rosy lights tinting the fainter smoke wreaths and touching the white slopes into a dream of fairyland. The snow lay as low as in January, covering the cold black lava of many yesteryears.

Then rain washed the ashes from the vines and everything jumped forward into summer life. The vine leaves were of a most wonderful, delicate, beautiful green. Wistaria was in luxuriant flower. Spring roses everywhere blossomed. The hills were orange-colored with marigolds. Below me the lemon garden, and then the village with tiled roofs yellow with lichen; then the young green of the almond trees, punctuated by dark, straight firs; then the rocks of Theater Hill, yellow here and there with spurge; at the top the dull red of the Theater, and beyond, the blue sea—all this I saw——

And so around once more in the mighty sweep of the vision to the Mountain—and I knew the meaning of every tiniest wisp of rising smoke, its cost in tears and anguish!

CHAPTER II

Messina Six Months After

WHILE I was waiting at the wooden shed that served Messina for a Post Office, I saw a little dust-covered Sicilian coming up, pulling the bridle of a donkey loaded with fresh figs and lettuce. Two trim Americans of the teacher type followed, each armed with Baedeker and camera.

"Vossia——," began the Sicilian. But one of the Americans interrupted:

"We want some figs, but what stuff is she talking?"

The bent little woman was patiently repeating the prices.

"Three for a soldo," I translated.

"That's three for a cent, isn't it? Could I get them any cheaper?"

A minute later the purchase had been made and the woman was moving away with a parting blessing.

The American looked at me with round eyes. "That's Sicilian for 'May God reward Your Ladyship,'" I explained.

"My Ladyship! That's good!" said the other. "Do they all talk like that? But come on, Josie, we never shall have time to see the ruins and catch the train."

To this had come Messina! Six months after the earthquake of December 28, 1908, the Smiling City had become the hunting ground of tourists in search of a new sensation in a new Pompeii. The search never failed, for half a year had changed Messina chiefly in adding the grotesque and the pitiful to the appalling.

Under the great sepulcher lay perhaps 30,000 dead. Camped close among the mountainous graves were not far from 40,000 living. The peaceful summer sky of Sicily, the moveless waters of the Strait, the outlines of the Calabrian mountains, were a dream of blue. Waking, you breathed the poisonous dust of death hot with the scent of orange blossoms.

The disaster left, aside from immediate relief, two problems: the temporary and the permanent rebuilding of Messina, Reggio, Palmi, Bagnarà, Tre-Mestieri, Alì and dozens of other towns along the Sicilian and Calabrian coasts. The barracks, the building of wooden sheds provided imperfectly for the first difficulty. At all plans for permanent reconstruction the ghastly piles of ruins, here chaotic, there imposing, grinned much as they grinned in December.

Of the one thousand three hundred houses allotted to Messina, three hundred not yet built are to stand to the north of the old city toward the

Faro, the famous lighthouse many times destroyed. The other one thousand lie a little to the south, not far from the railway station. This village, approaching completion, is to Messina the "American street"; to its American superintendents "The White City."

To reach this bright spot that relieves the horrors of the great sepulcher you pick your way from the port, crowded with lumber-laden ships, to the little wooden Post Office at the corner of the Via Primo Settembre and the Viale San Martino. Here you are at a rag-fair among the graves. All about rise disemboweled houses, their crumbling walls, gay with scarlet poppies, threatening to fall on wreckage or on the gypsy huts hastily put up in the first days of agony by the Italian and Russian sailors.

The street is as busy as before the earthquake. You are jostled by peddlers whose push-carts are full of small wares saved from the ruins, and by donkey-carts piled high with blood-stained mattresses, bound not to the fire that should consume them but to be sold, with or without disinfection, throughout Sicily. Bumping these are the carts of fruit and vegetable sellers and the venders of lemonade and ices. Here is a great ox-cart laden with lumber and there the carriage of a chance tourist from Naples, gaping at the strange sights. Everybody except the tourist wears a soiled, grimy black, powdered by daily dust storms. Everybody from the bootblack to the tourist wears huge protective eye-glasses.

In the old days the Viale San Martino was a broad boulevard shadowed by locust trees. Now it is a narrow, treeless lane flanked by double, sometimes triple lines of wooden structures, ranging from huts of six boards and a mass of old clothes to trim little restaurants and barber shops. Every one of these shelters is a barrack, and to make a barrack you need nothing more than a bit of sailcloth stretched between two shanties. Here on the ground sleep perhaps four or five persons, while by daylight the space is given over to a tailoress with her sewing machine. Nothing at once more grotesque and more pitiful than the Viale San Martino has been seen since civilization dawned. The barracks are roofed as it may happen with tar paper, bamboo or old boards. All the older ones and some of the newer are without fire-places. Four to six bricks or a couple of stones in front of each door support the cooking pot, and among a people for ages used to stone or cement houses it is a miracle that fires are not as common as the daily earthquakes.

Behind the barracks are the mountains of ruins. Slowly, in the Italian fashion, the wreckage is being removed as far back as the curb and a few streets are being opened. On one side of the Viale little iron tip-carts are run on temporary tracks; on the other side donkeys and boys are doing their poor best to clear the city.

Following the Viale south, one comes to the first new brick house begun since the earthquake. I remember seeing two months ago a stick thrust into the ruins with the sign "Occupied by the Owner." The owner has now run his back wall perhaps twenty feet high against a mass of rubbish, such as no one who has not seen the wreckage of Messina can imagine, a mountain of broken brick, plaster, iron beams twisted as you would twist a straw, bamboo, mattresses, iron beds and broken furniture. At each side the tottering walls of tall houses promise to come down before many days to wipe out this little stroke of energy.

A few steps more against the poisonous dust that always sweeps the Viale and you reach a house that stood the earthquake without injury. It is a beautiful mansion of one story in reinforced concrete, standing in a rose garden. Its elderly owner spends hours daily on a terrace overlooking the city, and I sometimes wonder if he is glad of the lesson in construction he has taught his fellow citizens, or if, like so many others, he has lost friends enough to say, "We who are so unfortunate as to survive."

The clamor is like that of another Naples. Around a little spigot bored into an old aqueduct fifty people are literally fighting for water. The braying of the donkeys and the screeching of women offering lettuce and huge purple figs, fresh from the country, that already—or is it fancy?—exude the acrid stench of Messina, deafen the ears. Messina is rising again—but through sufferings!

Constantly rising, one comes to the plain of Mosella, a suburb of the city where the first lands were expropriated for building on a large scale. Sorry barracks are most of them, sheds divided into rooms twelve feet by twelve feet without windows, often without doors. Passing these rapidly, at the height of the long slope is a bridge crossing a torrent where the way is stopped by guards. Beyond the bridge shines a white village under the Stars and Stripes.

An American passes with a quiet "Buon giorno," and then is almost at home. Not quite; the intense blue of the sky and the overpowering scent of lemon and orange blossoms do not chime with the little Yankee houses all in white trimmed with green. Yet—yes; he is at home!

The village has been built under the architectural direction of John Elliott, artist, son-in-law of Julia Ward Howe, with Lionel Belknap, representing Lloyd Griscom, American Ambassador to Rome, as Superintendent in charge. It is away from the ruins; it stands on healthy, uninfested ground; shaded by such trees as could be spared, orange, figs, olives and acacias.

The village is laid out roughly as a square with broad streets running East and West, and narrower side streets grouping the houses into blocks of twelve. Each house is sixteen by twenty feet and stands apart from its neighbors, though the space is not so wide as it should be. Each is clapboarded and roofed with zinc. It has a little attic with ventilating louvre boards and is divided below into two rooms with a small annex for kitchen. Outside it has two coats of white paint and a little notice in white and green enamel, "U. S. to Italy, 1908." The kitchen would hardly be recognized by an American even as a kitchenette. Its only furniture is a brick fireplace built solid to a convenient height. A brick wall is carried up at the back and side but the wise Sicilian smoke finds its way out through a chimneypot in the ceiling. The front room is often divided further by hangings into bedroom and living room while the back room serves for dining-room and, often, a second chamber.

When completed, this village will be given to the City of Messina. At present several hundred houses are occupied by families in special need, as when an invalid must be removed or a child is expected. In addition to the barracks a church in the form of a Greek cross and a hotel of seventy-five rooms, placed East of the village toward the station, are well under way.

By the wish of the United States Government, all this work is being done by Sicilian laborers; largely by survivors of the earthquake. Six hundred men are employed now and they show no signs of the apathy of which Messina has been accused in the

QUEEN ELENA'S VILLAGE

"KITCHENETTE," AMERICAN VILLAGE

Italian Parliament. "Faithful and intelligent" are the words of Mr. Elliott.

As for the future, in the minds of commissions, sub-commissions and sub-sub-commissions, everything is done, because plans for everything have been endlessly discussed. There is a key-plan for the laying out of a new city with commercial and residential quarters, the essential quarters consisting of streets ranging from ten meters for those of less importance to twenty for the main avenues; the houses to range from seven to twelve meters in height, each standing in its own garden. This plan, aside from the bureaucratic difficulties expected in Italy, encounters two obstacles: It cannot be carried out without the removal of the mountains of ruins that encumber the city and without the founding of special credit for builders' loans.

Messina has complained with reason about nearly everything that has been done and has not been done for her during the past six months, and especially of the lack of schools. There is no school yet in the American village, but it might surprise those Americans who think of Sicily as a country of ignorance to see schools in barracks which are little more than dens, barracks that seem to cancel twenty centuries of civilization. The only schools that do not bring tears to the eyes are those of the village built by the Italian sailors and soldiers and called by the name of Queen Elena.

Inferior in some respects to those of the American village, these houses pay far more attention to picturesqueness of appearance. They stand well North of old Messina among olive and lemon groves and near the sea. The life of the village centers around the Piazza Vittorio Emanuele III, a public square adorned with a little wooden church and with a fair supply of gymnastic apparatus. The barracks are of one and two rooms each and are built for the most part roof touching roof, almost in solid blocks but always with the prolongation of the roof above a porch in a manner almost Swiss, which gives a sense of cheerful homelikeness not to be found elsewhere in Messina. As in the American village, every house is staring white, and the village has a workshop with sixty sewing machines and a public kitchen.

It devotes two barracks to elementary schools, one for boys and one for girls. The girls' school is furnished with rough benches, a blackboard and pictures of the King and Queen. On the blackboard was written, "A dirty and ignorant girl is scorned by all." Intent on spelling out the syllables stood a child of the dark, almost wild, Moorish beauty so often seen in Sicily, in this case domesticated by the uniform of the school, a long blue and white pinafore. Five minutes later girls and boys together were scampering up and down the street, skipping rope, turning handsprings and watering the roses that grew in their gardens.

This is the bright side of Messina. Another

school I visited flourished under different conditions. To reach it, an alpenstock and hob-nailed shoes would not be out of place, for you take one of those mountain paths among the wreckage which are still the ordinary means of communication in Messina, climbing now to the second story of a house whose front wall has fallen, leaving almost intact the furnishings of the upper floors, now descending through debris of every sort to the broken pavement. I came to a little square bounded on two sides by ruins, on the other two by barracks, life touching death everywhere here. Among the scattered stones, the wrecked chairs, the torn mattresses that had fallen from the ruins a dozen or twenty girls were dancing in a circle and singing something as pretty and nonsensical as our old nursery rhyme:

> [14] Swing around, around me!
> A loaf and a round loaf, see!
> A handful of blue pansies
> I would give to her who fancies—
> And who fancies is Sandrina.
> Down; kneel down, the littlest!

As, obedient to orders, the smallest girl dropped on her knees the Sister of Charity in charge said to me in her sweet Southern Italian: "The little ones do not know." Her glance went from the ruins about us to a table inside the nearest barrack where

[14] Gia, gia tondo! Un pan' ed un' pan' rondo! U mezzo di viole Lo vi dare a chi lo vuole; E lo vuole la Sandrina. S'inginocchi la piu piccina!

stood a jar of flowers that carry to all Italians a meaning, the flowers of patience.

But it is not patience that is keeping a once proud and turbulent city so quiet during its months of agony. It is grief, it is physical and mental fatigue, the result of unhygienic living, and it is a powerful wrath that becomes despair. A few weeks ago there was started a weekly journal called "L'Iniziativa," edited by Giacomo Marocco, a survivor of the earthquake, whose object is to call the attention of Italy to the red tape that strangles the new life of Messina, and to sing the song of the moment:

"Beautiful is Life, and holy is the Future!"

From the first number I take a paragraph which, exaggerated or not, expresses the feeling of Messina against the government of Giolitti:

Under the ruins lay our dear ones, wounded and calling for help, and you sent us 12,000 soldiers, not with hooks and ladders to save us, but with rifles to hinder us from approaching our houses, under which we still could hear the groans of our families. You justified your work by saying that it was necessary to guard private property. Setting aside the fact that we would have given everything we possessed to save the lives of our relatives, only bureaucracy could have conceived the idea that among the wreckage and in the dark any sort of watch was possible.

I remember San Francisco. As soon as the fires which completed the destruction of the business part of the city were extinguished, the people, who lived for the most part outside the business section, came flocking into town, laughing, calling to each other "I've nothing to wear. I don't know where to get my next meal. But we're all alive. We're here; we're here!"

Hardly fair. San Francisco kept her people. Messina lost her best. The tall palaces of her men of substance and of energy, the heart and core of a commercial city, perished; the low houses of the slums escaped. Catania is sheltering six thousand refugees, the largest number of any city in Italy, and a census of these unfortunates shows that only seventy-five are above the class of the day laborer.

To be a refugee from Messina has become a trade. It suffices to put on black and, to the anger of all Sicily, to revive the custom of hand kissing, which since the days of the Bourbons Messina has fought, side by side with Palermo, to extirpate as a relic of feudalism. The custom will dwindle again as the disaster recedes into history, but at present it is pathetic to be unable to pass through a village without being mobbed by a crowd all struggling to kiss your hand or arm, and all crying: "I kiss your hand, Your Excellency" or "I kiss your hand, dear pretty young lady." Foolish private charity has done this mischief, has done so much mischief that intelligent Sicilians are beginning to measure its evils against its good. The multiplication of private committees and the lack of statistics of families have made it possible for a diligent refugee to receive help from half a dozen committees while persons not accustomed to asking relief have had nothing.

This offense to their dignity the best of Messina is feeling, and against the clamor of beggars rises a protest. One day I heard an old sailor tell a story with much bitterness. Awhile ago a couple of little beggars, ragged and barefoot, were begging through the streets of Rome and playing a hand organ. A lady threw them a pair of shoes so worn that they hesitated to take them, but a woman of the people called to the lads: "I'll take them; they'll serve a year for 'Pro Sicilia.' "

"What's not good enough for beggars will do for us Sicilians," he said wrathfully. "And whose fault is it if not our own that for every little misfortune —tidal waves, earthquakes and the like—we beg the rags of all nations? We who have survived the earthquake and those who have the courage to return—we have no need to beg, even of the Government! We are sufficient to ourselves."

There will be a new Messina, not because the domination of the Strait is necessary to Italy, not because in 1908 Messina was eighth in importance among the ports of Italy; but because her people love the city. When in January it was proposed to bombard the ruins the people rushed to the port crying: "Kill us too! Let us die with Messina!"

A few days ago as I stood by a ruined church, since brought to the ground with dynamite, there came to me a man and a tottering old woman, strangers to each other, who told me the story of the church, of its great convent suppressed years ago by the Government, of its wealth and of its beauty. Finally the woman said: "Ah, what beauty is gone forever! If the lady could have seen that she could have seen our city!"

I told her that I had seen Messina before the disaster and the woman, smiling as if I had given her a fortune, turned away saying: "God reward you! She knew our city!"

Love of the city will rebuild it. It is easy to see the difficulties. But also easy to see that the noble impulse of brotherhood that gathered the survivors on shipboard and trainboard and scattered them from Naples to Genoa and from Taormina to Palermo went too far. Well for the wounded that there were hospitals; well for orphans and widows and the old that they could find asylum. But for able-bodied men with families stranded in cities where they could not speak the language—Sicilian dialects are foreign to Northern Italy—the natural relief was the soup kitchen. When funds were exhausted and the kitchens closed, the cry "Send the Messinians back to Messina" found the barracks full to overflowing, and work on the ruins taken largely by Northerners. Houses are going up now with speed, though they cannot keep pace with the flood of population; people are sleeping on the lower floors of ruined houses likely to fall in upon them.

Some weeks ago I met a poor creature in black carrying a baby and leading a donkey laden with a few poor articles of furniture. She had lost her entire family except a brother in New York. In the first hours under the ruins she and her husband had talked together. Later, she had said to him: "Let us not lose strength speaking. When I press your hand, press mine, and we shall know both live." After a time her husband ceased to return her pressure, and later still when rescue came husband and three children were dead. She was taken to a hospital in Palermo and when she had recovered strength went to her brother in New York. But in New York she was unhappy because of her mother and sisters still under the ruins. So the brother gave her what little he could spare and she returned—to find that April was nearly spent, and that after the beginning of May digging in the ruins would for sanitary reasons be forbidden.

CHAPTER III

In the Sulphur Mines

CASTROGIOVANNI, the most picturesque town in Sicily, is as good a point as any to set out for the place to which descent is swift, as dimly foreshadowed for us by the sulphur mines. N—— and I went together, local belief being that it was unwise to set out alone into that wild and desolate country.

The transformation in the appearance of man and his habitations was dramatic enough; at the very edge of the town we passed grottoes dug in the rock of the cliff-side and still inhabited by cave-dwellers, as we were to see them at Caltanisetta and elsewhere. But once out in the country, the way was bare, through limitless plains of wheat and beans for miles.

The few people whom we met were kindly and interested. An old shepherd was watching sheep on a slight rise to the left of our road. I jumped from the carriage to photograph him. He was manifestly pleased by the process and asked if I could not wait while he went to his hut to get a ricotta for me, anxious above all things to prove his hospitality.

That little break in the journey past, nothing interrupted the monotony.

It was more than a two hours' drive to Bonanno. The desolation of the sulphur country is unspeakable—a blasted region of yellow earth, with little holes pecked into the ground, about which the smell of sulphur ever hangs. The Bonanno mine is small and still uses the old-time kilns, so that from a distance one sees the conical furnaces walled up on the sides, but open at the top except in the actual process of burning, when the sulphur with which they are filled is covered with earth and refuse. Fusing can take place only in settled weather; at that altitude, only in summer. Rain has free entrance.

As I expected, permission to enter was refused. The superintendent was most kind and showed us the smelting and other exterior operations, but seemed inflexible in his refusal to go further. He said that the galleries are so deep in water that they would be quite impassable for me. I assured him that I understood the conditions and took my own risk, and chatted a little in Sicilian, that being the easiest way to get on terms with sub-authority. Pointing to the line of wretched little "carusi" coming out, each with an abominable back-load of stone, I said I was sure I could go once where those boys went twenty-four times a day. Finally he agreed, and I took off my hat, wrapped my head in a scarf, took off my coat to replace it with a workman's canvas jacket, pinned my skirt high, and was ready.

MINERS AT VILLAROSSA

The superintendent detailed two master workmen to accompany me, each with a little terra cotta lamp fastened at his forehead. The law prescribes that safety lamps must be used but in practice they are not, except immediately after an explosion of ammonial gas. The tunnel down which we started was in no place much more than two feet wide and we had often to flatten ourselves against the slimy stone wall to permit the passage of boys laden with sulphur ore—wretched, wrinkled, yellow little bodies bent double under their yellow load.

The law forbids inside labor before the age of thirteen, but outside the boys begin at eight and ten, and who is to know if they go into the mine? There is nothing to prevent except the fear of accidents to boys too young to be licensed. Each boy must make twenty-four trips daily with sulphur rock on his shoulders. The pick-men work twelve hours. Caution money of thirteen hundred lire must be paid to the parents of boys; in theory this is simply a loan, to be repaid when the work is given up. The boys are bent and wrinkled like old men.

Very seldom could I stand erect, the roof seeming not much more than three or four feet high. The descent was almost perpendicular, down broken stone steps deep in mud, water constantly dripping from the top and sides. The two men constantly warned me not to slip, strengthening my conviction that I should.

After a little we began to pass side galleries where because of the intense heat men were working naked; they dodged out of sight as we approached, but it was easy to guess that they cannot stand erect at their task but must work in a crouching position. We went down and down, the heat every minute more suffocating; my clothing was plastered with mud. Finally we came to the mouth of a gallery where someone was screaming with pain. We found that a mass of rock had fallen and apparently broken the arm of a miner. It is unlawful to use dynamite in the mine because the roofs are precariously supported by slender props, but it hastens production and the owners wink at the process. This was the result of a blast, I used my scarf to make a tourniquet and bandage—there was nothing else to do. They did not dare carry him out until quitting time for fear of raising a riot. So there we left him, in that inferno, to wait another half hour; I felt as if I were leaving my own brother, but there was nothing I could do except sacrifice my muddy scarf. I had left money and food with N——

So I climbed back up the broken, slimy steps, the water dripping on my head, through darkness to daylight, emerging, I was told, white-faced and nerve-shaken as well as muddy.

One of the more primitive mines was hardly a fair sample, perhaps. So, three days later, off we started for one of the six or seven largest mines in

Sicily, the Lucia, three hours from Girgenti. I had a letter of introduction from a man who had been paymaster of a neighboring property but had been thrown out of work by the flooding of his mine. We were warned at Girgenti that the road to Lucia was unsafe and that we must have a good driver with a gun; we let the hotel choose him, and he proved a sensible fellow. After such precautions, less experienced island travelers might have been made nervous when, an hour out of town, a group of countrymen taking their ten o'clock luncheon by the ditch at the roadside ran toward us waving their arms and calling on us to stop. The driver pulled up and the rough-looking fellows offered him and us their flask of wine and some hot beans. I put my hand into the bean dish and held out my glass for the wine, winning from the driver compliments upon my Sicilian manners. For it is custom, and very old custom, thus to offer food and wine; to refuse is an insult that, in the case of a man, is sometimes the cause of feud and bloodshed and is always grave discourtesy. But with these chance acquaintances of the roadside we parted most amicably, exchanging courteous good wishes.

The Lucia mine belongs to the Principessa Pignatella di Napoli; the director, Signor Savona, entertained us at luncheon. To his stock of food we added our own, and duly complimented the cook upon his adaptability and skill.

Signor Savona was unwilling that we should enter

the mine, but while we sat at table, arrived most fortunately the young son of the lessee with a friend. They both fell in love with N——, as everyone does, and insisted that if we wished to see the mine, the mine we must see. So the reluctant superintendent had us shown to a room where we put on waterproofs and later were conducted to the shaft where the elevators were bringing up cars of sulphur ore—for in this mine there is considerable machinery, and a force of one thousand men where there are but eighty or a hundred at Bonanno.

We stopped on the cage, or lift, a dirty iron platform hanging from four steel ropes, which met so close above our heads that it was necessary to crouch on our knees to avoid them. These elevators are commonly used only to hoist the sulphur; the men go up and down on foot. We went to the second level, about two hundred meters below ground, with the superintendent and three workmen. I found a gallery seven or eight feet wide, with a narrow track for dump-cars and room to walk beside them; the height ample, the way comparatively dry. Here N—— sensibly stopped, while the men and I walked on in the darkness almost endlessly—I forget how many miles of passages there are—the way narrowing little by little as branch galleries leave it at either side; and finally, after following through water a tortuous side branch, we came to the end of the track and were in a part of the mine much like that at Bonanno, with narrower galleries and steep, broken stairs, where men were slaving naked, and from which yellow little boys carried big weights of yellow-veined rock on their shoulders to the track. Here also there were the channels of drilling for dynamite; for the superintendent said that, law or no law, they could not mine sulphur without it.

I felt as if I had lived a lifetime underground. It was impossible to imagine the light and the air. Here was a world of human beings, dwarfed and stunted, snatching up their jackets at my approach, or hiding behind jutting rocks; yet there was no sense of impropriety; the men seemed a race of gnomes. The heat was so intense that the natty superintendent had stripped to his shirt. We came to a pause, and a man brought water to bathe our faces and wrists.

"If I cannot endure this two hours," I asked the superintendent, "how do men and boys endure it all their lives?"

"Poor devils," he replied, "I don't know. The mine is big, but not rich in sulphur, so the earnings are low. They work in shifts, but for the most part from 5 A. M. to 3 or 4 P. M., and they never have a soldo. When they are paid on Saturday they are so"—the Italian word means so driven by fatigue and desperation—"that they are mad drunk over Sunday, and knife for a word. They come back Monday moody and melancholy and work all week as patiently as mules, but as sullenly as bears until another Saturday."

Not without reason are the mine bosses averse to visitors. The men are given to little jests like cutting the ropes of the elevators. A year ago they killed an engineer. He had done nothing. He was not responsible for conditions in the mine; his duties lay outside, in the power house, but the miners were desperate and craved excitement. Later I learned that a considerable guard had been put on in our honor.

When we had regained breath we climbed to the level—two levels are almost exhausted and they are now digging down to a third—and in a few moments rejoined N—— and the young men. They gave us their arms as punctiliously as if at a ball, and I reflected upon the caricature of life afforded by two women picking their way with the polite help of cavaliers through the water, while gaunt, wrinkled men were sweating out their lives in every side gallery and peering at us from the darkness with their little lamps flickering at their foreheads. Some of the men dressed hastily and ran out to offer us bits of sulphur for money, and I affected not to understand their blasphemy when they were ordered back.

By and by we came again to our elevators and waited until a man had been sent up to make sure that all was ready for our ascent and to stand by

IN THE SULPHUR MINES

the gear. When we emerged I was for a time blinded by the sudden daylight.

The men were coming up early from their work, for it was Saturday and pay-day, and I thought I would see what they really were like. I asked a number if I might take their photographs and they were as pleased as children. They crowded about me so eagerly that it was difficult to use the camera, but I could not have found people more kindly, more anxious to see my camera and more good-natured. The superintendent and the young men at first tried to take me away, but presently saw that all would go well, and I used every film.

"You Americans are queer people," said the superintendent; "you are not afraid of these miners, and yet if you went to their village, and put yourself in their power—well, I wouldn't answer for the consequences."

I am a coward, but I am not at all afraid of Sicilians. I immediately asked the coachman to take us home by way of the miners' village, and the party divided, some going with the young men's carriage direct to Girgenti, while I took the longer route, with a miner on the box-seat with Jehu, and a "caruso" hanging on behind. Of course I did not meet with the smallest incivility. On the contrary, an old woman whom I picked up on the way told me quaint stories to add to my gatherings. Naturally I was well scolded at the hotel, but the coachman defended me, reminding them of the Barone G——

and the Barone A——. These two men own much land about Girgenti. One never stirs out of his house without six or eight mounted men to protect him. The other goes on foot alone everywhere and is safe because everybody feels that he is a friend. And yet—it is a sad thing to stand on a mountain and not be able to see beyond the land of one man!

Next day we went again into the country to Siculiana, four hours from Girgenti, along roads not supposed to be too safe, but they seemed as peaceful as Long Island. We attended a festa where one man in every six or eight carried a gun, but unless rabbits are plenty it was hard to see why he needed it. We bought roasted chick-peas and peanuts and were as happy as children. I did not see a beggar and the courtesy was in striking contrast with the rudeness often encountered in Naples or Rome.

We went also to Caltanisetta, where we visited a mud volcano and another group of mines. I did not go in again but watched the smelting. A good furnace smelts sulphur in thirty hours. At Lucia the furnaces are twenty-four in number, with four compartments each. The fire is started with a little coal, and spreads from furnace to furnace, for all are connected. The old-fashioned furnaces consist of circular walls of stone-like lime kilns within which the sulphur is piled, and covered with refuse sulphur rock or slag. In these the fire smoulders for three or four days.

"Carusi" Child Labor
The Little Sulphur Miners

IN THE SULPHUR MINES

It was not imagination that made me see the sulphur workers as occupational dwarfs. In a grave report of the Minister of War, printed in Rome in 1909 and retailing observations of the military classes born in 1887 as called up for service, it is stated that the largest percentage of boys above five feet nine inches came from Udine and Lucca. The greatest percentage below the height of five feet one inch were from Cagliari, Sardinia, and from the sulphur districts of Sicily. In Caltanisetta one youth of every six is undersized.

Yet it is an interesting place. The old hotel is buried in a huddle of streets, the new one fine and brave. Many of the mines about this town are closed because of obstinate fires and a bad explosion in one of them four months ago that injured sixty men. The hands doing outside jobs, such as shoveling loose sulphur rock into cars, paint dark pictures of their life; but there is one ray of hope. "As fast as we can," said one of them, "we escape to America." The "carusi" have bright faces and go to their work laughing, though they may come from it crying. And they play about the great scales in which the sulphur is weighed as if it was a giant swing.

The piazza of the town is too pleasant a place to be obliged to "escape," with the Sicilian swallows twittering about, the band playing—in Sicily a bank may maintain a brass band as good business—and the miners, goat-herds, peasants and town gentry taking their evening ease together.

Ought I to feel aggrieved that in this town a mass of mud thrown through a restaurant window struck my face? Assuredly not; since I was solemnly told that it was meant for quite another person; since by it I made the acquaintance of a noted Anglo-Sicilian authoress; since the Mayor most humbly apologized in person, and since the suburbs contain some of the finest cave houses it has been my happy fortune to behold, yet not inhabit!

CHAPTER IV

Hearth, Distaff and Loom

Gna Tidda was preparing this morning to set up her loom for a new job, to weave a wider cloth. She was adding to her "lizzu"—the English "healds" is as foreign a word—by slipping on old threads that had been used before, keeping a record of the additions by taking a grain of Indian corn from her apron for each twenty-five threads and putting it in her lap.

Gna Tidda is grown very gray and old and patient and sad. She lives alone in her room at the left of the street. Her children are married and gone. Her husband died four years ago, and she has a horrible photograph of him dead in bed. Behind the room is the tiniest kitchenette possible. She eats a pennyworth of bread in the morning and another at noon; at night, if she has anything to cook, she cooks it, but her ovens did not look as if they had been used for a month, and there were no olive-prunings for fuel. I never pass the house without hearing the clack of the loom, and seeing her bent figure in shabby black sitting in the loom seat, her stockinged feet on the rough treadles. Her shoulders are bent almost to a hunch.

Gna Tidda has to keep her loom in repair, which may not be easy, as it belonged to her cousin's mother and is fifty years old. She must pay the woman who comes to fill the spools, and can only charge so many pennies a yard for weaving. Taking one day with another, she may clear seven to ten cents. She is working now on an order from a woman who has a little girl eight years old and is already preparing the stuff for the child's dowry. Little by little the mother saves the money for cotton and linen. Perhaps she has spun the thread herself. She has ordered three pairs of spreads for a big bed, and this homespun, half cotton, half hemp, is preferred to machine-woven stuff because it is more durable. It is not fine enough for pillow cases or underwear.

Gna Tidda is always tired; has no longer the will to work; the cotton keeps breaking and her chest hurts. She suffers, suffers, but compels herself to go on. But little attractive as loom and life are, both must be protected. She unfastens her dress to show me that she carries on her neck figures of various saints, including the Madonna della Rocca and the Madonna di la Grazia. On the old loom hang red rags, a little bag of "sacred things," a bunch of olive sprigs, several small palm crosses and a handful of wheat from the piatti—plates— of Holy Week. These plates are of all sizes, but each contains sprouted wheat rooted in wet cotton-wool, and reminds us of I know not how ancient

GNA TIDDA'S LOOM

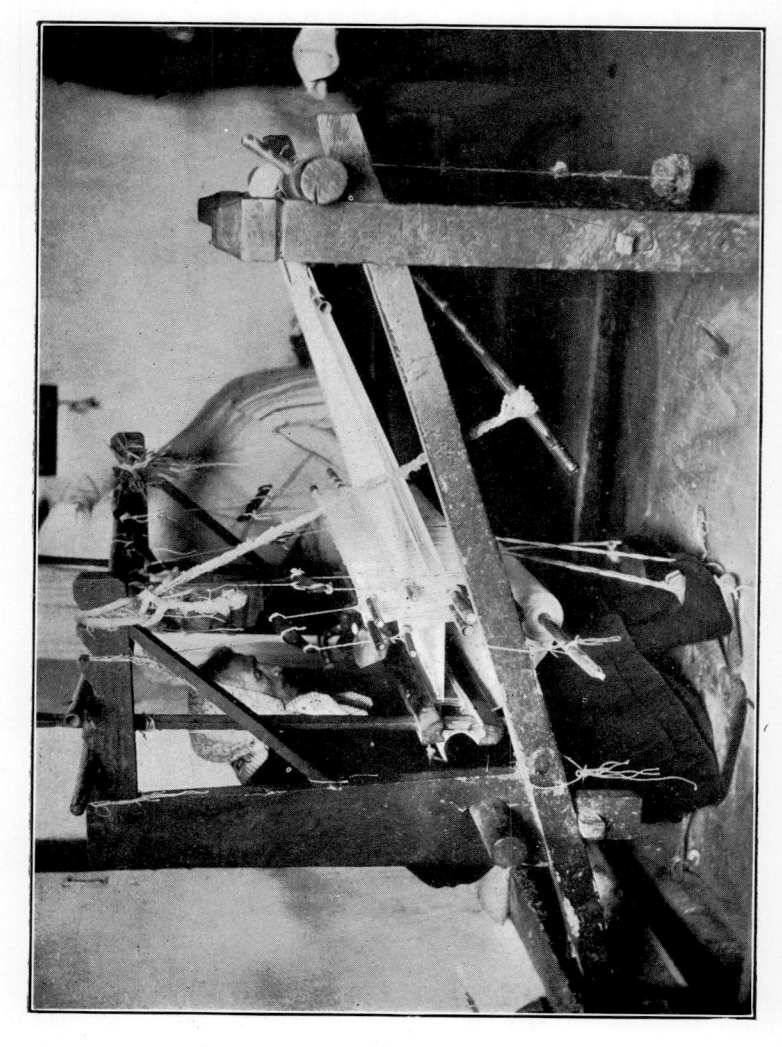

customs of honoring the old gods in the season of nature's resurrection. At the head of her bed Gna Tidda has more wheat from the plates and her rosary.

Her loom must differ little from those used in our country in Colonial days. Blankets and carpetbags are made much as our rag carpets are still— woven by hand in odd corners here and there. The tension is kept right by a rope wound around the beam and weighted with a stone.

At the head of the stair-way street is another old woman who uses the hand-loom for fringes, braids and the like. The garters of the contadini who still wear knee-breeches are woven on the little handloom. But this old woman is weaving fine cotton and the work goes slowly. She is very old, and cannot work all day; a little in the cool of the morning and the evening. The hand-loom is as old as she is. When she was a wee thing it was new. Now that she has a bad chest the loom is sick, too, and trembles. Never does she or any right-minded weaver begin a task without making the sign of the cross.

In the dusty, dark, low cellars of Limina I came upon younger weavers. One of these had a brown face with straight wrinkles across the forehead from perpetual peering at warp and woof, and eyes that looked tired. She was making cloth for her own dowry at odd times, and weaving for hire as well. And she weaves all that the family wears, bed and body. The black and white "scampittu" worn so gracefully as a mantle is woven on the same loom in summer, after sheep shearing.

The colored ribbons that I see in mountain villages, on the hand looms, red, blue and yellow, must mean complicated arrangements of the threads, for mechanism so crude. Silkworm women weave coarse stuff while tending their charges. Sicilian silk is yellow, suitable for soft satins. In reeling it the filaments should come off evenly in one long smooth thread. The method is to float the cocoons in basins in boiling water, brush them until filaments which will unwind to the center of the cocoon are found, then wind them into hanks upon the reels. Much of the inland silk must go into the silk-and-cotton mixture of Palermo factories.

Spinners of spells are all these women of reel and loom and spindle; but the wisest are of course the old. If one needs a very special spinning, where could one better go than to seek La Scimone as, bent double with asthma, she gathers minestra at the foot of the garden.

La Scimone feels well enough by daylight, but at night cannot lie down and rest, and she is afraid. Medicines do her no good. She can eat nothing but eggs and a little milk. She has prayed to God, to the Madonna and to the good people, and yet she is not well.

The air is breathless and warm; the mountain is covered with blue veils one above another, through which the mountain villages show dimly. There is just a fringe of surf at Giardini; the water near the shore is greenish-white; further out a whitish blue and bluish purple. But there is little air in the old woman's room.

La Scimone's devotional table changes with the seasons and Saints' days. Recently it was made up of pictures of S. Pancrazio, Sant' Alfio, the Madonna del Carmine and the Madonna della Catena. She has a prayer in seven sections; so long that when she tries to tell it to the priest, he says in section 1, "Enough!" Also she has salt and oil for evil eye, and never fails to say "Bless you!" under her breath when she has met a person and has thought of her, "How fat!" or any other unpleasant thing. Now why should one who is so exemplary have asthma?

La Scimone's husband was a sailor. For thirty years she "did the tongue" in church to ensure his safe return, but he died five years ago. She makes brooms for sale, and her door charms against witchcraft are complete and exhaustive. But she cannot make the round of the great church festas because of the asthma and the cost of travel.

I asked La Scimone about the conjuration with a thread, and she said it must be a thread of wool, and at once proposed to make me a sufficient protection. Going to a corner of the room where there was a sheepskin, she pulled out some flocks of wool and shredded them in her fingers, making them soft and pliable. She looked admiringly at the stuff and said she would card it and make me a "lacciu"—a lasso or snare.

When at night I went back a minute, the beautiful soft wool was on the distaff and in my presence she spun, winding the thread about it. She did not finish because the church bells began ringing the benediction; she must go to church, where they would say "many beautiful things of God"; after that——

The snare later proved to be a braid of three strands of wool. She could not tell me how or why it is useful against the evil eye, but there can be no doubt of the fact, for when she was a child her parents told her the evil eye had no power when it was worn. She said I must make a bag and wear it inside my dress.

La Scimone does not forget the church in her veneration for the old ways. In a Worcestershire sauce bottle she has holy water from the three fonts of the Mother Church; she is waiting a chance to send it down to the wife of the man who tends the dazio, whose mother is dead, so the house must be sprinkled anew.

La Scimone has never combed her hair on Friday, and she says there are many women in the country hereabouts who have never done so. For there is a curse——

> Cursed be that woman's hair
> For which on Friday comb shall care!

A Sicilian Kitchen

Some who respect this ancient wisdom wear a kerchief, so that no one knows the difference. There are young girls, even, who do not comb on Fridays. Some stay away from the lace schools a day for that reason.

Even in America there are people who do not like to begin a journey on Friday!

As I came down the path with La Scimone's licciu fending off all evil a day or two later, Cumari Ciccia was heating her oven—for in Sicily as elsewhere the oven and the distaff are not far separated; bread and the needle; baking, weaving, spinning—these are the trades of the home-matrons.

Cumari Ciccia's stubby, calloused feet were bare, her grizzly hair in disorder; her dress was open at the throat, and the sweat was trickling down her round, seamed, brown face.

"Walking in this heat, Signurinedda!!" she exclaimed, brandishing a handful of the vine-cuttings she was drawing from the writhing heap outside her door. "Sit down a minute."

As I entered she opened the wooden shutter of the little square window about the oven to let out the heat, and went on breaking up the vines. Gna Ciccia's hearth, like that of every contadina fortunate enough to have one, is of masonwork, its mouth opening between the two ovens that serve for everyday cookery, the one a fire-hole for bits of wood, the other for charcoal when steadier heat is needed. Under the shelf is a recess handy for odds and ends or for chickens at night; at one side is a dish-rack. There is no chimney.

When the flames had quieted a bit Gna Ciccia thrust in a poker with a hook on one side and a rake on the other and drew out the nearer red embers, catching them on the iron plate that serves as oven door. Dropping these on the floor she dipped a broom in an earthen dish of water and wet them down, "for the brazier, when Uncle January sends us cold weather." Home-made charcoal. Then she broke and bunched more cuttings and fed her fires.

"How often do you bake?" I asked.

"Every twelve days; and the bread, does it get dry? Hard as a stone to kill a dog; too hard to eat without grinding teeth." She opened her mouth to show me a few straggling yellow fangs. "But at night if there is no cooked food one boils water with a little garlic and dips in the bread. That is good."

She wiped her face with her grimy apron. The hen sitting in a basket nest of rags under the bed gaped in the glow.

"How long does it take to heat the oven?" I asked, pushing my chair as far away as possible.

"Half an hour in August but in winter, when the walls are damp, perhaps an hour."

A Colonial housewife used to piling wood into her brick oven would have rebelled if expected to bake with no fuel but grape prunings, but in Gna Ciccia's land these are good fuel; the woman who bakes with thorn twigs or brambles is the one to pity.

Again and again Gna Ciccia brought in waving lengths of the red-brown cuttings, doubled them and poked them into the flaming cavern. "The oven is ready," she said at last, drawing out and wetting down another heap of glowing coals and bending to sweep the inside walls with her black, charred broom.

The loaves were still "abed," literally in the family bed. Many times I have watched Gna Ciccia knead her dough, spread a dark bread blanket on the bed, set her round loaves in rows and cover them with another blanket. Once, when her husband had been driven home from work by rain, I saw him roused from a nap to give place to the batch.

All the older women have charms to insure a good baking, one to be said when mixing the dough, another when the bread goes into the oven.

"Tell me again," I begged Gna Ciccia, "what does one say over the bread?"

There was soot on her white bristling eyebrows and lashes as she turned good-naturedly. "What does one say?" she repeated, arms akimbo, leaning on the broom, "One says:

[15] "Rise, dough, grow,
  As grew little Jesus in his swaddling clothes."

[15] "Crisci, crisci, pastuni,
  Comu crisciu Gesuzzu 'u fasciuni."

Then she took from its place against the wall a long-handled wooden shovel, which she carried to the bedside, lifting with it a great round loaf. "I'm forgetting the salt," she said, and shifting the shovel to her left hand, she took a pinch of brownish salt from a dish on the rack and threw it into the oven. Then she signed a cross before the oven door and recited the second charm:

> [16] "Saint Rosa and Saint Zita,
> Good of crust and good of crumb!"

She slid the shovel into the oven, dislodging the loaf far inside. Another and another she carried, until all twelve were in place; then she ranged a few hot coals at the front and set the iron door in place.

"It's hot!" she sighed, dropping on a stool and beginning to retell the gossip of the neighborhood. After fifteen minutes or so she took down the door, examined and moved every loaf and closed the oven again with a satisfied "They must bake a while longer. If you wait until they're done we can eat this noon some hot bread dipped in oil."

Gna Ciccia's bread charms may not be the best. Very common is "Santa Rosalía, white and red, like you," referring to the reddish-brown bread crust and the white within; or "Santa Margherita, make it pretty as a zita," a bride. But you must use

> [16] "Santa Rosa e Santa Zita
> Beddu di crusta e beddu di muddica!"

some charm, even if you bake bread every day for the neighbors.

Seeking the mill that ground Gna Ciccia's flour, one runs the gauntlet of street industries. Most familiar are the old men and women past more active work who make fish-nets, trailing their long lines by the blank walls, and the blacksmiths and tinsmiths who set up forges in the street. The bellows blows up a little fire kindled in a hole in the pavement. So one forges nails, or even considerable pieces of iron-work, or dismembers the square kerosene tins of Zu Vanni Rockefeller and makes of them a surprising variety of useful objects.

In an old factory down by the water, a long and dusty shed, we come upon the making of citrate. Three girls bending over a trough cut with one quick motion the pulp out of half a lemon. The peels fall on the floor and are taken by a boy who presses them for juice to make essences. The pulp is ground in a big hand-mill and then piled under a press which is turned by levers. The juice runs in channels under the floor to another room whence it is pumped into tanks and boiled with powdered lime-rock; the fluid is run off into vats and the rock is squeezed dry. The soft gray residue is spread on shelves in a drying room where a stove fire burns three or four days, when the finished citrate is packed for exportation. Nearby, halved oranges and lemons are put into casks with salt water to be shipped to Germany for marmalade.

A little farther, at the macaroni factory, the search for the mill grows "warm." There is a mill of a sort that grinds the special hard wheat used for "pasta"; then it goes into revolving sieves where the bran is taken out. It is then fine flour. In one corner of the room is a huge stone, a little hollowed by use, in which the dough is kneaded, making rather a hard, yellowish batch. A suitable piece is cut off and put into a cylinder, in the bottom of which is the mold, a metal disk punched with holes to graduate the size of the spaghetti or vermicelli as it is forced through. This mold would turn out only solid pasta. Above it a clumsy hand press is adjusted so that a woman, pressing hard against a wooden beam, toils from one side of the room to the other, bending forward, a patient animal, as in a treadmill, and the pasta issues at the bottom in strings. The man adjusts them deftly along a rod, cuts off the skein at the top and hangs the rod outside the house to dry in the dust. It takes from a day to two days to dry the pasta; and whether volcanic sulphur in the air betters the taste I know not, but in the lee of Vesuvius, as of Etna, the suburbs are whitish-yellow with drying pasta, like a floury wash-day.

And now we are at the real mill of Giardini, small and hard to find, but a pretty picture against the background of the steep hill. It is almost the only one remaining of many that used to function along the torrent. The wheat is brought by peasants who have patches of ground or who get grain as part wages. I often see women sifting wheat preparing to send it down to be ground.

The mill is overshot. The grain is weighed and poured into a feeding-trough from which it is run between two small mill-stones and issues into sacks. And, as the miller says the saints make good flour, others may wish to know with what pictures the hopper is covered. They are the Madonna della Catena, a crucifix, San Giuseppe, Alfio and his brothers, Filadelfo and Cirino, and others—good workmanlike saints, all of them.

CHAPTER V

Speed the Plow!

Mark, too, when from on high out of the clouds you shall have heard the voice of the crane uttering its yearly cry, which both brings the signal for plowing and points the season of rainy winter, but gnaws the heart of the man that hath no oxen.—Hesiod, Works and Days; Banks's Trans.

Retracing Gna Ciccia's flour from her oven back to the mill and thence to the sower and the plow was a long trail.

It led back to Rome and Egypt; across the sea to the United States; back again to Sicily with the returning emigrants. It united the most incongruous seeming elements of old and new.

Consider merely the plow—not the symbol; the tool. You may see in many parts of Sicily the ancient Egyptian plow described by Maspero in "The Dawn of Civilization"; a larger hoe, drawn by oxen. A bas relief from the tomb of Ti shows one less primitive than that of Sicily often is. It actually had two handles!

In plow-making the bend of the wood is utilized. Two sticks fitted and spiked together at one end to form the proper angle at the other, the longer and lighter one turned up and smoothed to a handle—

PLOWMAN HOMEWARD BOUND

this is a plow. The end is sharpened at the point and hardened by fire or shod with iron. A brace is set between the sticks a little back of the coulter. A ruder plow may be made of two branches or the natural knee of a tree; the bigger stem, placed lowest and smoothed at the bottom, serves as the share; an upright stick is the handle.

Like the Egyptian fellah or the rayah of Asia Minor, the Sicilian peasant sows by hand and plows or scratches in the seed. To restore fertility to great areas impoverished by latifundia since Roman times, resort is made to fallow, which Hesiod calls "a guardian from death-and-ruin and a soother of children."

When plowing is finished the plow is reversed; the share catches on the yoke of the animals that draw it, and with the end of the handle trailing on the ground it is taken home. As in Ovid

> . . . what time the laboring hind, released,
> The plow reversing, yokes it to his beast.

Pliny describes the plowshare as "a lever furnished with a pointed beak; while another variety, used in light, easy soils, does not present an edge projecting from the sharebeam throughout, but only a small point at the extremity"; but he speaks of a newly invented plow with two small wheels used in the Grisons—much as an Italian of to-day would describe a gang-plow made in Chicago and bought by a Sicilian co-operative association.

The thrashing floor derives as anciently and honorably. Varro says it "should be on high ground so that the wind can blow upon it from all directions, preferably round, with the middle slightly raised. It should be paved with well-packed earth, best of all clay, so that it may not crack in the sun, and water collect." And so it is made now. The sheaves are brought on the backs of mules or donkeys. Threshing is done by treading the grain beneath the feet of animals, men stirring it with wooden forks. To winnow the grain, it is tossed in the air—and we see why Varro wanted free access for the wind. The heavier grain falls straight, the chaff is blown away. A sieve is used for more careful screening.

Crude? Well, a great American farmer, George Washington, wrote to Gen. Harry Lee: "The model (of an English threshing machine) brought over by the English farmers may also be a good one, but the utility of it among careless negroes and ignorant overseers will depend absolutely upon the simplicity of the construction—I have seen so much of the beginning and ending of new inventions that I have almost resolved to go on in the old way of treading until I get settled again at home and can attend myself to the management of one—I have one of the most convenient barns in this or perhaps any other country, where thirty hands may with great ease be employed in threshing. Half the wheat of the farm was actually stored in this barn in the straw

THRESHING

by my orders for threshing; notwithstanding, when I came home about the middle of September, I found a treading yard not thirty feet from the barn door, the wheat again brought out of the barn, and horses treading it out in an open exposure liable to the vicissitudes of the weather."

The anonymous "Virginia Farmer" who has described for us "Roman Farm Management" has set down many such curious parallels. In Varro's time the peasant sowed and reaped substantially the same amount of wheat per acre as the American farmer to-day. Varro's shrewd advice that you should "reserve ground for planting hemp, flax, rush and Spanish broom (spartum) which serve to make shoes for the cattle, thread, cord and rope" reads like the appeal of a State agricultural college in our own South for diversified farming.

There are processes more primitive. Many islanders have tiny patches of wheat snuggled in among other crops, the yield of which is reaped, like nearly all Sicilian grain, with the sickle, beaten out in small quantities at home and winnowed in a sieve on the doorstep. When the contadino who has emigrated to the United States comes back to Sicily he buys a small farm. For a time he rather puts on airs; does not want to work. Gradually the soil draws him back. He may enlarge his acres by hiring, like his neighbors, from the great landowners through their agents on the share-and-share system, the landlord furnishing the seed, the man the labor. Or, more likely, he will seek the "co-operative" and modern crop machinery.

From the door of my hotel in Siracusa I set out in a carriage one day at dawn to follow the city-dwelling peasants out to their patches of ground; and to discovery beyond. As we neared the bridge over the Ortygia the street was full of men and women going out to work. Sometimes they spend as many as three hours going to their tasks and returning for the shelter and companionship of the town. Some were on foot, with a bag across the shoulder and perhaps a cricle of bread hanging with a wide straw hat from the other arm; some were on mules or pattering donkeys.

As we left the city and turned toward Canicattini, I began to see peasants already at work, reaping with sickles. Their heads were bound with red kerchiefs, their faces burnt almost as black as Moors. With dexterous movements others bound sheaves of cut grain. Behind the reapers and binders followed gleaners, as in Bible times, each woman with a huge canvas apron or sack at her back. The heads they gathered seemed scanty. Each wore her red kerchief; each was as dark as the men. The proprietors expect the workers to be in the field by daylight and to work, with intervals for food and rest, until seven at night. Some give only a money wage; others supplement it with cheese, olives and other bread-accompaniment, with wine at discretion.

The plain below Epipolæ was luxuriant with

olives and almonds, lemons and vines—the strong perfume of the grape blossoms filling the air. But after a little we began to climb into less fertile country, so stony that I ceased to wonder that reaping is done by hand. "Machines destroy themselves," said the driver. It was a marvel that any grain could be raised; yet where the outcropping was most obtrusive was always the yellow wheat, with undergrowth of poppies between the stones. Here and there were stone walls six feet high to keep off hungry animals. On fallow land overgrown with thistles and white morning glories were grazing sheep and goats. By the roadside were wild artichokes in abundance; the driver called them "time-killers," they are so small.

Up the ladder of Canicattini we went, so called because it climbs swiftly through country so barren that even olive trees become scanty. Then again we came into wheat fields and vineyards through which we fared to the one long street of the town, all white houses one story high, each with door and single window frame. Then up again through more rock desert, ever climbing, ever watching the reapers at their hot work, winding through the passes of the hills of Palazzolo and finally to the rock cave tombs of Monte Pineta, pierced in the sides of cliffs so steep that one wonders how bodies were ever laid there to rest.

The landlady of the little inn has had twelve children and lost seven. She called me Little One, and spoke of far-away America, to which so many of this place have gone. So few tourists come that she and the custode of the tombs remember them all for years—but there are links with America, none the less; for, passing through Floridia on our return, we found the greatest building activity I had seen in Sicily, the masons at work after seven o'clock at night. Streets and streets of new houses were going up, each white, of one story, with a frontage of fifteen to twenty feet; clean, neat houses, if tiny. They were built by the returning emigrants from America, and such new quarters are called "the American houses." They are surrounded by luxuriant vineyards, olive and almond orchards and the inevitable wheat filling the gores between. In time these staring new houses will be wreathed like their ancient neighbors with low arbors of clinging vines.

And they told me that at Belvidere, a mile beyond Epipolæ, only one thousand were left of the one thousand five hundred inhabitants; five hundred men and boys were in America! There will be more little white houses when some of them come back.

Everywhere the same story. Following the plow to Monte San Giuliano in an antomobile bus which strangely contrasts with sickles and threshing floors, we stopped at a rare steam mill to deliver bags of wheat and take in bags of flour; but even from such advantages the men thereabouts emigrated hundreds at a time. In America they make fortunes in

THE "AMERICAN HOUSES"

MORE HOUSES OF RETURNED EMIGRANTS

two or three years; sometimes they come home and stay; sometimes they make a second voyage; in the end they buy a bit of land and settle down; so that in the same region there are both small proprietors and the estates owned by rich nobles.

In San Giuliano itself I was reminded at once of the steam mill and of Gna Ciccia's painful labors by three old women working a hand mill for the grinding of wheat; an ancient quern of little mill-stones in the shape of larger ones, the flour issuing in driblets into a crock on the floor. The women grasp a bar to turn the stones, as they do in Palestine, as the twelve slaves did in the palace of Ulysses, as the Greeks of the Archipelago do now.

There is much money at the Post Office, sent from America. Emigration interferes with the marriage of the girls, though the returning men marry, rather later in life than if they had stayed. The custode of the castle, who carries a gun, wanted to know if I could not recommend him as armed guard to some rich American family; half a generation of tourists could vouch for his honesty.

The boy called Candela who acted as guide at San Giuliano never ate meat except at carnival and on holidays. In the morning he had bread and olives; at noon bread and finocchi; or once or twice a week salt fish; at night minestra. "Signora mia," he asked, "what should I do with meat? It is for you others, not for us." Candela had been at school and could read and write. He had learned a few words of English from some ladies who stayed a month on the mountain—he thought because they had so much knitting to do they could not finish it. He showed me a five-cent piece given him by a tourist and pointed to the head of Liberty: "America, then, is not a republic?" But republic or not, all the countryside was going there.

How, in returning, the adventurers aid in the stirring up of Sicily I wished to hear now, not from reapers and gleaners singly, and little boys dreaming of America, but at headquarters of intelligence. The Advocate lo Vetere, a specialist in urging and arranging for co-operation on the soil, was of such information an authoritative source, and to him I went. There were at that time, he told me, three hundred and forty-two co-operative societies in Sicily, mostly in the provinces of Caltanisetta and Girgenti. Perhaps forty had taken land to work co-operatively. A majority of their members were men who had come back from America. There is intelligence at work in these associations, but money is lacking. To be sure, there is the "credito agricolo," but the amount that can be loaned one group is limited. There should be money to buy up the great estates and split them into holdings. There is water; deep, but it can be had. Machines are coming in slowly, though much of the land is too rough for machine sowing and reaping. Emigration, says lo Vetere, is a great good, since it brings into the country not only money but intelligence.

The co-operative societies lessen crime; only men of good character can belong to them. Boys lie about their ages to go to work, and age fast; but so do the men who go to America. They work so hard to get money to come home with; perhaps they do not eat as much as the American climate demands. They come home tired. But they bring money and ideas.

The venerated and lamented Giuseppe Pitrè, besides his labors as a savant, with some forty volumes on folk-lore and kindred topics to his credit, and his wide labors as a practicing physician, was a Senator and a statesman. Describing conditions which the war must have changed greatly, he told me that emigration to America had become an intoxicant. It unsettled people, though not so much in Catania and the large places—for the immigrant who in America huddles in tenements is in his own land a farmer. Home wages were raised by the drain of labor until land owners did not know what to do. Taxes frequently ran to forty per cent of income. The American Sicilians sent home big sums of money, preferring to deposit in their home banks, but many districts were too poor to pay the school tax; the compulsory education law could not be enforced.

Whether the emigrants take Socialism to America or bring it back from there is like the old question whether the bird or the egg came first. It is a power in the towns, and is becoming a power behind the plow. Deputy Giuseppe De Felice, middle-aged, a little gray, stout, big for a Sicilian, not much given to Latin oratory, earnest and sincere, is one of the great leaders of the movement and a powerful man in Sicily.

Him I asked about conditions in Catania and in the great Etna-enriched plain to which its city-dwelling laborers go out for work upon the fields. He was basing great hopes which the war must have rudely shocked upon the labor leagues and the Catania Chamber of Labor. The city gives rooms for the league meetings rent free, with lighting and a little money for expenses. The members hire a doctor for each league, who is paid perhaps five hundred lire a year. Each quarter of the city has its public doctor, but workingmen prefer the physicians employed by their leagues.

De Felice favored emigration. It had, with the action of the leagues, raised wages for those who stayed, while those who go and come back are not the same people. Away, they pour a stream of wealth into the country; returning, their minds are quicker and they join in co-operative and other forward movements—if they stay. Illiteracy one cannot estimate, since the last census was taken in 1901. In all Sicily it may be forty-five per cent, including the smaller centers.

But was not De Felice, here, too optimistic? Girls are not sent to school as generally as the boys who figure in the army statistics. Other authorities set the percentage lower. Nothing could be finer

Pictures Made for "Babbo in America"

in spirit than the Francesco Crispi school which I had visited in Palermo, with its eleven hundred pupils—the Sicilian parallel of our "little red school house," since most peasants live in towns. Here are none of the beautiful gymnasiums and assembly halls of American city schools; but what American school has classes in fencing? And how many teach, once a week, "rights and duties" in the true Mazzinian spirit—one's duties toward his country and his fellow men?

The children look intelligent; many of them beautiful, with fine oval faces. They read, it seems to me, with more expression than American children of the same age and are more fond of reciting poetry. They are neatly dressed and have been carefully trained in politeness. They rise with one accord as one enters the room. Always in such a school are some children who made the beginnings of school education in New York, or near the aqueduct works of Mt. Kisco or the steel mills of "Pittisborgo."

De Felice spoke frankly of such festivals as that of Sant' Alfio as relics of paganism, commercialized, with which one must be patient a little longer. Italy has neglected the South; it should have given the communes all the proceeds of the sale of the lands of the religious congregations for public works. Naturally De Felice did not favor dividing commune lands among small owners, because they would be obliged to sell them again and the big owners would pick up the little farms one at a time as they have done in the past. So Arthur Young, studying French farming just before the revolution of 1790, did not favor dividing the estates, as was so soon to be done, preferring the efficiency of larger operations.

De Felice is of the fertile coastal plain, the tillage lands. Castrogiovanni is in the grazing country of high hills; and Napoleone Colaianni, the veteran Deputy, is its prophet and spokesman in the Roman Congress. He says—and I thought at once of the cattle reivers of the Scottish Border and other fierce bands in hill forays—that one reason why Sicily has but one hundred and sixty-four cattle for each one thousand inhabitants, while France, Germany and Great Britain have, or had before the war, from two hundred and sixty-eight to three hundred and eighty-three, is the activity of cattle stealers, carried on under a system which subjects the owner, if he seeks to prevent or punish the theft, to the danger of having his remaining stock killed, himself shot at or taken for ransom, and his buildings burned. How are capitalists to be attracted to an industry, however lucrative, in which they are likely to lose their all without redress?

"I remember," says Signor Colaianni, "two plucky young men from Argentina who on their return from that far-away land, where they had saved up forty thousand lire, full of faith bought thirty-two animals of the finest breed from fanciers at Caltavutoro and other villages to devote themselves to stock-farming. They were fancy farmers exactly one week and one day. Eight days after they had taken the beasts to the grazing ground came the word that all their stock had been taken by bandits."

Colaianni tried to do something for the young men, but without success. How should these returned emigrants of modest means hope to escape a toll which was laid upon great landlords, like Baron Lombardo of Canicatti and Baron Sabatini of Petralia; on resourceful lawyers like the Advocate Algozine of Leonforte—the very town where the young Argentine adventurers came to grief—and the Advocate Pace di Bella of Bronte? No; the plucky pair went back to Argentina to make another fortune. Cattle stealing will lessen with better courts, roads, detective service, schools, hygienic service; they had only one lifetime to spend and could not wait.

The Sicily that is a garden, the Sicily known chiefly to the tourist, the smiling shore of the sea, is only one-quarter of the island. The frowning interior, of the wheat fields and the wide estates and the big landlords with their armed and mounted guards, is three-quarters of the whole area. Here the estates that existed even before Roman times, intensified by the Norman baronage, modified now for the better, now for the worse, in constant three-cornered struggles between serfs, kings and nobles, exist to our day. The fall of feudalism, so far as it did fall, made it easier for a careless owner to lose his property, but also easier for a more niggardly master to gain it—and no easier at all for the workers to secure its division.

The modern land question met Garibaldi at Marsala, marched with him into Palermo, dogged him to the Strait. Franchetti writes that the North Italian government has misunderstood Sicilian conditions, much as England misunderstood Irish land systems a century ago; and that the confiscation of church properties made matters worse. The lands fell into the hands of large owners, and the peasants suffered a disaster, losing age-old privileges and being driven from their homes.

As in France, the new legislation aimed at creating small proprietors, but the auctions of church lands took capital out of circulation, so that peasants who took small holdings could get no advances to work their grounds and fell into the hands of usurers. Usually they lost their lands, the estates became wider than before, rents rose and owners fattened, while the peasants, no longer allowed to live in the feuds, to gather wood, to pasture their animals, bore a rule harder than of old.

Inevitably there followed secret organizations, revolts, bloodshed, until public opinion began to take the Sicilian land question seriously. Emigration supplied a harsh remedy, so far as wages went, but found or forced no cure for lack of water; for the closing of ancient rights-of-way by new owners; for the absentee system, caused as often by fear as by greed; for the armed rural guards who play upon the timidity of city owners to prolong their hold; for the flocking of peasants into town to find more congenial labor.

And all this is as much an American question as was the famine in Ireland in 1847. It has an immediately practical bearing not only upon the immigration of Sicilians into the United States, but upon their proclivity for shooting robins when they get here, in the country; and in the city their cynical views about the police and the courts of law. With them they bring their unwillingness to seek legal redress for wrongs suffered; their fear of testifying against desperadoes; their "mafioso" code of honor. Upon American soil their tribute to the brigand scarcely ceases, and for the landlord the "bosso" and the padrone furnish a substitute to be feared or hated.

To understand is to pardon. To teach is to win. Something we may teach ourselves. The Italian is possibly the only element in our immigration whose children are less healthy in the new country than in the old. The men, coming from the farms, may suffer less on the canal and aqueduct, in spite of the bad housing of labor camps and loneliness for home faces and the beauty of the old land. The women and children, accustomed to live in the open air, huddle into swarming tenements and work in city factories. Even in mining regions, factories follow the "labor supply" to congested towns. In New England the factory itself is a family affair, and there are at least fewer domestic tragedies of alienation, desertion, bigamy.

But how quick the children are in school! How the Latin genius shows in handiwork shaming our clumsier Northern fingers! How the little ones bring to their schools the gift of song and the sunshine of affection! They are the true immigrants; they see, as their parents cannot, what America really means, the good and the bad alike, the hardships, but also the opportunities. Through them we conquer prejudice and suspicion.

And the fathers and mothers, unlettered as they are, and inevitably the prey of exploiters and agitators of their own race—have we tried to teach them also? Have we shown proper gratitude and appreciation in treatment? Have we granted them the courteous address which is essential to their honest pride? Have we any conception of the debt we owe to their patient toil in the darkness of the mine, the danger of the trench, the service of the rising walls of new homes?

The United States itself is a League of Nations. Let us look to the justice and the love that should bind it close.

THE END